MILITARY INCOMPETENCE

Why the American Military Doesn't Win

MILITARY INCOMPETENCE

Why the American Military Doesn't Win

Richard A. Gabriel

𝕀𝕟 **HILL and WANG**

A division of Farrar, Straus and Giroux
New York

To PAUL, JIM, DAVE, and JOHN,

who covered my back in the fighting . . .

and thus became my brothers

PREFACE

THE idea for this book emerged within six months of the invasion of Grenada by United States forces in October 1983. Like most Americans at the time, I regarded that military action as a necessary means to secure American strategic objectives in the Western Hemisphere. Probably more than most, I welcomed its success as an indication that the American military had finally gotten its act together and was able to carry out a modest military operation with precision. After all, it had been a long time since American military force had been decisive in fostering the country's national interests. With Grenada, the Vietnam legacy finally seemed to be receding.

In the months after Grenada, I had opportunity to visit the Pentagon, where from time to time I am asked to present my views on various aspects of military policy, and to speak with a number of military officers of different ranks. Our conversations began to reveal to me that the Grenada operation was something less than a textbook application of military force. Worse, as my brother officers told it, it was marked by a number of serious mistakes that seemed reminiscent of Vietnam. On Capitol Hill, a number of respected military analysts whom I have known for years not only confirmed that the Grenada operation had gone wrong but added horror stories to the list. It gradually became clear that what the American public was told about the Grenada invasion by the White House and the Pentagon public-relations office was, in many important aspects, simply untrue and that the application of military

force in that operation was marked by a number of shortcomings so serious as to bring into question whether the American military had learned anything from the lessons of Vietnam.

If I had any doubts that something was still wrong, they rapidly vanished when I began talking to officers and men who were actually involved in Grenada. Most of these were old friends or people to whom old friends introduced me. They included officers and men in the Rangers, the 82nd Airborne Division, Delta Force, and other units that had taken part in the invasion. While Grenada had presented the military with an opportunity to demonstrate that it could conduct a sizable military operation with some degree of proficiency, the facts suggested otherwise.

I have been a student and observer of military affairs for almost fifteen years, and a student of military history for much longer. I tend therefore to bring a historical perspective to my analysis of military operations and to view them against the reasonable standard of how well other armies of the West would have performed in similar situations. By this standard, Grenada was a failure. Moreover, as an officer who served during the Vietnam era, I remain acutely sensitive to the causes of military failure. Anyone who was on active duty during Vietnam and saw firsthand the innumerable errors and the at times gross incompetence in that war understood then, and understands now, that if the military does not reform itself and learn to plan and mount military operations with greater precision, it will risk failure again and again.

The record of military success and competence between Vietnam and Grenada has been less than spectacular. The United States mounted a number of military operations in those years; all of them failed or were marked by serious errors. Between Vietnam and Grenada, we failed to rescue our POWs in the Sontay raid, we produced a microcosm of military disaster in the *Mayaguez* incident, almost lost our credibility as a military force after the Iran mission, and lost over two hundred men in Beirut in what surely must count as one of America's most incompetent military operations. And so, after Grenada, I decided to review these operations and determine just why it was that we seemed to have learned nothing after our searing experiences in Vietnam.

This book is highly critical of the American officer corps, which is the primary cause of what I have called American military incompetence. It will cause some in the military to bridle. The incompetence causes me to be angry as well. Although a number of my books and articles have been critical of the military, and I am cited by some as a "critic of the military," the fact is that I am not anti-military or "out to get" the military. During the twenty-one years I have been an officer on active and reserve duty—three of them on active duty during the Vietnam war—I have been involved in a number of assignments and have commanded units. My work has brought me into frequent contact with senior and middle-level officers who have commanded men in battle, watched them die, or been responsible for planning operations that sent men to their deaths. Those who know me well know that my intention is to point up the military's shortcomings, to bring them to the attention of those who are in a position to bring about reform. My criticisms of the officer corps are presented more in sorrow than in anger. All officers are, after all, brothers in arms. Each of us must try to ensure that we carry out our responsibilities as best we can, so that our military forces succeed in combat and men in our charge are not lost needlessly. I am certain they will understand.

Moreover, anyone who has been as closely associated with the military for as long as I have knows that there are a great many officers who are competent, dedicated, courageous, and self-sacrificing. They bear the burden, trying to bring about change, sometimes at great risk to their careers. No one who knows the senior officers at the top of the military pyramid, especially the current crop, who were junior officers during the Vietnam war and saw firsthand what military incompetence can do, can honestly question their sincerity. The problem is seldom with individual officers. The problem is with a system that seems to prevent good men from exercising their talents in the service of their men and their country. The system is deformed and it hamstrings the men who serve in it. We have many fine officers, but the system must be reformed to allow their abilities to be brought to bear on the conduct of battlefield operations. Otherwise, their talents will continue to be squandered.

Many, many officers quietly cry out for reform of a system that they know in their guts does not work well. This is demonstrated in any number of ways, but no more clearly than in their willingness to ensure that the truth about military operations reaches the public and our political leadership. This book could not have been written without the help of officers and men who provided me with information about what really happened in the military operations in which they were involved. The fact is that much of the information necessary to determine just what did happen at Sontay, with the *Mayaguez*, in Iran, Beirut, and Grenada is still hidden from public view by the Pentagon's declaring secret anything which might cause it embarrassment.

Other information was provided by individuals who, while not directly involved in the actual military operations, were in a position to know what went on and were willing to share that information with me. In all cases, I have guaranteed anonymity. Whenever names of officers and men appear in this book, it is because they have been mentioned in open sources by other analysts. I have pointedly refrained from mentioning the name of any officer or public official who is still on active duty or holds office, except where his name has already been mentioned by others in public sources. So be it. I will not betray the trust of officers who, in helping to make the facts public, are truly living by their oath of service, which, I note, is to the Constitution and not to the temporary occupant of the White House or the office of the Secretary of Defense.

I have, where possible, visited the areas where the military operations actually took place. I was in Beirut while the Marines were under siege, and I have visited Grenada. It is, of course, quite impossible to visit Iran, North Vietnam, or Cambodia. During my visits to Lebanon and Grenada, I saw the terrain in which American military forces had to fight, and interviewed scores of civilians and military men of other fighting forces (including militia leaders in Beirut), many of whom witnessed what occurred. Moreover, my contacts in other areas provided me with very useful data. I was, for example, able to obtain a copy of the operations plan that was carried aboard one of the Marine helicopters during the

Iran raid and captured by the Iranians. To the best of my knowledge, this plan has never been published in the United States. While in a number of places I must protect the anonymity of my sources, I am confident that what I report is the truth.

There is one thing that this book is not about: I have not entered the political arena, either to question or to praise the purpose for which we have sent our military into dangerous engagements. That's someone else's book.

I hope that *Military Incompetence* will help the military and the public to focus attention on the need for reform. As an officer, I feel the responsibility to help because it is other officers who will die along with their men if something is not done to improve our ability to plan and execute military missions. As a citizen, I am acutely aware that the nation's security depends ultimately on maintaining a credible military force capable of carrying out the orders of its elected government. Thus, this is no gratuitous attack on the military—any more than my previous works have been— but the effort of one citizen-soldier to tell the truth.

Writing a book of this sort takes a great deal of help and encouragement. After all, much of the material contained in it is not usually available to the average student of military affairs. Moreover, because it is critical of the military, there are some who might misunderstand its purpose. Those who helped me—especially my fellow officers and the men of the fighting units—will understand that its purpose is to help the fighting services understand their problems so that they will not repeat their failures.

I am in debt to many experts and researchers who gave generously of their time and expertise and insight. Among these I count Bill Lind of the Military Reform Caucus, my friends in Delta Force and the Rangers, and my brother officers in the Army. In addition, three journalists contributed much: Scott Minerbrook of *Newsday*, John Fialka of *The Wall Street Journal*, and Frank Greve of the Knight-Ridder chain all shared much of their information and expertise with me.

A great debt is owed Bob Windram of NBC Nightly News and

his colleague, Fred Francis, NBC's chief Pentagon correspondent, for helping me piece together a number of events which are described in the book. Thanks is also owed to the many people of the NBC Today Show, ABC Nightline, CBS, and the CNN television network who took quite a chance in presenting some of the findings about Grenada and Iran in this work when it was risky and unpopular to do so. My gratitude also extends to a number of academic and military institutions which provided forums to test and explore my ideas. Among these are the National Defense University, the Army War College, the U.S. Army Command and General Staff College, and Tufts University.

There are my friends Paul Savage, John Windhausen, Jack Lynch, and John Feick, all of St. Anselm College, who read the manuscript and suggested changes. Terry Boissenault, my secretary, and Cari Colangelo, my assistant, labored hard to transcribe and type the manuscript. Thanks are also owed to St. Anselm College in Manchester, N.H., which has for the last decade provided me with a peaceful and secure haven from which to teach and write.

Manchester, N.H.   *Richard A. Gabriel*
March 1985

CONTENTS

When an officer accepts command of troops, he accepts not only the responsibility of accomplishing a mission, but the guardianship of those who serve under his command. The military hierarchy exists and can function because enlisted personnel entrust their well-being and their lives to those with command authority. When those in command authority either abdicate that authority or neglect that guardianship, more is lost than lives. Lost also is the trust that enables those who follow to follow those who lead.

Representative Dan Daniel,
U.S. Congress, in hearings
on the Beirut tragedy

MILITARY INCOMPETENCE

Why the American Military Doesn't Win

1

WHY THINGS GO WRONG

THE ability of a nation to work its will through military force is one of the vital elements of national power. The credibility of a state's military forces (based on its record) is an important factor in its ability to gain its foreign-policy objectives *without* the use of force. The threat of force is often sufficient to gain policy objectives. As a corollary, when a nation has a record of successful military operations, the available options of its adversaries are often self-limiting. It was, for example, the excellent reputation of the British Navy during World War II that prompted Hitler to call off the invasion of Britain when strong evidence suggested that the invasion could have been successful. And it was the reputation of American naval and air forces that convinced Nikita Khrushchev during the Cuban missile crisis of 1963 that Soviet ships would be engaged if they attempted to pass the American naval blockade. The threat of military force operates best when it is aligned with specific foreign-policy objectives whose goals are militarily obtainable. The injunction of Clausewitz that military applications of force should always be subordinate to well-defined political objectives remains as valid today as it was one hundred and fifty years ago when he first stated it.

The reverse is true of a nation with a record of failure and incompetence in its military operations. Such a state puts itself at a great disadvantage. A pattern of repeated military failure can prompt or encourage an adversary to embark upon policies designed to take advantage of this pattern. A reputation for failure

encourages a nation's adversaries and increases the possibility of military confrontation. This axiom is more true of conventional wars and the use of military force in the service of limited objectives than it is of nuclear war. Thus, a nation that acquires a reputation for its inability to execute successful military missions increases risk to itself.

It seems almost beyond doubt that since World War II the United States has acquired a reputation for failure and inefficiency in its military operations. This well-deserved reputation is supported by the evidence. The truth is that the application of military force has not been decisive in furthering American foreign-policy goals since World War II. The Korean conflict resulted in stalemate, and while it could be credibly argued that U.S. forces performed reasonably well, the fact remains that U.S. forces were pushed out of North Korea by the massive weight and determination of Chinese armies. Only after the Chinese had inflicted a series of military defeats upon U.S. forces and pressed them back against a line roughly equivalent to their position prior to the hostilities did the conflict settle into a political stalemate. U.S. forces did not achieve most of their battlefield objectives during that war. After Korea, there was Vietnam. For ten years, American military forces engaged an elusive enemy and in the end withdrew from the conflict. The performance of American combat forces in that war left much to be desired in terms of military technique, quite apart from the larger political reasons for the withdrawal of the United States. The American military effort was characterized by the improper use of ground tactics, combat units that did not fight well, officers that led badly, the fragging (assassination) of officers, and the application of enormous rates of firepower delivered by highly complex systems that simply did not succeed in breaking the will of the enemy to resist. By any standard, the Vietnam adventure must be classified as both a military and a political defeat.

It has been a decade since American forces left Vietnam and almost a dozen years since American forces began systematically to withdraw from battlefield operations and turn over responsibility

for the fighting to the South Vietnamese. Since the drawdown in Vietnam, the American military has launched no fewer than five major military operations to apply military force in support of Washington's foreign-policy objectives. These operations are: (1) the raid on the Sontay prison in North Vietnam to rescue seventy American POWs held there; (2) the rescue of the crew of the *Mayaguez* in Cambodia in 1975; (3) the mission into Iran in 1980 to rescue the hostages held at the American embassy in Teheran; (4) the participation in the multinational force in Lebanon from 1982 to 1983 in support of the Gemayel government; and (5) the invasion of Grenada in the Caribbean in 1983 in order to topple a hostile regime and replace it with one more accommodating to U.S. interests. In every instance, the U.S. military either failed to accomplish its mission or else mounted operations characterized by serious shortcomings in military technique. The result has been to bring the credibility of American military forces into question in the eyes of America's friends and adversaries both. No less an authority on successful military operations than the former chief of staff of the Israeli Defense Force, Rafael Eitan, remarked in response to U.S. criticism of Israeli forces that he found it difficult to take seriously the advice of military commanders who could not even protect their own Marines at the Beirut airport.

MILITARY INCOMPETENCE

The record over the last fifteen years of American military ventures has been demonstrably one of failure bordering on incompetence. The critical question is why this has been so. What factors contribute to military failure and the development of incompetence? Is there something about the American military that tends to produce leaders who cannot plan and cannot lead? Are there systemic institutionalized practices and values that increase the probability of military failure? The answer seems to be yes. Moreover, when military failure becomes as frequent as it has, the chances of success are diminished by the system itself. When the

military as a matter of course produces people who cannot do their jobs, then the system is corrupt.

Military incompetence can be defined as the inability of military leaders and forces to avoid mistakes which, in the normal course of things, should and could be avoided. This definition says nothing about those contingencies that cannot realistically or reasonably be planned for or foreseen and therefore avoided. All war involves the "fog of war," and the fog of war can never be totally overcome. Chance and folly play major roles in any military operation. But military competence is a result of avoiding the avoidable; planning for reasonable contingencies and being able to produce and execute plans that have a reasonable chance of success; and exercising control over events rather than being buffeted about by them. In short, military competence means the application of prudential judgments which minimize foreseeable risks, thereby increasing the probabilities of success.

There appear to be a number of institutional conditions engendered by the American military structure itself which increase the probability of military incompetence. How the impact of any one of these conditions will affect any particular mission cannot, of course, be determined in advance. What can be said is that these conditions certainly increase the probability of military failure and incompetence. Military decision-making is, of course, never flawless. Victory and success go not always to the brilliant but to those who make the fewest mistakes. My contention is that certain institutional practices of the U.S. military increase the probability of failure: planners will make more mistakes than could reasonably be expected under normal conditions.

THE OFFICER CORPS

The responsibility for military planning, direction, and execution falls most heavily on the officer corps. What is it about the American officer corps that seems to produce officers who fail to succeed on the battlefield? It should be pointed out that the problems which characterize the officer corps today were first manifest

in Vietnam. They had devastating effects on the ability of U.S. forces in the field to conduct battlefield operations, and they continue to have great impact on operations as the record of military operations since 1970 seems clearly to indicate. Worse, it is likely that without serious reform, these shortcomings will lead to future military failures.

The officer corps is critical to combat operations. It is the institutional memory of an army, the living repository of its history, its experiences, and, above all, its lessons. It is the officer corps that reflects the values and characteristics of the military. If the corps is corrupt or incompetent, the whole army will be also. If the corps is of high quality, then it is possible to forge a good army. The officer has three chief obligations: to be technically competent, to be an example to his men and his junior officers, and to provide solid judgment. Without role models, effective combat units cannot be built. Without an officer corps that sets the example for behavior in battle, an adequate corps cannot be developed, since there is no clear line stretching from the past through the existing corps to the corps that must meet the future. An officer corps that is incapable of good battlefield judgment will be unable to avoid defeat.

SIZE OF THE OFFICER CORPS

One major problem of the American military officer corps is that it is too large. The ratio of an officer corps to its men is historically associated with its ability to perform well. There may even be an optimum size. Experience suggests that a corps that ranges between 3 and 6 percent of total strength is the most effective in battle. Historical examples abound and include the Roman Army, the Waffen SS, the German Army in both world wars, the British Army, the French Army in Indochina, and the present-day Israeli Army. American Marine units fought better than Army units in Vietnam in part because the Marine officer strength never exceeded 6.4 percent of total strength, whereas Army officer strength exceeded 15 percent.[1]

The reason that size is important is not difficult to discern. To

limit the size—ratio—of the officer corps is a recognition that leadership is a relatively rare quality. When rigorous intellectual and physical standards of leadership are set, only a few can meet them. Historically, successful armies have tended to employ only qualified officers rather than to lower standards. American policy, both in Vietnam and since, has been marked by exactly the opposite policy; standards have deteriorated because there is an inflated officer pool, inflated staffs, and excessive school assignments.

The size of an officer corps contributes to good leadership and planning in another sense. A small corps is likely to develop a professional brotherhood—a sense of camaraderie and cohesion. A sense of profession, besides creating esprit, establishes within the corps an information network through which one can learn of an officer's reputation and abilities. In such a network, bureaucratic incompetence cannot be easily hidden. Members of a small corps, as in the Israeli Army, are likely to know one another and make it easier to develop mutual trust.

Small size also encourages officers to assume responsibility. Larger corps diffuse authority and thus diminish responsibility. It is interesting that despite the fact that the U.S. military has conducted five major military operations since Vietnam, all of which were failures, not a single officer has ever been removed from his command or position as a consequence of these failures. The ability to avoid individual responsibility and to blame "the system" is a major shortcoming of a large officer corps.

If the size of an officer corps is an indication that we produce officers who are not good planners and combat leaders, then the American military seems to be in great difficulty. During the Vietnam war, officer strength comprised about 17.5 percent of total strength.[2] Since Vietnam, the percentage of officers has fallen to 11 percent (84,447 officers) of total force strength. Curiously, however, as the number of officers relative to enlisted strength has declined since the war in Vietnam, the ratio of general officers to troop strength has increased by 31 percent. The Army has more general officers relative to the number of troops it can put in the field than it did during Vietnam. And the same is true of the Navy and the Air Force as well. Today, Army troop strength is less than

half of what it was during Vietnam. Although the number of officers has declined, the percentage of officer strength is still far too large and maldistributed by rank. Historically, in effective combat armies, the percentage of officers to men almost never exceeds 5 percent.[3] By this standard, the American officer corps is twice as large as it has to be in the Army, and at least a third as large in the Navy and the Air Force. During Vietnam, the Army fielded one officer for every 8.5 soldiers, a ratio that was far too high and even exceeded the high World War II ratio of one officer for every 9.4 soldiers. Today that ratio is even more disproportionate, with the Army fielding one officer for every 6.8 soldiers.

The American officer corps is an association of strangers in which officers, even at the top, rarely know one another well. Its primary virtue seems to be that its size increases the possibilities for promotion when things go right and reduces the probability that anyone will be held directly responsible when things go wrong.

TURBULENCE

Historically, there is one thing worse than a large officer corps for engendering incompetence, and that is an officer corps in a state of perpetual motion. Stability of assignments is important to combat effectiveness. The period of assignment for officers has ranged, historically, from the extremes of the Roman Army (twenty years) to the modern Canadian and British Armies (five years). The greater the stability of officers in command and staff positions, the greater the likelihood that they will develop a close knowledge of their men and their units' abilities. When officers remain with their units for long periods, they can develop, learn from their mistakes, and grow in competence. But when an officer has only eighteen months with his unit, a common occurrence in the American military, every decision and mistake becomes crucial to his promotion and his career. These conditions are intensified by an evaluation system which requires officers to be almost perfect, on paper at least, to qualify for the next promotion or assignment. Thus, officers

rarely learn from their mistakes. Few dare to admit that they made any, for fear of being passed over for promotion.

Officer-corps stability is also important to the development of unit cohesion, without which combat effectiveness and military competence simply cannot exist. The bonding of men in battle can occur only when subordinates see their officers as competent, trustworthy, and dependable leaders. These perceptions and attachments require long tours of duty with the same unit. The American officer corps is afflicted by excessive personnel turnover—turbulence. In 1980, 81 percent of the Army's officer and enlisted personnel changed assignments. A 1975 study of the 2nd Armored Division in Europe found that, in a seven-month period, the turnover rates were 119 percent for platoon leaders, 113 percent for company commanders, and 98 percent for platoon sergeants. In the same division, among the staff for the S-3 section, the crucial operational planners for the division, turnover ranged from 177 percent to 217 percent for senior staff officers and noncommissioned officers. The assignment turnover rate for the entire division in all ranks ranged from a low of 177 percent to a high of 388 percent.[4]

Things have not changed very much. A report on combat readiness produced by the House Armed Services Committee of the U.S. Congress in 1985 emphasizes the problem of increased assignment rotation in all military services as contributing greatly to a decline in combat readiness. It would appear, from a detailed review of the committee report, that the single most important factor, next to the lack of equipment and training time, in reducing readiness is the turnover in assignments of the officer corps. The high rate of turnover of officers makes it impossible to develop long-term strategies and, more importantly, to hold anyone responsible. The high rates of turbulence are evident not only in the officer corps but in the enlisted ranks as well. According to the House report on DOD appropriations,[5] the average turnover rates in individual units range from 14 percent per month to 25 percent per month, and in some units it is almost a hundred percent a year. This situation refers only to external turbulence—that is to say, to turnover of officers and men who rotate in and out of their

units—and does not take into consideration additional internal turbulence, the movement of men within their units. As a consequence, for all practical purposes, most American units turn over
almost once every three months.

Not surprisingly, it is difficult to develop any sense of confidence, competence, or cohesion in such units. They are comprised
of and led by men who are strangers to one another. The 1980
Army Training Study made the simple but important point that
any unit which manifested a rate of assignment turbulence of 25
percent per quarter was simply impossible to train to an adequate
level of combat effectiveness.[6] This rate, regarded by the military
as an extreme, seems to be typical of American units today, since
it reflects the rate of turbulence in the officer corps and among the
enlisted ranks as well.

The turnover of general officers is equally rapid. From 1960
through 1980, the average length of time on station for a four-star
general in the Army was only twenty months. For a three-star
general, it was twenty-one months, and declining rapidly to nineteen months. For most lower-ranking general officers, the average
assignment was less than twenty-four months.[7] Even at the highest
staff level, the rotation in assignments was excessive. Over the
same twenty-year period, Lewis Sorely analyzed positions at the
highest level of the Army General Staff. He found that the average
time all these officers were stationed together so that they could
function as a complete staff unit was only 4.8 months.[8] Although
this figure is up somewhat from the 3.8-month average found during
the Vietnam war, turnover was still excessive. The comparable
figure for the Soviet General Staff during the same twenty-year
period was fourteen years! Thus, even the major planning mechanism at the highest level of the Army is in a state of continual
turbulence, a fact which has led Paul Savage to conclude, in his
article on the Joint Chiefs of Staff, that it is simply unfit and un-
structured either to plan or to command major military operations.[9]
At least three of the major military operations which failed between
1970 and 1983 were planned within the office of the Joint Chiefs
of Staff.

The severe turnover is the logical consequence of other in-

stitutional practices which require that the officer corps change assignments frequently in order to prosper within the military's increasingly bureaucratic environment. One major cause is that the military has too many officers to begin with, and far too many field-grade and general officers. The increased number of staff officers, coupled with the unrealistically short twenty-year-retirement system, compels young officers to move through at least seventeen different assignments in order to qualify for promotion to general officer. The military does not allow captains, majors, and lieutenant colonels to serve long periods in their posts without having to compete for promotion and new assignments. This up-or-out policy forces an officer to pass through a number of gates or to punch "tickets" in order to continue to be promoted, and even to qualify for retirement benefits. An officer cannot remain on a specific assignment for a long time as his Canadian, British, French, German, Israeli, and even Soviet counterparts do, so he can stay on to perform effectively in that assignment. The emphasis is on numerous different assignments rather than long-term service in one or two fields of expertise. Command positions, so necessary to success, are far fewer in number than there are officers, and so, to ensure that each officer gets an opportunity to command, assignments are reduced to the shortest possible duration, frequently less than twenty-four months. The tremendous competition for these assignments adds to instability of the corps and increases the isolation of officers from one another, since they are continually forced to compete with each other.

This chronic instability at all levels of the officer corps, most particularly at the higher levels, has made it almost impossible for American military forces to develop a general-staff system. The system should be built around a corps of permanently assigned officers who have great expertise in their own fields. This corps should be selected from young officers, usually captains, and should have to endure slow promotions. In other armies, general-staff officers tend to be the best and the brightest members of the corps, and their value rests in providing a cohesive group of trained experts permanently in place. That allows experience and expertise to be brought to bear on the planning and execution of military

operations. They become the "nervous system and brain" of the military structure, a repository of the lessons and traditions of military service and history, as well as the locus of experience and expertise. Although the French, German, Israeli, Canadian, British, and Soviet Armies all have a general-staff system, the American military does not. As a consequence, the American military structure lacks a stable central nervous system which can continue to send orders and ideas to the fighting arms of the service.

Unfortunately, since we have no general-staff system, the American military has no institutional memory. There is no place where the lessons of past wars are brought together and analyzed for dissemination throughout the corps. Although one would think that some institutional mechanism to do this would be evident within the office of the Joint Chiefs of Staff, in fact it is not. Further, the education of officers is such that they do not, as a rule, study the failures of their own history, especially if those failures tend to be recent. Consequently, there seems to be a marked tendency for military commanders who plan and execute military operations to repeat the mistakes of the past. As one wag remarked with regard to this tendency in Vietnam, "We were not in Vietnam for ten years; we were there for one year ten times." It has been said that the corrupt Bourbon monarchy remembered everything and learned nothing. The same is true of the American military high command.

OFFICERS AS ENTREPRENEURS

Excessive rotation also produces an entrepreneurial officer corps. Competition and careerism make every officer look out for himself. Such a system engenders values corrosive of any concept of the military as a special calling requiring special service and sacrifice. It encourages attitudes and values in which one's men are seen as instrumentalities of advancement, and thus erodes any sense of special moral or ethical obligations. There is no place left for the competent officer who wishes to have a career in a given

field of expertise and who is willing to forgo promotion and rotational assignment. Linking retention to promotion, instead of linking retention to competence and experience, is a serious flaw in the system.

Military experts have been replaced by managerial technocrats who have little interest or feel for the human dimension of war. In fact, as Jeff Record has pointed out, the few surviving combat leaders remain because they were also able to master management skills so demanded by a bureaucratic system.[10] One general officer (Yasotay) has gone so far as to suggest that "ours is an army of clerks, not fighters, and they are running the show."[11] This general officer, still on active duty but writing under a pseudonym, makes the point that personnel managers are actually in charge of the system and they have redesigned the system of military promotion and rewards to reward managerial bureaucrats while penalizing the warriors. He notes that the Officer Personnel Management System (OPMS) was created by administrative non-warriors for managers, at the expense of combat leaders, who ran the military during its more successful days. He goes on to charge that the Army promotion boards in 1983 were chaired and controlled mostly by officers who were not front-line soldiers but who served in combat support or administrative positions for most of their careers.[12] Paradoxically, the OPMS system was designed in the mid-seventies as a reform, to give the non-warrior an equal chance to remain in the Army and to prosper. The system, it seems, has been stood on its head. As a consequence, the officer who succeeds within the military bureaucracy is more often not a trained combat leader who has studied and practiced the arts of war but more likely an experienced bureaucratic infighter who has studied the art of management and knows how to survive in a bureaucratic system that rewards non-inventiveness, compliance, a willingness to follow rules without question, and an ability to protect bureaucratic turf and, above all, not to rock the boat. These are not the qualities of successful combat leaders or the qualities of successful military planners. A large number of American officers, especially at the highest ranks, are more fit for the boardroom than for combat command.

AMATEURISM

An additional problem is that many American officers are amateurs. Only a few have managed to make use of their combat experiences while at the same time acquiring the skills necessary to survive the bureaucracy. Amateurism is, of course, directly associated with rotational turbulence. Officers who move frequently are just about reaching a level of expertise where they can stop learning their job and carry out their tasks effectively when it is time to move to another assignment. Moreover, the need to spread oneself thinly throughout a wide range of different assignments and skills of short duration inevitably affects the quality of experience that the officer takes with him from one assignment to another. The recent reform to create a staff school for junior officers (called CASS CUBE) is ready admission that the military does not expect to keep junior staff officers in their positions long enough to learn the job. The theory is that officers will hit the ground already trained in staff skills, even if it means sending them to staff schools at the expense of reducing the time available to train them in combat skills. The fact is that many American military officers, especially at the higher levels of command and staff, are simply not expert in the military arts. Most high-level officers have not had troop command for many years and have spent a good part of their careers within the confines of staff assignments or at the "puzzle palace," the Pentagon. It is interesting that most of the higher-level command and staff schools throughout the services have courses on how to respond to congressional requests for information and how to testify before a committee hearing. In short, the frequent turnover of officers through a multiplicity of assignments, most of them not associated with the attainment of military war skills, almost guarantees that any given officer in place at any level of the military at any given time, but most particularly at the highest planning levels, will likely be an amateur in the sense that he is still learning his job rather than being able to carry out his responsibilities on the basis of experience.

BUREAUCRACY

The problem of bureaucracy interfering with military planning has reached outrageous proportions within the American military. And, indeed, it is a problem that begins at the top, with the Joint Chiefs of Staff. It is difficult to imagine a military organization and staff which cannot effectively and continuously control resources, implement war plans, allocate funds, direct operations, or enforce its discipline over operational commanders. Neither can the JCS control the direction, quantity, or quality of weapons and material available to the fighting forces. The JCS is prohibited from all of this by law. While the law can be circumvented, as it often is by Department of Defense directives or by order of the President, the authority granted is often both temporary and tenuous. The JCS is but one of a number of planning staffs that compete for a share of the defense budget and for influence at the highest levels. These other staffs, including the office of the Secretary of Defense, the Departments of the Army, Navy, and Air Force, the National Command Authority, etc., are often very large and very powerful. While there are 1,082 officers in or directly supporting the JCS the office of the Secretary of Defense has 1,120, including nineteen general officers. There is presently a ratio of one general officer to every 1,735 enlisted men. In short, the JCS, as the highest planning agency in the American military, is a bloated and overburdened bureaucracy.

The consequence is that the number of staffs, study groups, and sub-group interests proliferate greatly, as do committees and sub-committees, with the result that decisions eventually reached by the JCS represent the least common denominator among competing bureaucracies. Such decisions tend to reflect two common pathologies: first, group think, the tendency to go along with plans and policies even when expertise and experience suggest that the plans may be in error or the policies flawed; and second, component thinking, a tendency to plan operations piece by piece, with little consideration to whether the pieces can be integrated into an operational whole. The results are often failure. Today the staff organization of the U.S. military forces is superburdened by large

16

numbers of officers, powerful sub-staff elements, and, of course, paper flow. The execution system is characterized by commanders who often neither trust their subordinates nor are trusted by them. Officers in high-level staff positions clearly understand that a single mistake may be the kiss of death to their careers, and, as a consequence, tend to develop a propensity to act like bureaucrats rather than military leaders.

Historically, a military staff is a collective intellect for the military services that assists and advises the commander in the accomplishment of missions assigned to him or his forces. Generally, there are four dimensions to staff work: operations, logistics, personnel, and intelligence. These dimensions are designed to do two things. The first is to prepare for war; that is, to see to it that the forces are in the highest state of preparedness permitted by the resources available. The second is to assist the commander in war in such a way that the overall strategic and tactical interests of the nation and the fighting units are preserved and that operational plans are realistic and achievable. Both the commander and the staff operate according to two central ethical imperatives: anything that contributes to combat readiness is good, and anything that detracts from it is bad. A commander and staff who are not permitted to act by these rules for reasons of self-interest, organizational maldesign, political obstruction, external corruption, or even conditions beyond their control will inevitably find themselves producing military plans which simply do not succeed.

The Joint Chiefs of Staff, the highest planning agency of the American military, is a historical curiosity in that it fulfills few of the conditions for rational and effective staff work. In the first instance, the JCS has no operational authority at all. In creating the JCS, the Congress authorized its existence but limited its authority and power to planning and coordination and, above all, transmitting the military orders of the commander-in-chief to subordinate commands. It is denied any operational role at all. Thus, the JCS was not and is not in the chain of command and, since 1953, can act only when authorized to do so under signature of the Secretary of Defense. This leads to a number of serious and difficult problems. Since the chain of command for operations runs from

the President to the Secretary of Defense to the five unified commands and the three specified commands, the JCS cannot originate orders. It can only transmit orders given by its superiors, and even then, not always. Moreover, in the absence of a single national strategic plan as there is supposed to be, the JCS can scarcely plan with much effect in any case. There is a National Command Authority centered in the President, who surrounds himself with individuals who are personally loyal to him regardless of their professional role—most of whom are not military men at all. Since cronyism is inevitable in such circumstances, coupled with the fact that few civilian authorities around the President last a full term of office, the National Defense Authority itself is characterized by the same amateurism in military matters that is found at the top of the military bureaucracy itself. Worse, it is an amateurism far more sensitive to political considerations than to military ones. Thus, for example, the average term of a Secretary of Defense between 1960 and 1980 was only 2.3 years, while the average term of the military staff officer in the JCS was between twelve and fifteen months. There seems to be an evident failure to evolve a coherent national planning mechanism for directing military operations within the larger requirement of civilian control. Paradoxically, none of this has stopped civilian leaders from placing operational responsibility for planning and execution of military operations on the JCS when they have felt it politically expedient to do so. Note, for example, that it was the JCS, under General John Vessey, which planned and executed the Grenada operation.

The members of the JCS face a dilemma. Reaching their present positions depended heavily on their ability to work successfully within their individual services. Support of his subordinate commanders, who, after all, control the operational resources, is directly proportional to the degree to which the individual member of the JCS is prepared to support his subordinate interests in interservice rivalries. While the JCS service chiefs are individually influential within their own services, they are often forced to choose between conflicting interests: the classic interservice rivalry and the interests of overall force planning to meet the military needs of the nation. If they act responsibly, they must almost always go

against the short-range, pressing interests of their respective services. And yet, if they do this, they will lose the support of their constituencies. If, on the other hand, they act primarily in the interests of their respective services, they will almost surely sacrifice the interests of the nation. The fact is that since every member of the JCS must wear "two hats," as a member of the JCS and as chief of his own career service, there is an almost inevitable conflict of interest.

When these bureaucratic interests clash with the requirements of balanced long-range operational planning, it seems inevitably that the interests of the individual service take precedence. One consequence is a military structure that is often burdened with personnel and training programs and weapons systems that do not work and, devastatingly, often work at cross-purposes to the development of a cohesive, well-led, and competent military force capable of successfully executing military operations. It takes little imagination to suggest that a great deal of the responsibility for failure on the battlefield rests at the top.

If one requires more evidence regarding the inability of the JCS to plan and execute successful military operations, one need only consider the fact that of the five military operations carried out since 1970, all of which failed or were marked by extraordinary shortcomings, three—the Sontay raid, the Iranian debacle, and the Grenada invasion—were planned and coordinated within the JCS. It is perhaps also worth noting that in at least two of these operations, the Sontay raid and the Iran mission, the JCS itself found the planning so uncoordinated and ineffective that it created ad hoc planning agencies within the JCS to plan and execute these missions, a move which, ironically, contributed to the failure of the missions.

If the JCS is neither empowered to act nor responsible for failures, then they are quite useless as a planning group. If they are responsible, they should have been punished. Failure at the highest levels to be ready for war is perhaps the greatest military sin: deliberate failure to plan for realistic contingencies; in short, negligence. While the members of the JCS collectively are not responsible for force development, they are responsible as the

heads of their respective services. If there is a failure in readiness and military competence, the Chiefs have at least a moral responsibility to disclose this condition and make a protest. The same obligation exists for the Chiefs in their capacity as heads of their career services.

As one respected analyst has noted: "If the function of the JCS is in some measure to sort all this out and to introduce rational planning, procurement, reliable combat equipment, and adequate levels of military readiness, then they have clearly failed. If, on the other hand, they are unaware of the state of affairs, then they have not done what is expected of them. If, on the third, they are aware and have neither protested nor moved to correct it, then they have failed in their duty."[13] These conditions seem evident in the operations of the JCS as a planning and execution group. The corollary of these circumstances, of course, is that the military operations the JCS plans or oversees generally fail.

The tendency to sacrifice operational requirements to bureaucratic interests and consensus has been evident in every one of the five military operations conducted by the United States since 1970. As we will see, each operation shows how the need to reconcile conflicting bureaucratic pressures within the planning structure dictated operational considerations. The Iran raid is a case in point.

This propensity to compromise operational standards for bureaucratic considerations leads to another major difficulty: group think. Group think may be defined as a condition in which the major assumptions of an operational plan go unexamined by the planners in order to protect the bureaucratic consensus. In the Iranian raid, once the decision was made to use Marine pilots (to satisfy the Marine Corps demands for a role in the mission), that decision was no longer subject to scrutiny or question. This remained so even though in the six months of planning prior to the raid, the Marine pilots never successfully mastered the technical skills required to put the plan into effect. From one point of view, there are great virtues in group think and in sustaining the bureaucratic consensus. If things go wrong, the entire planning staff has a vested interest in defending each component. This, in

turn, minimizes responsibility, or deflects it altogether, reducing the probability that any individual or component will be penalized for failure to execute the plan successfully.

Another characteristic of the military planning process since 1960 is a tendency, once a consensus has been reached, to plan the details in a component fashion. Allowing each component commander to develop his own operational prerogatives in executing the mission gives the higher planning authorities an excuse to avoid responsibility if things go wrong: the plan was sound, but the combat force failed to perform adequately.

These conditions can be readily and accurately characterized as military incompetence. The process itself seems to contain very basic institutional pathologies which produce something akin to a civilian bureaucracy rather than a military force capable of conducting operations that have a success rate at least greater than 75 percent. By even this modest standard, the historical record of U.S. military operations over the last fifteen years has been miserable.

COMBAT READINESS

The poor quality of senior military leadership and, indeed, the generally poor quality of leadership at the lower levels is recognized by soldiers in the ranks. One of the remarkable findings of the Vietnam years was that the incompetence of the officer corps was readily perceived by the common soldier. In the U.S. Army alone, over one thousand officers and NCOs were killed or wounded by their own men.[14] In peacetime, of course, things rarely go so far. Nonetheless, the perception of the soldiers that their officers are not of good quality remains evident in the Army and, one suspects, in the other services as well. In a study conducted annually since 1974, the data show that Army officers are perceived by their men in a rather poor light. Since 1974, the overall perceived quality of officers by their men has declined. In 1974, 58 percent of the soldiers interviewed believed that their officers were competent; ten years later, that number had fallen to 48 percent.

In that decade, despite some significant attempts by the military at reform, the soldier's perceptions of officer leadership declined. Moreover, the quality of junior NCOs continues to be the major problem it was in the mid-seventies: 55 percent of the soldiers feel that their NCOs are competent while 45 percent think they are not. While the trend has remained relatively stable over the years, the number of soldiers who lack confidence in their officers and NCOs is, in absolute terms, very high, compared to other Western armies.

Among the officers interviewed in the survey, 77 percent felt that the quality of junior NCOs is a major problem, and most strikingly, it is among unit commanders that the perceptions of low-quality NCOs seem to be most severe. Equally important is the soldier's impression that his officers do not truly care for him. About 42 percent believe that the officers truly care for their men, a general decline since 1974, when 58 percent felt that the officers cared for their men. In addition, only 50 percent of the soldiers think their NCOs care for them, about the same number as a decade ago, but in absolute numbers still very low.[15] The soldiers' perceptions that the officers are of poor quality stand in sharp contrast to the perceptions of the officers themselves, who, in general, believe they are doing an adequate job of establishing a bond with their men. Perhaps what counts most in terms of fighting ability is the perception of the soldiers. As the Army report noted: "Recent Israeli research on cohesion indicates that the most critical factor influencing unit morale is leadership competence. But, correspondingly, it appears that because a soldier's perceptions of leadership competence are declining, so too are perceptions of unit morale and esprit, namely cause and effect. . . . Nonetheless, the level of a soldier's performance is largely determined by these perceptions."[16] In short, the Army seems to admit that its studies of morale and leadership have reached the same conclusion for a decade: soldiers do not hold their leaders, officers or NCOs, in particularly high regard.

Morale and esprit de corps is relatively low. Only 28 percent of the soldiers felt that the morale in their units was high, while 31 percent said that they were proud to be members of their units.

Both indicators are down by almost ten points from 1974. Equally startling, only 62 percent of the soldiers believe that their units would be ready to go to war within a week, about the same level as a decade ago, but still very low. Only 43 percent of the soldiers think that their units would do well in combat, a decline of more than fifteen points from the 58 percent who thought similarly a decade ago.[17]

While the American military seems to be meeting its manpower goals for the first time since the All-Volunteer Force was created in 1973, the fact is that, due to the bureaucracy, the military force still remains short of trained combat soldiers. Weapons crews are often understrength; in many cases, crew-served weapons go completely unmanned, although they may appear on official reports as fully manned. There are also critical shortages in combat-support units and technical military operational specialties. The result, according to the House of Representatives Committee on Military Appropriations, is that "there are weapons unmanned, squads unfilled and maintenance unperformed and a general inability to accomplish training objectives."[18] Paradoxically, while many infantry squads and platoons are at zero strength or understrength, the Army actually has an overage of 7,700 trained infantry combat soldiers! Why are these soldiers not in the positions for which they were trained? The answer seems to be that the military gives priority to staff assignments. When a choice has to be made, the administrative position is filled first. Moreover, there is a tendency to put a soldier trained in combat skills into an administrative position for which he is completely untrained. This happens most frequently with NCOs. It is standard military practice. In 1984, for example, the headquarters company of most division staffs was overstrength, while some of the fighting units did not have enough people to fill the war requirements. The headquarters company of the 2nd Infantry Division in 1984 was 104 percent overstrength, while the 82nd Airborne Division was 221 percent over its authorized staff strength. The 1st Armored Division was 147 percent overstrength in staff, while the 25th Infantry Division was 181 percent overstrength.[19] Moreover, many of these posts were filled by NCOs, which further exacerbated the shortage of NCOs in

combat units. In the words of the House Committee: "The army has not placed enough soldiers in tanks, squads, and maintenance shops, where they belong."[20]

The NCO corps is also encountering problems. There is a critical shortage of small-unit combat leaders within the NCO corps; the combat army is short of the trainers of new soldiers. As the old saw has it, the NCO corps is the "spine" of the Army. The Army's own public reports note that the Army has about 96 percent of all the NCOs it needs. But within combat units, the Army has only 89 percent of the NCOs necessary to go to war. The Committee on Military Appropriations uncovered the fact that, among the services, the Army has only 80.4 percent of what it says it needs to meet its combat requirements.[21] While somewhat better than a few years ago, the NCO shortage is still present. One result of this shortage is that troop training and equipment maintenance are below standard. There are simply not enough trained NCOs to go around, to supervise and train soldiers in critical specialties. Worse, the shortages and poor quality are greatest in the combat units.

In one division which the House Committee did not identify, in 1984 out of 231 tank crews and 184 artillery firing crews, only twenty were together long enough to participate in two consecutive field training exercises.[21] The military solution to the problem is administratively to define it out of existence. Thus, the Army has invented "battle rostering," an administrative redefinition of the number of men required to operate a tank or man artillery. A tank crew in battle, for example, requires four men. By battle rostering, the military simply redefines the number of men to two who are "actually essential": the tank commander and the gunner; if it becomes necessary to fight, the Army can only hope that a loader and a driver can be found somewhere. In reality, of course, the shortages exist. In one battalion in 1984, out of fifty-four tanks, the commander could only field fourteen with full crews, although under battle rostering the battalion can be reported to be at full strength.[22] A large number of tank and artillery crews (and crew-served weapons systems) will simply be unable to fight.

Equipment shortages continue to plague the military. Our NATO forces are short the following equipment: cargo tracked

vehicles to equip ten field-artillery battalions; ammunition trailers to support sixty-four field-artillery battalions; five-ton trucks to comprise forty truck companies; armored personnel to field thirty mechanized infantry battalions; tanks for two tank battalions; missiles for twenty-two mechanized infantry battalions; and electrical equipment to staff fourteen maintenance battalions.[23] Forces committed to NATO alone are short ground aircraft support for 293 aviation battalions. And these shortages reflect the needs of only one of the Army's present missions. The sad truth is that some units do not have enough rifles or small-arms ammunition, TOW anti-tank missiles, or anti-tank shells to perform even half their mission requirements. In addition, about 60 percent of the Army's combat support forces are in reserve, and they have only 74 percent of the equipment they need to fulfill their mission.[24] Much of the existing equipment is old and unsupportable, because there are no spare parts to keep it functioning.

In order to deal with the problem of spare parts, the military resorts to the same type of administrative sleight of hand that it uses to conceal personnel shortages. The military has adopted the administrative practice of "exemptions" and "in lieu of" items, to account for equipment which it simply does not have. For example, if a unit is supposed to have a specific number of tanks and does not have them, trucks are counted as "in lieu of" items. The result is an administrative nightmare: "The Army has lost control of its equipment inventories."[25] As the House Committee on Military Appropriations found out to its horror, the Army's logistical commanders have no idea how much equipment they have on hand or even where it is located. Nor can they provide a complete inventory of either their stocks or their battle needs. One of the paradoxes is that equipment shortages not only affect old items but tend to be most severe with regard to new items. Thus, while the old M-60 tank is continually short of spare parts, the fact is that the newly deployed M-1 tank suffers from far worse parts shortages. Most of the money allocated goes to pay for the tank, with the expectation that the money for spare parts will be appropriated in future budgets. Therefore, for a period of five years, new combat weapons systems often are deployed without adequate spare parts.

Much of the inability to maintain a proper inventory is due to inadequately trained personnel, especially NCOs. It is also due to the poor quality of the soldiers being graduated from military technical schools. Moreover, the military's penchant for purchasing equipment that is unnecessarily complex means that much of its equipment is subject to breakdown.

Many of the electronic components of weapons systems such as the TOW anti-tank missile fail to work at least 30 percent of the time. Indeed, some of the equipment seems never to work at all under actual field conditions. In 1981, for example, the Cobra helicopter gunship was short of ten critical maintenance items needed to keep it combat-ready. Two years later, that list had grown to twenty-five.[26] As one critic noted, this condition turned one of the more effective field weapons into a very expensive observation platform!

War stocks needed to supply and support just the forces committed to NATO are less than half of what the wartime requirements are projected to be by the Army itself. In addition, the Pentagon admits that "there are not enough war reserve stocks to sustain currently planned combat operations."[27] In short, the equipment problems of the American Army border on the disastrous. If the Army is forced to battle, it will most likely be unable to sustain itself as a combat force of any size for very long, perhaps only ten days.

The quality of Army training is low and considerably below that of our NATO allies. Training suffers as a consequence of reductions in funds, turbulence, and the lack of good officers and NCOs. These conditions are often compounded by equipment shortages. As more and more of the defense budget goes toward purchasing new equipment, less and less goes into funds for training. The 1984 budget showed a 6 percent reduction in operations and maintenance funds, funds used for training and maintaining the force, while the drop in O&M funds for the reserve was 5 percent. In short, the Army is training less and less as the defense budgets get larger and larger.

As a result, there is a lack of basic "go to war skills," to use the argot of the Pentagon. At the National Training Center, for

example, after-action briefings continually stress that the commanders of units make the same mistakes over and over. The 10th Special Forces Group has considerable difficulty in training its troops to read tactical maps, to say nothing of following them in nighttime. Some units, such as the TOW anti-tank missile crews, only fire one round a year (when they get to fire any at all), because of the expense of each round. The rifle qualification training of the soldier on his basic infantry weapon has been reduced to about forty rounds a year, down from four hundred rounds only five years ago, when even four hundred rounds was considered insufficient. The Army, in the words of the House Committee on Military Appropriations, "is simply inadequate to perform its required combat mission."[28]

THE AIR FORCE

If conditions in the Army are less than desirable, they are no less so in the other military services. The Air Force has severe problems in training and readiness as well, according to the House Committee on Military Appropriations. The Air Force in 1985 has about 7,200 aircraft in its inventory, which include 900 long-range bombers and tankers, 3,000 combat tactical aircraft, 1,660 training aircraft, 830 transport aircraft, 400 reconnaissance aircraft, and 500 support planes, including helicopters.[29] This is a large amount of equipment to sustain at military readiness, and, not surprisingly, the Air Force has failed to sustain it. There are so many aircraft that there are not enough forward area bases to deploy them. In Western Europe, the number of bases is insufficient to handle the number of combat aircraft that are expected to deploy to them in the event of a crisis with the Soviets. Those bases that do exist are insufficiently equipped with fuel, ammunition, repair facilities, control towers, etc., to keep any additional aircraft in action. Even the Air Force admits that aircraft deployed to the European theater can't be maintained on the ground or in the air. Indeed, it notes that many of the deployed aircraft will become tempting, unprotected targets for the enemy.[30] In a paradox of the first order, the

Air Force finds itself in the position of actually reducing the combat power of the forces in Europe by deploying more aircraft to support it!

The manpower structure of the Air Force, like the Army's, presents a number of serious problems. There is a serious shortage of mid- and senior-level personnel, especially NCOs. This shortage is made up by an overabundance of junior-grade personnel, who lack both the experience and the training to keep sophisticated aircraft systems combat-ready. On some complex weapons systems, over 90 percent of the people maintaining them are either untrained or have insufficient experience. Service-wide, more than 84 percent of all maintenance personnel have less than three years' experience on the systems they must keep flying.[31] It is not surprising, then, that the Air Force suffers from a high rate of aircraft breakdown and unreadiness.

Added to a lack of trained personnel is the fact that spare parts needed to keep the aircraft combat-ready are often unavailable. Some aircraft parts are so scarce that there is a constant cannibalization of war reserve stocks in order to keep aircraft flying. The Air Force's war reserve stocks in 1984 were about 65 percent of the capacity required to perform its mission in a shooting war.[32] Cannibalization is so normal that additional aircraft are routinely assigned to bases to be used for spare parts. These "hangar queens" are often counted as combat-ready, thus giving the Air Force—and the rest of us—an inflated concept of the number of aircraft that it can use in wartime. The logistical system is so confused and inefficient, and delays from production to deployment so long, that six spare engines are needed within the logistical pipeline in order to ensure that one engine is available to combat units only 80 percent of the time.[33] Our ability to sustain aircraft at a reasonable level in time of war is marginal at best.

If the Air Force would have difficulty sustaining its aircraft in wartime, it already has great difficulty sustaining them in peacetime. The fact is that the flying hours budgeted in 1984 amount to only about 65 percent of what is really needed to meet mission requirements.[34] Many Air Force pilots cannot get sufficient flying time because their machines are not fit to fly, due to mechanical

breakdown. And the Air Force lacks adequate personnel to perform maintenance functions. Like the Navy, it has had to employ civilian specialists, who have become a permanent fixture on American bases. The Air Force has become almost totally dependent on these civilians. In the event of war, however, these civilian technicians are under no obligation to deploy to the battle area to keep the aircraft flying. The Air Force confronts an interesting paradox: as long as there is peace, it can rely heavily on civilian technicians to keep its aircraft flying at least 65 percent of the time. But in the event of war, this ability will decrease so that combat-ready aircraft will decline perhaps to 20 percent.

If spare parts are a problem, so is the shortage of munitions that are supposed to make American aircraft among the deadliest in the world. Air Force munition shortages, as noted by Congress, include shortages of air-to-air missiles, air-to-ground missiles, conversion kits, ammunition, storage and assembly points, and even loading equipment. There are extreme shortages in chaff* and flares, two systems absolutely vital to deceiving attacking enemy aircraft.[35] In addition, the reliability of many of these munitions is in grave doubt. A recent Government Accounting Office (GAO) report found that 35 percent of the Sidewinder missiles and 25 percent of the Sparrow missiles do not work.[36] Moreover, the Air Force has limited ability even to determine the weather conditions over a battle area. In fact, this ability is close to non-existent. The ability to observe, collect, and process "real time" weather information over target areas is seriously deficient, even when the target areas are under friendly control.

Finally, any plan for fighting in Europe requires that the Air Force play a key role in airlifting reserves to the battlefront within ten days of the outbreak of hostilities. The inability to provide and sustain sufficient airlift will guarantee the defeat of U.S. forces. Airlift capability is absolutely vital to any realistic wartime scenario. And the Air Force does not have enough workable aircraft to perform the airlift mission. The shortage of deployable planes is due

---

* Aluminum strips deployed over the fleet to confuse the tracking radars of enemy planes and missiles.

largely to lack of logistical support, as well as to the limits placed on the performance of the aircraft themselves. Some of these restrictions have been imposed by the Air Force itself in recognition of the fact that some of their larger transports cannot perform in practice what they were supposed to when originally ordered. The defective wing roots of the C-5A,* which make it impossible to fly with a full load, are but one example. In the event of conflict in Europe, it is highly unlikely that U.S. forces will be able to reinforce with more than two divisions; much vital equipment will simply have to be left behind. Throughout the 1970s and early 1980s, no fewer than three major exercises designed to test the ability of the "aluminum bridge" (airlift capability) to perform up to requirements proved that airlift was not sufficient to meet mission requirements.[37] If this condition is not improved rapidly, and there has been no improvement in the last decade, it is almost impossible to imagine a non-nuclear war in Europe in which U.S. forces will not be rapidly and decisively defeated.

The readiness and battle worthiness of the Air Force is no better than the Army's. A congressional investigation into Air Force readiness concluded in 1984 that "U.S. air forces are not capable of sustaining conventional war operations against the Soviets. The support elements required to sustain a conventional war simply do not exist. Wartime taskings cannot be met because of a shortage of aircraft spare parts. This shortage is not the result of funding but is the result of ineffective planning and the acceptance of shortages as the normal conditions of command."[38] In light of the billions of dollars that have been spent on the Air Force over the last ten years, one can only question the competence of the military command which has allowed these conditions to develop. It is not unfair to suggest that officers whose responsibility it is to ensure that U.S. air forces are combat-ready have not performed well. Moreover, they have legitimately earned the epithet of military incompetent.

---

* The C-5A Galaxie is the world's largest military transport and central to the U.S. military's strategic airlift capability. The U.S. has fewer than one hundred of these aircraft, which have been plagued by a number of operational problems. It requires five hundred flights of the C-5A to airlift a single Army division to the battlefield.

THE NAVY

The Navy is no better prepared than the other two services. Although the Navy reports that it has 98 percent of authorized personnel, the quality of personnel tends to be low, as it is in its sister services. Navy personnel are also maldistributed, with priority given to filling staff slots. As a consequence, the Navy, too, is suffering from critical shortages of men and material absolutely vital to wartime missions. One shortage is of well-trained petty officers. This shortage means that, in many instances, normal maintenance takes too long to perform, and in many instances cannot even be performed by the crew. To correct this situation, the Navy has been forced to hire civilian technicians, called CETs (contractual engineering technical service personnel). Without CETs, the Navy cannot operate. Again, a congressional committee found that "the Navy has become totally reliant upon these CETs to keep its more sophisticated complex weapons systems operating."[39] One commanding officer of an aircraft carrier noted that, "without my CETs, I don't sail at all."[40] In 1983, the Navy spent $166.2 million for CETs. But in the event of a war, the CETs are under no contractual obligation to deploy with the fleet. The Navy is having great difficulty keeping its ships deployed and combat-ready and will almost certainly be unable to do so in time of war.

The Navy's combat skills are inadequate. It lacks the trained manpower to provide adequate fleet air defense. There is a lack of skilled people to man and maintain the search radars, the fire-control systems, and the missile launchers. In addition, there are significant shortages in weaponry. For example, there is an absolutely critical shortage of air-to-air and air-to-ground missiles.[41] Further, what is in the inventory is unbelievably expensive; each Phoenix missile costs over $900,000, and some fighter pilots will never get to fire a single missile in training in their twenty-year careers. About 30 percent of the weapons which are available to the fleet are inoperable on any given day, moreover, because of technical breakdowns and lack of spare parts. The Navy is also short of chaff, which is vital to successful air defense. In testimony before Congress, both the Atlantic and the Pacific fleet commander pointed

out that their ships lacked sufficient air-defense capability. The Atlantic fleet commander described his air defenses as "meager," while the Pacific commander said his ability to defend his ships from air attack was "minimal."

A crucial element in a successful air defense of the fleet at sea is the ability to scramble and sustain combat aircraft to intercept attacking enemy planes at long range. While the figures themselves are classified, congressional staffers for the House Armed Services Committee estimate that, on any given day, probably no more than 60 percent of the aircraft aboard an attack carrier can be put into the air. The remaining aircraft are "grounded," either because of a need for spare parts or because they have been cannibalized to keep the rest of the aircraft flying.

The House Committee concluded its analysis by stating that "the U.S. naval fleet's readiness to defeat a Soviet multi-dimensional threat is seriously degraded by existing equipment, logistical and manpower deficiencies. These deficiencies exist not only in the U.S. Navy's ability to defend itself against a 'first-strike salvo' but also in its ability to sustain full combat air and surface operations for more than two weeks in duration."[42] As part of a multi-service force, then, the Navy will likely be unable to carry out its combat tasks in support of ground and air operations in the event of war. And such a situation can have come about only as a result of the inability of high-level commanders over a decade to carry out the obligations assigned them not only by law but as a consequence of their rank and position.

THE MARINES

The Marine Corps is in slightly better shape than its sister services, largely because it's a small force which relies on the Navy for its logistical support. The Marine Corps, after all, must sustain only 195,880 men at any given time, about a third of whom are routinely deployed at sea as part of the Fleet Marine Force (FMF). Although the combat readiness of the Marines is generally better than in the other services, an examination of their ability to sustain

themselves once deployed shows that things are not too different for them. For example, the shortage of air-to-surface missiles which plagues the Navy comes home with a vengeance for the Marines. It seems to be Navy practice to strip the Marine air wings not only of their aircraft but of their weapons and other munitions, and the Navy mission of defending the fleet takes precedence. Thus, the critical shortage of missiles in the Navy falls heavily on the Marine air wings, which often have no missiles for carrying out their missions. Because Marine aircraft have no cannon for defense against other aircraft, they are defenseless. More important, the primary role of the Marine air wing is to provide close combat air support and air cover for the Marines deployed on the ground. Because their aircraft have no cannon and are short of missiles, the Marines risk having their ground forces subject to merciless air attack. Since Navy aircraft will be busy performing their own missions, the Marines will be defenseless from the skies.

The Marines hope that some of the shortages in combat air support will be compensated for by the use of naval gunfire to destroy targets on the ground, but, clearly, naval gunfire is of little help in solving the overall problem of air attack. Naval gunfire cannot support the Marines once they are deployed.

The Navy's own assessment of its ability to provide close air support for the Marines is devastating in its honesty. Official reports state that "the Navy is not now effective in the close air support role."[43] What this really means, of course, is that once Marine units are deployed on the beach, they are unlikely to be able to control the air over the battlefield. As any number of wars have shown, including the 1982 Israeli invasion of Lebanon and its concomitant conflict with Syrian troops in the Bekaa Valley, ground forces without combat air support to interdict enemy aircraft and to silence ground positions are likely to be decimated.

CONCLUSION

In examining the ability of the military services to carry out their missions with some probability of success, it seems clear that

none of them is in a position to do what it is required, should it be forced to battle. This is not a new condition. And it is important to state that these conditions are not the result of insufficient funding. Quite the contrary. Both the House Committee on Military Appropriations and the GAO reports have found repeatedly that the monies appropriated over the last decade have been, for example, more than sufficient to purchase the spare parts to sustain a modern force. The real problem is that the military has created a logistical and support system that is so complex that it cannot operate well, and at times not at all. Billions of dollars are spent every year on spare parts, but the military has failed to devise a system that can get the parts to the fighting units in a timely manner in order to keep these units combat-ready. It is a condition for which the high-level military commanders can be blamed more than their political masters. It is the military commanders who are given the task of planning and ensuring that U.S. forces are combat-ready. By all indications, however—and the evidence is overwhelming—they have failed to fulfill this responsibility. That the competence of such leaders should be brought into question as a consequence of their own actions is hardly surprising.

The real test of the officer corps and the military system is this: Can they plan and execute successful military operations? The question, then, is simply: How well have U.S. military forces done in battle? Five times in recent years, our forces have been engaged in battle overseas. An examination of the five military operations carried out by the United States since 1970 suggests strongly that the American military has failed that test. Even in those few instances where the success of military force was never in doubt, as in Grenada in 1983, the operations seem to have been conducted in such a manner as to raise serious questions about the quality of both the planning and the execution ability of the forces themselves. These operations, in short, have been characterized by a high degree of military failure and incompetence.

2

THE RAID ON SONTAY PRISON

AT mid-morning on November 18, 1970, a small group of military officers and their political superiors met in the Oval Office of the White House. The purpose of the meeting was to listen to Admiral Thomas Moorer, the new chairman of the Joint Chiefs of Staff, who presented a plan to the President to rescue American POWs being held at a prison camp at Sontay, deep in North Vietnam. The planning for the raid had been under way for almost six months, and the President and his staff had been informed about it. The reason for the November 18 briefing was to secure final approval from the President to go ahead with the mission. At the time of the meeting, the raiders had already deployed from their U.S. bases to their staging point in Ta Khli, Thailand, and were awaiting the final order from the White House. The target of the raid was the POW camp located in the provincial capital of Sontay, twenty-three miles west of Hanoi.

As Admiral Moorer delivered the briefing to the President and his advisors, he described the camp as "the only confirmed active POW camp outside Hanoi."[1] He went on to say that intelligence sources had confirmed that the camp held seventy American pilots. Sixty-one had been tentatively identified, as the result of ten months of extensive intelligence efforts. Of the seventy prisoners, forty-three were Air Force pilots, fourteen were Navy, and four were Marines. When questioned by the President about the probability of the mission's succeeding, Admiral Moorer assured Mr. Nixon that "the ground commander is positive that the

operation will succeed."[2] Less than six hours after the meeting adjourned, the President phoned the Secretary of Defense, Melvin Laird, and ordered the rescue team into action. Mr. Laird then contacted Admiral Moorer and gave him the final order to execute the raid on November 19, 1970.

The idea for a rescue attempt had originated almost six months earlier. Today, long after the war, it may be difficult to picture how desperate the situation was for the American pilots being held prisoner and how complex the political problem it posed. In 1970, there were 462 airmen being held by the enemy somewhere in Southeast Asia. Despite American efforts during the peace talks in Paris to get the Vietnamese to resolve the POW issue, no progress was being made. The North Vietnamese understood that the fate of the prisoners was a difficult issue for the President and that it was creating great political pressure on the Administration. The North Vietnamese negotiators in Paris correctly assessed the POW issue as one of the main cards they had to play in the complex negotiations. They were in no mood to resolve the POW issue until a larger agreement securing the withdrawal of the main U.S. forces from Southeast Asia had been concluded. They continued to stall in the face of American inquiries about the fate and condition of U.S. prisoners.

As the talks dragged on, the North Vietnamese allowed a few peace groups to enter the country and meet with a few POWs, under carefully controlled conditions. These groups were encouraged to make public statements that the prisoners were being well treated. From time to time, the government in Hanoi would provide the names of a few prisoners which these groups could make public—something the intelligence community had been unable to accomplish. Pressure increased on the Nixon Administration to do something about the POWs.

American military intelligence knew that many of the POWs were injured. Indeed, almost 80 percent of the pilots had been injured in the process of ejecting from their disabled aircraft, and others had been injured when they parachuted to earth.[3] Some had been terribly hurt at the hands of the hostile peasantry, who were often the first to reach the downed airmen. The intelligence

community had a far different view from the peace groups concerning the conditions under which the POWs were being held. It was known that the prisoners were being badly fed and were often tortured, facts confirmed when the prisoners were released. The military feared that their comrades would either die or be driven insane by the inhumane treatment. A number of Americans had been held for almost four years. The military felt powerless in the face of these conditions and for years had been searching for some military solution to rescue their comrades.

The idea for a raid on the prison camps came from a group of intelligence officers of the 1127th Air Force Field Activities Group stationed at Fort Belvoir, Virginia. Their ongoing mission was to collect information about the POWs on an all-source, worldwide basis. A secondary mission was to devise programs and tactics to help pilots escape and evade their captors if shot down over North Vietnam. The major problem confronting any attempt to rescue the POWs was the simple fact that, except for the "Hanoi Hilton," located in downtown Hanoi, the intelligence community didn't have the foggiest notion where the prisoners were held. By 1970, the intelligence community had made the task of discovering an active POW camp outside Hanoi one of ten top-priority missions. One aspect of this effort was to photograph every building and compound in North Vietnam that had a wall around it. The scope of this work was staggering. Vietnam had innumerable pigsties and water-buffalo pens, and thousands of photographs were taken of walled compounds in the country, from the Chinese to the South Vietnamese border. The attempt to rescue the POWs had originally been formalized in 1967 with the creation of the Inter-Agency Prisoner of War Intelligence Committee (IPWIC). By 1970, after almost three years, the American intelligence community had still failed to identify a single active POW camp outside Hanoi.

But in May 1970 three intelligence analysts of the 1127th thought they had solved the puzzle by analyzing the entire intelligence data for three years. They concluded that there might be two active camps outside Hanoi, located almost side by side, some twenty-three miles west of the capital. One of these camps was Ap Loa, and the other was located in the provincial capital of Sontay.

The information from the 1127th was passed in a formal report to the Assistant Chief of Staff for Intelligence (ACSI) of the Air Force. When the ACSI was formally briefed, he too came to the conclusion that the 1127th had indeed quite possibly located two active camps.

But the ACSI's job was to find the POWs, not to rescue them. The rescue effort was the responsibility of others. Therefore, the ACSI passed on the information to the Assistant Chief of Staff for Operations, Air Force Brigadier General James Allen. General Allen was formally briefed on the intelligence estimate and concluded that there was a chance that both Ap Loa and Sontay were active prison camps. Five days after General Allen received the information he passed it on to the SACSA for further action. SACSA was the Special Assistant for Counter-Insurgency and Special Activities, located in an office in the Pentagon basement. His office came under the direct command of the Joint Chiefs of Staff. The head of SACSA was Army Brigadier General Donald Blackburn. Blackburn, after receiving and analyzing the intelligence assessment, called in Colonel Ed Mayer, his chief of the Special Operations Division, and asked his opinion. Mayer concurred with his chief and the idea for a rescue mission against both Ap Loa and Sontay was born. In the end, it would be Blackburn and Mayer who would plan the raid on Sontay.

Practical difficulties surfaced early. In his last days in office in January 1969, President Lyndon Johnson had ordered that all special ground operations against North Vietnam be terminated. This restriction included even the resupply and rescue of agents and agent networks in place in the north. The restriction had outraged the intelligence community, especially the CIA, who were forced to watch helplessly as their agents were picked off one by one for lack of support. As far as anyone knew, when Blackburn began planning for the Sontay raid, the order not to "thrash about" in North Vietnam was still in force. If any raid was to be attempted, it was clear that special authorization would be required even to conduct preparatory reconnaissance of the target.

General Blackburn and Colonel Mayer knew that lifting this restriction would require permission of President Richard Nixon, and access to the President would require the consideration and

support of the chairman of the Joint Chiefs, General Earle Wheeler. Accordingly, General Wheeler was briefed on May 25, 1970, just days after the Nixon Administration ordered the invasion of Cambodia. After examining the material presented by Blackburn and after receiving assurances that large numbers of troops would not be needed to carry out the mission, General Wheeler gave his permission to set up a small planning group to continue exploring the possibility of rescuing the POWs at both Sontay and Ap Loa. Blackburn now took his case to the Director for Operations, the J-3 of the JCS, and informed him of Wheeler's decision. He told the J-3 that he needed the resources to put together a team to conduct a feasibility study of the rescue mission. Blackburn and Mayer then set June 1, 1970, as their deadline to formulate a tentative plan and present it to the JCS for approval. The plan was code-named Polar Circle, a name chosen from the Pentagon's computer that generates random code names for military operations.

Early on, it was decided that the major responsibility for intelligence support would rest with the Defense Intelligence Agency (DIA). The military planners apparently felt much more comfortable using their own intelligence agency rather than relying on either the NSA or the CIA, which are outside the military chain of command. As events developed, however, both the CIA and the NSA would have significant roles in intelligence collection and the analysis process. But for the record, DIA was to be fully responsible for collecting all-source data about the target and for conducting the analysis.

Blackburn and Mayer met their self-imposed deadline of June 1, and on that date, tentative guiding principles for the plan were established. One of these was that the intelligence community should be as certain as possible about the conditions and activity in the camps. However, while it was important to have the most current data available, the increased surveillance effort could not be so heavy-handed as to tip off the North Vietnamese that a rescue might be in the offing. It was also clear from the beginning that any operation would have to stage out of Thailand. It would not be possible to use bases in Laos, especially Site 32, an old CIA camp on the Laotian–North Vietnamese border. Fighting had in-

creased in the area, and the North Vietnamese continued to make clandestine cross-border raids against U.S. installations in Laos. Therefore, the operation would have to based at the big U.S. Air Force installation at Udorn, Thailand. It was also evident that any operation against Sontay would have to involve some sort of diversion with Navy and Air Force attack aircraft flying over Hanoi. This would present a significant problem, since a bombing halt was in effect and no one had dropped bombs on the North Vietnamese capital in almost two years. It would take Presidential authority to lift this restriction.

On June 5, the chairman of the JCS was briefed on the general outline of the plan as well as its guiding principles. He approved the concept and ordered a further and careful feasibility study to work out the details of the mission to be conducted simultaneously against the camps at Ap Loa and Sontay. The raid would be the first major military operation planned directly by the office of the JCS. Blackburn and Mayer set about forming a fifteen-man staff and planning group drawn from all military services and including representatives from the major intelligence agencies. The staff's job was to begin to formulate and coordinate not only the plan but the intelligence effort that would be necessary for its successful execution. The planners were haunted by history; except in the Civil War, and despite scores of later attempts, there had never been a successful rescue of American prisoners from any prison camp in American military history.[4] On June 10, the fifteen-man team assembled at Arlington Hall Station, the headquarters of the Defense Intelligence Agency. In a secure room "behind the green door," they began to plot their strategy for the rescue of American prisoners in the camp at Sontay.

Intelligence support would be handled exclusively by DIA, with such help as might be needed from other intelligence agencies. DIA, accordingly, leaned heavily on its own resources and relied almost exclusively on military intelligence, and on a number of SR-71 overflights. The SR-71 Blackbird can fly at 80,000 feet at more than three times the speed of sound, taking high-resolution photographs. SR-71 flights are controlled by the Strategic Air Command, and liaison was immediately established with SAC. Its

reconnaissance pilots were not told the purpose of these missions. Since high-altitude missions often fail because of weather or cloud cover over the target, it was decided to conduct seven Buffalo Hunter missions over the Sontay camp in a period of three months. Buffalo Hunter was the code name for the Air Force's remote-controlled reconnaissance-drone program. These pilotless drones could fly at very low altitudes directly over the camp and secure additional photographs. One such mission was particularly important because it was to provide a detailed view of the camp at very low level: photographs needed to plan a detailed ground assault. In addition, technical intelligence was to be gathered in USAF RF-4 Phantom overflights. These could be called up at almost a moment's notice and could fly both high- and low-level missions, although the latter involved great risks for the pilots.

The deadline for developing a preliminary plan was June 30, and the planning group was unable to meet it. Ten days later, on July 10, the planning group briefed the JCS and its new chairman, Admiral Thomas Moorer. At this briefing, Blackburn and Mayer were given permission to begin recruiting, assembling, and training the force that would conduct the raid on Sontay. At this point, President Nixon and his advisors were brought into the planning process. They were told that a rescue mission was being organized for the coming months, to secure the release of seventy American prisoners at Sontay. The White House was enthusiastic and gave its approval. The selection and training of the Sontay assault team got under way.

Blackburn and Mayer next had to choose a ground commander to lead the Sontay force. They chose Army Colonel Arthur "Bull" Simons. Simons was one of the Army's oldest and most experienced special-operations ground commanders. He had led special operations behind enemy lines in World War II, had fought in Korea, and had commanded a number of special operations, White Star missions, into Laos and even North Vietnam. Simons had a reputation for being tough, fearless, and, above all, a brilliant tactician and commander. He was also regarded as an excellent officer, who never risked his men needlessly or put them in a situation that he was not willing to endure himself. His men worshiped and feared

him. On July 13, Blackburn and Mayer met with Simons at Fort Bragg and over lunch offered him command of the mission. They told him that, though they wanted him in command, they could not at that time tell him what the mission was. Simons, ever the ready soldier, simply nodded agreement: he would accept the assignment.

Most of the ground-force elements for the rescue team would come from the Special Forces Group stationed at Fort Bragg. The air and helicopter support units would be drawn from Eglin Air Force Base in northern Florida. Eglin was also chosen as the training and stateside staging area for the group. The planning group was redesignated the Joint Contingency Task Group (JCTG), and the operation renamed Operation Ivory Coast. Its point of contact within the JCS would be General Bruce Palmer, who personally approved the choice of Simons as the ground commander, and who assigned Air Force Brigadier General Leroy Manor to oversee command of the entire operation. General Manor would report directly to the JCS through General Palmer. Manor's mission was to ensure that the assault group obtained anything they needed to make the mission a success. The JCS approved.

The timetable called for developing a training plan by August 20. The actual plan of operations was to be completed by August 28. Training would begin at Eglin Air Force Base on September 9 and be completed by October 6. By October 10, the raiding force would be ready to deploy to Thailand and await the order to execute the raid. From the beginning, it was clear that the assault on Sontay was "weather-sensitive." Meteorological analyses indicated that the first "weather window" in which conditions of moonlight, rainfall, and cloud cover would permit a combat assault would be between October 20 and October 25. If the raid did not come off at that time, the raiders would have to wait until mid-November before another "weather window" would open up. General Manor and his deputy would be responsible for the selection and training of helicopter and air crews, whose job it was to fly the raiders in and out of the Sontay camp. The planned raid on Ap Loa was canceled because recent intelligence photos had shown that it was empty. Colonel Simons hand-picked his ground assault force of fifty-six

men. The total ground force consisted of fifteen officers and eighty-two enlisted men, organized into combat and combat-support elements. While the overall mission commander was General Manor, it was Simons who was responsible for ensuring the readiness and effectiveness of his men. He even had final authority to certify the readiness of the air crews. Simons's complete control over all elements of the force would later contribute greatly to its near-success.

Bull Simons early on selected Lieutenant Colonel Elliott "Bud" Sydnor to be his deputy commander. Simons chose Captain Richard "Dick" Meadows to command the compound assault team. Both officers had long and distinguished careers in special operations, in which they had shown both brilliance and bravery. Dick Meadows was one of only two men who had received a battlefield commission during the Vietnam war. Both officers had served with Simons before and knew him well. In early August, the three men flew to Fort Bragg to select and assemble the assault force from the Special Forces units stationed there. Unobtrusive notices were placed on company area bulletin boards announcing that Colonel Simons was putting together a unit for a "moderately hazardous" assignment. Volunteers were told to report to the post theater the next morning. About five hundred Special Forces soldiers turned out to hear what Simons had in mind. Simons told them that there was some risk involved in the mission but that he was not at liberty to say what the mission involved or even in what area of the world it would take place. If anyone wanted to be part of it, they would simply have to trust him. Throughout the assembly and training phases of the operation, the raiders were never told where they would mount the operation or for what purpose until they had already deployed to Thailand!

Simons told the assembly, upping the ante, that anyone who volunteered would not receive separation pay, which the Army provides when a soldier is away from his wife and family. Moreover, Simons went on, there would be no hazardous-duty pay. Simons was only interested in attracting men who had adventure in their souls, the few natural warriors who are drawn to battle by the excitement and risk. The meeting ended with Simons's instructions that anyone still interested in this "interesting" operation should

return to the post theater after lunch. At 3 p.m. that afternoon, about two hundred soldiers showed up. It was from this group that the final assault force was chosen. Each man in the group had his personnel records examined, with particular attention paid to his skills and combat performance, and each man was given a personal interview by a team of three men, including the commander and a psychiatrist. By the end of August, the final selection had been made. Of the men chosen, one-third had served with Bull Simons before and knew him personally. The rest knew him by reputation. By early September, the Sontay assault force had been formed.

The training of the assault force was held at Auxiliary Field #5, deep in the interior of Eglin Air Force Base, one of the country's largest training facilities. The problem of operational security (OPSEC) was paramount. A major concern was that a Soviet satellite, Cosmos 355, passed directly over Eglin at least twice every twenty-four hours. In addition, a Soviet electronic-surveillance (ELINT) trawler was routinely posted off the Florida coast. It had the ability to monitor the flying and radio activity of the helicopters and other aircraft that would be involved in the raid. The chief concern was that, with their satellite cameras, the Soviets might discover the nature and training of the ground assault force. Simons intended to construct a full-scale mock-up of the Sontay compound, to use in training his troops for the assault. Soviet photo interpreters pay particular attention to any new construction on American military bases, and once the mock-up was built, the Soviets would probably spot it. If they were clever enough to recognize it as a type of construction not usually found in the U.S., they might try to identify it, and might eventually associate it with Vietnamese architecture. If they managed to put the pieces of the puzzle together, the element of surprise might well be lost.

The problem was solved rather ingeniously. The entire mock-up was built in sections, from ordinary lumber, each section comprised of painted canvas much like that used in theater scenery. The mock-up was reconstructed in detail from reconnaissance photos supplied by DIA from a number of overflights. Each day, it was unfurled in sections and placed in postholes in the ground. Daylight training was limited to two four-hour periods each day.

After each session, the entire mock-up was disassembled and stored under cover until the Soviet satellite had passed overhead. Even the postholes were covered each day, to prevent the Soviets from discerning the outline of the camp. In order to duplicate the terrain around Sontay, earth was moved with bulldozers. Forty-foot-high trees were transplanted from other areas of the base and put in position exactly as they would be found by the raiders when they landed around the camp.

Photo reconnaissance of the Vietnamese camp, handled initially by the CIA and the Strategic Air Command, produced generally good results. Not only was the camp photographed from every conceivable angle, but photos were taken of the air and ground routes in and out of Thailand, Laos, and North Vietnam over which American pilots would have to fly. With the photographic intelligence in hand, the ground units, helicopter pilots, C-130s, and A-1 Skyraiders could now begin their training in earnest. All during the training period, the Air Force continued to fly SR-71 missions at high altitudes, and seven Buffalo Hunter missions for low-level reconnaissance were carried out at intervals, so as not to alarm the enemy. To aid in the training, the CIA produced a $60,000 model of the Sontay camp, code-named Barbara. The model, which fit on a tabletop, was fitted with variable lighting and special eyescopes so that the assault team could see how the camp would look from different angles at different times of day or night. Each man in the assault team would know and memorize the position on the ground that he would occupy during the raid. Nothing was overlooked.

THE PLAN

The plan called for airlifting a fifty-six-man ground assault team by helicopter into the camp at Sontay. The force would stage from Udorn, Thailand, and would fly in five HH-53 (Jolly Green Giant) heavy-lift helicopters and one modified H-3 Seaking, used by the Air Force as a rescue helicopter. The helicopters would be led by three C-130 Hercules aircraft. One of these, an HC-130, would

assist in the early stages of navigation over Thailand and Laos and would refuel the helicopters in mid-flight so that they would have enough range to reach Sontay. The C-130s would refuel the helicopters again on the way out to provide them with enough fuel to reach their staging bases on the return leg. Two C-130s were special Combat Talon aircraft equipped with sophisticated navigational equipment, enabling them to fly the low and tortuous route to the target. Combat Talon aircraft would act as mother ships, flying a precise route, with the helicopters "in draft," to the target. The route over Thailand, Laos, and North Vietnam had been mapped by satellite photos and by overflights by DIA and NSA. The route called for flying "nap of the earth" (NOE) approaches around mountains and through valleys, carefully avoiding enemy radar positions. Flight checkpoints were timed to coincide with the swinging of enemy radar dishes, so that the flight would pass in front of a radar site while its dish was pointing in the other direction. The plan called for precise and careful timing. A few minutes early or late at even one checkpoint and the raiders might easily be detected by radar and air-defense positions.

The Combat Talon aircraft were equipped with forward-looking infrared radar (FLIR), which was used in combat for the first time during the raid. This new technical device allowed the pilots to fly a strip approach to their target by looking through special scopes that made the ground strip below them appear almost as it would in broad daylight. One C-130 would lead the flight of helicopters directly to the prison compound and drop flares over the camp. It would then turn south to a position four miles from the camp and drop its "firefight simulators" to deceive the enemy into believing that a major ground assault was under way far from the camp. The second Combat Talon aircraft would act as a mother ship for the flight of A-1 Douglas Skyraider aircraft which would accompany the assault team. Once over the target, this second Combat Talon would act as a tactical air controller to direct strikes against any enemy forces that might try to relieve the camp. The major mission of the A-1s was to keep reinforcements from reaching Sontay. They would also provide air cover against any aircraft that rose to intercept the heliborne assault force on its way in or out of the Sontay camp.

There were enormous technical problems in flying such a mixed bag of aircraft in so tight a formation for so long a distance. Each type of aircraft had different minimum and maximum operating speeds, its operating envelope. The C-130s, for example, would lead the flight but not fly faster than 105 knots, only ten knots above stall speed. In order to stay in the air at so slow a speed, the C-130s had to fly with 70 degrees of flap extended, a flap setting usually reserved for landing. Moreover, at such low speeds and with its flaps hanging out, the aircraft became very unstable and difficult to turn. Flying under these conditions, very low to the ground and along a route calling for precise twists and descending turns, took great skill and courage. The reason for the reduced speed of the C-130s was that the HH-53 helicopters could fly no faster. Indeed, at 105 knots, the helicopters were giving all they had, and they could not fly at that speed for very long without endangering the structural integrity of the machines.

To make matters even more complex, the A-1 Skyraiders could not fly slower than 145 knots without stalling. Their flight pattern, therefore, involved flying in circles and S-turns all the way, so as to stay behind the C-130 mother ships and the helicopters. All in all, it was very complex and dangerous flying. In practice runs, the air crews flew a total of 1,017 hours in 368 separate sorties, to hone their skills. Flying time to the target would be 3.4 hours, and radio silence had to be maintained.

The members of the ground assault team required no less skill and bravery. The team was divided into three components. The first, the compound assault team, was led by Dick Meadows. It was armed with CAR-15 silenced automatic weapons with folding stocks, chosen because they would take less room in the cramped helicopters. The compound assault team was to land within the compound, rush the prison cell blocks, and free the POWs. But the compound was too small for the large HH-53 to land in and then be able to take off when the mission was completed. Some thought had been given to using a UH-1 Huey helicopter, which was smaller, but the idea was quickly abandoned because the UH-1 could not carry the fourteen-man assault force. In the end, it was decided to find a pilot willing to take an H-3, a smaller version of the HH-53 and used extensively by the Navy and Air

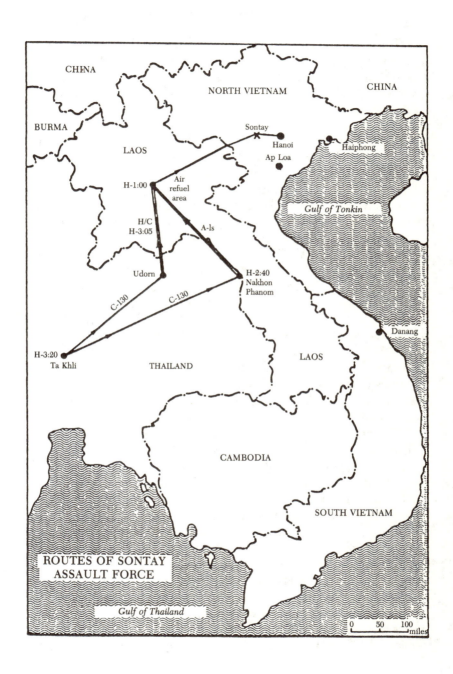

CHINA

NORTH VIETNAM

CHINA

BURMA

LAOS

Sontay

Hanoi

Haiphong

Ap Loa

Air
refuel
area

H-1:00

Gulf of Tonkin

H/C
H-3:05

A-ls

Udorn

H-2:40
Nakhon
Phanom

C-130

C-130

Danang

H-3:20
Ta Khli

THAILAND

LAOS

CAMBODIA

SOUTH VIETNAM

**ROUTES OF SONTAY
ASSAULT FORCE**

Gulf of Thailand

0   50   100
                miles

Force for search-and-rescue missions, and crash-land it through the trees in the small prison courtyard. The helicopter would be mined with explosive charges. Once the compound assault team was in command of the prison and the prisoners rescued and loaded aboard the HH-53 waiting outside the prison walls, a timer would set off the explosive charges to destroy the helicopter within the compound. It was a bold plan for fourteen men and a helicopter crew to crash-land in a very large helicopter in the middle of an enemy prison camp. If anything went wrong, there would be no way back, and in all likelihood the men would be killed.

Colonel Bud Sydnor would lead the second component, a twenty-man command and security team. Their mission was to land outside the prison walls and position their M-60 machine guns to cover any enemy forces attempting to interfere with the compound assault team. They were to ambush, delay, and destroy any North Vietnamese troops trying to reinforce the camp. Colonel Simons would lead the third component, a twenty-two-man support group. Its mission was to land outside the camp within seconds after the compound assault team had landed its helicopter in the prison courtyard, and blow a hole in the compound wall. Simons's men would then rush through the hole and in the confusion kill or wound the men who garrisoned the camp. Meanwhile, Meadows's men would go from cell to cell and free the prisoners.

Seconds prior to the Meadows assault, a helicopter equipped with two 7.62mm six-barrel Gatling guns, capable of firing ten thousand rounds a minute each, would strafe the guard towers, knock them to the ground, and kill their occupants. The helicopters carrying the assault forces and the POWs would then return to the designated helicopter rendezvous, roughly a mile away, where they would join the other helicopters and await further instructions. When the assault was completed and the POWs were in hand, the commander of the group would radio the helicopters to come in, land outside the compound wall, and evacuate the prisoners and the rescue team. The plan called for the entire assault to take no more than twenty-six minutes from beginning to end.

Bull Simons left nothing to chance. The three elements of the assault team practiced the attack on the compound at least one

hundred and seventy-five times before the raid.[5] Each element had an alternative plan of action in the event something went wrong; each team was cross-trained in the mission of the other two elements. The transmission of a single code word by radio would enable the units to reverse roles and missions. The assault units were equipped right down to lock picks and hacksaws to cut the hand and leg irons on the prisoners in their cells. Even baby food had been loaded aboard the helicopters to feed the prisoners, whose diet had been so poor that solid food would have made them ill. The pilot who was to crash his helicopter into the center of the compound had practiced his mission no fewer than thirty-one times. Communications linked all elements of the team to the helicopters and to the C-130s and A-1s overhead. In addition, the teams could communicate with an orbiting command post in a holding pattern over Monkey Mountain near Danang in South Vietnam. The communications pattern was so complex that the team carried ninety-two radios, about the same number carried by a full infantry battalion deployed in battle.

The operation was planned to take place during the first available weather window, between October 20 and October 25. If the operation was postponed, the next launch window would not be until mid-November. Suddenly, for reasons never made public or even explained to the team, the White House decided to cancel the mission for October.

Although the mission was postponed, the White House gave approval for the team to continue preparations for an attempt in November. On October 27, the Joint Chiefs of Staff told General Blackburn that he could deploy his coordinating staff to Thailand, and on November 1 the staff was deployed. On November 10, the mission task force itself was flown across the Pacific to Ta Khli air base in Thailand and was immediately closeted in some old barracks on the outskirts of the base. Coordination began with the Navy and Air Force to launch a diversionary air attack over Hanoi. On Thursday, November 12, the White House issued the final order for the units to deploy to their staging base at Udorn and to execute the Sontay mission on the order of the JCS. The assault force waited at Ta Khli, Thailand, prepared to execute the mission within ten

hours of receiving the order. The code name was changed again, this time to Operation Kingpin.

While the rescue mission was under way, the Navy and Air Force were to mount a diversionary attack over Hanoi. The Navy aircraft would come from the carriers *Oriskany, Hancock,* and *Ranger,* deployed on Yankee Station in the Gulf of Tonkin. Other Air Force aircraft would stage from five separate air bases in Thailand, in support of the diversion. The problem was that no air strikes had been flown over Hanoi since October 1968, when the bombing halt had been announced. Moreover, the U.S. government was deeply involved in peace talks with the North Vietnamese. The White House was concerned about the disruptive effects any renewed bombing of Hanoi might have on the negotiations. In order to satisfy both the military requirements and the political sensitivities of the White House, a plan was developed that would place more than one hundred aircraft over Hanoi at the same time but none would be allowed to shoot or bomb anything. The aircraft would drop flares to light up the Hanoi area and confuse the enemy into thinking that a major strike was under way on the capital. The object, after all, was to deceive and confuse the North Vietnamese air defenses, rather than to inflict damage. Besides, if the raid was successful, that would be sufficient. Thus, the Navy and Air Force mounted the largest air attack on Hanoi in over two years and did not drop a single bomb. The pilots who flew the raid were not told the reason for it. They were told that they would go in unarmed, and some refused to fly the mission. As it turned out, the diversionary raid went off flawlessly, and while the North Vietnamese concentrated on the simulated air attack, twenty-three miles to the west the assault force flew undetected to the target at Sontay.

On Friday, November 20, at Ta Khli, the assault team was told for the first time what its mission was. There was great enthusiasm at the prospect of rescuing American POWs. As darkness fell, the men checked their equipment and weapons and then were driven in closed vans from their remote barracks to four C-130s that would ferry them to their staging point at Udorn. At 10:32 they left Ta Khli, and they arrived at Udorn in less than an hour. The assault force transferred from the C-130s and boarded three

of the five waiting helicopters. Also on the tarmac were two C-141 Starlifters, waiting to evacuate prisoners upon their return. At 11:18 on Friday, November 20, the last helicopter lifted off to join the C-130 Combat Talon orbiting above the base. After about six minutes, the flight formed up and turned north on a heading that would take them deep into Laos before turning east into North Vietnam. Four minutes after midnight, another Combat Talon and its flight of A-1 fighter-bombers took off from Nakhon Phanom airfield to rendezvous with the helicopters over Laos. Operation Kingpin was finally under way.

THINGS GO WRONG

As the C-130 mother ship neared the Sontay camp, having navigated 338 miles from Udorn to its target, it veered off and pulled away, leaving the helicopters carrying the combat assault team to make their final run to the prison compound. As it approached the camp, the lead helicopter drifted south of its target, coming very close to what DIA analysts had named "the secondary school," a walled compound believed to be a school or training facility. The pilot caught his error in time and banked sharply to the north to move in on the prison camp. This first helicopter, radio call sign Apple 3, began its assault on the Sontay camp. Its mission was to overfly the camp and rake the two guard towers with minigun fire, killing the guards and toppling the towers. In a six-second pass over the target, Apple 3 performed perfectly. Within seconds, the guard towers came crashing down, their wooden supports shattered by machine-gun fire. None of the guards survived.

But Apple 3 had passed too far to the south. The helicopter behind them, Apple 2, carrying Bud Sydnor's command and support group, also drifted to the south. Because they were in visual range of Apple 3, they caught their error and corrected their course to the north toward Sontay. They landed just outside the compound and began to take up their planned positions to intercept and destroy any enemy forces that might rush to the support of the

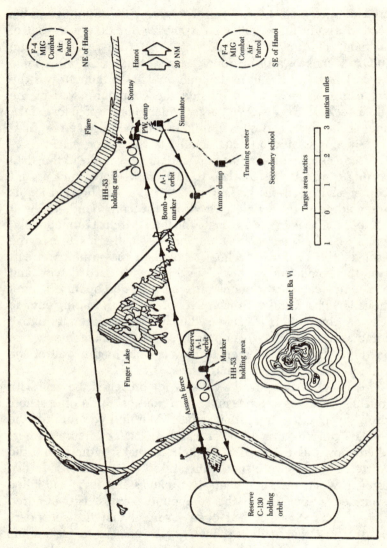

DEPLOYMENT OF THE RESCUE FORCE
AND AREA AROUND SONTAY

camp. The third helicopter, Apple 1, carrying Bull Simons and his compound assault force, followed Apple 2. But they were out of visual range of Apple 2 and did not see it turn away from the secondary school toward the Sontay target. Apple 1 held its course in the darkness and began to descend on what it thought was the Sontay camp. It landed just outside the compound wall of the secondary school. This was the target which, just days before, DIA intelligence analysts had warned might easily be mistaken for Sontay. The major assault force had landed in the wrong place!

As soon as Simons and his men landed, they realized they had the wrong camp. It was too late to turn back, since their assault helicopter had lifted off the landing zone and was headed for its secure holding point a mile away from the compound, to await orders to come back in and evacuate the force. Almost immediately, Simons's assault force came under heavy small-arms fire as the garrison of the secondary school reacted to the military threat. Worse, the compound was well fortified with barbed wire and reveted emplacements. Simons ordered his radio operator to get the helicopter back and to contact Sydnor, who was waiting outside the Sontay compound. He told Sydnor to execute the alternative plan and assault the POW camp with his men. Simons, never one to be timid, ordered his men to blow a hole in the wall of the secondary-school compound and attack.

The assault team moved swiftly. They breached the wall with their satchel charges and began a murderous assault on the school garrison, firing at anything that moved. Within five minutes, the place was "burning like a Roman candle,"[6] while enemy soldiers were cut down as they ran from their barracks. Others who did not react as quickly were shot while still in their barracks. In five minutes, it was over. The twenty-two-man assault team had killed or wounded every man in the compound—almost two hundred enemy soldiers. Since it had been assumed that the secondary school was just that, only a school, it was unclear to the raiders who was firing at them. When the mission was over, intelligence analysts learned that Simons and his men had probably killed or wounded two hundred Chinese and Russian advisors.

As the fighting at the secondary school was ending, Simons's

helicopter, recalled from its holding point, set down outside the compound, lifted off the assault force, and headed toward the Sontay camp, where the main assault was already under way. The attack on the wrong camp turned out to be a stroke of luck. U.S. intelligence had failed to show any enemy troops closer than ten miles from the Sontay compound. And the timing of the raid was predicated on the assumption that it would take enemy troops at least thirty minutes to react. The raid itself had to be completed in twenty-six minutes. But the garrison located at the secondary school was less than a mile from the prison and could have reacted in minutes, perhaps trapping the raiders in the prison compound. Quite by accident, Simons and his men had stumbled on the most important ground threat to the operation, and in less than five minutes had rendered it ineffective.

At Sontay, events were moving rapidly. Seconds after the first helicopter had strafed and destroyed the guard towers with its miniguns, Captain Dick Meadows and his fourteen-man rescue team crash-landed in the prison courtyard. Banana 1, the H-3 assigned to crash into the compound, made a deafening noise as its rotor blades cut through ten-inch trees on its way down. The rescue force raced from the helicopter. Meadows, using a bullhorn, called to the prisoners to stay down, that they were being rescued. As part of Meadows's team rushed the prison, the rest shot and killed everything in sight, as their comrades tried to pry open the cell doors.

Meanwhile, Sydnor's support group had landed outside the compound walls. Even before he received Bull Simons's radio signal to execute the backup plan calling for his men to assault the compound, he had figured out that Simons had missed the target. He had ordered his men to blow a hole in the wall and assault the camp. Within two minutes, Sydnor's men were inside, moving from position to position and silencing any enemy opposition as Meadows's men rushed the cell barracks. Within nine minutes of Meadows's initial landing, Simons's men had made their way to Sontay and were now adding their firepower to Sydnor's command. Simons radioed Sydnor to return to the original plan and once again assumed command of the operation. The prison was now safely in

the rescuers' hands as Sydnor's men redeployed around the camp to intercept and block any enemy forces moving toward Sontay. By now, the enemy garrison in the camp were mostly dead or wounded. At least twenty North Vietnamese soldiers were killed or wounded in the three-minute assault. Ten minutes into the raid, Meadows's prisoner-rescue force had completed its search of the compound. It was empty of any American prisoners. There were none.

Simons immediately radioed the helicopters waiting in the holding area. Fourteen minutes after the raid had begun, the first helicopter arrived to extract Meadows and his team, flew back to the holding point, and awaited rendezvous with the other helicopters. Ten minutes later, a second helicopter arrived to evacuate Sydnor's men. Simons's unit provided perimeter security as Sydnor's security force withdrew. At this time, four enemy vehicles came down the road toward the prison. They were immediately brought under fire and within seconds the vehicles and their occupants were destroyed. Exactly twenty-seven minutes after the assault had begun, Apple 2 lifted off with the remaining members of the assault force. Minutes later, the explosive charges aboard Banana 1 went off, filling the night sky with light. The helicopters turned toward Laos to keep their refueling rendezvous with the C-130s and then return to their staging base in Udorn. The raid had been swift and precise; none of the Americans was killed or wounded. But there had been no American POWs to rescue. They had been moved four months earlier—and what is unbelievable, the after-action report would show that DIA intelligence analysts were aware of that. In fact, perhaps the only people involved who were not aware that the camp was empty were the members of the force itself. They found out the hard way.

WHY THINGS WENT WRONG

When the attempted rescue at Sontay was made public, military men and political leaders, to say nothing of the general public, were outraged. How could the intelligence analysts have made

such a mistake? How could American military forces be committed to such a dangerous mission without accurate intelligence information? The truth was that the Sontay raid was neither the first attempt to rescue American prisoners in Southeast Asia nor the last. Nor was it the first to fail because the intelligence services had not provided accurate information to the combat forces.

Five years later, after the United States had left the Vietnam quagmire, the Pentagon revealed the extent of our efforts to find and rescue American prisoners. Between 1966 and 1970, no fewer than ninety-one attempts were made by U.S. forces to rescue prisoners in South Vietnam, Laos, and Cambodia. Sontay had been the seventy-first "dry hole" to turn up in these rescue attempts. Almost fifty of the ninety-one raids were prompted by evidence that Americans were being held in one location or another. Of the ninety-one rescue attempts, twenty-six succeeded in rescuing either South Vietnamese soldiers or civilians. But of the raids to rescue American POWs, only one succeeded.[7] On July 10, 1969, one Army enlisted man was rescued from a Vietcong prison compound in South Vietnam; he later died of wounds received at the hands of his captors. With that exception, not a single American was rescued from enemy hands throughout the Vietnam war.

All the rescue attempts were conducted by the Joint Personnel Center, the cover name of a special staff and operations section located in MACV headquarters in Saigon. Some of the raids failed because they had been compromised in advance to the Vietcong, who had successfully penetrated almost all elements of American military intelligence and operations. Most of the attempts failed because the prisoners had been moved or had never been there. After the Sontay raid, other rescue efforts were launched, and they all failed. From 1970 to 1973, at least twenty-eight rescue missions were undertaken—all to no avail.

The question was widely asked: How could intelligence have failed so dismally in providing accurate information about Sontay? After all, the mission had been planned almost six months in advance and had at its disposal the full resources of the entire intelligence community. The answer rests in a combination of bureaucratic complexity and the simple refusal of high-level com-

manders to believe the information DIA analysts had provided. Three months before the raid, DIA had produced a report indicating that the Sontay camp was probably empty. As with many "intelligence failures" throughout military history, the problem was not that the information was not available, for it was; but it was not taken seriously by commanders who, once committed to a course of action based on a bureaucratic consensus, refuse to recognize the validity of contrary data and abandon the operation.

Intelligence had been watching the Sontay and Ap Loa camps for signs of activity since May 1970. In early June, DIA had reported that the Ap Loa camp was empty, but still believed that the Sontay camp contained American POWs. The evidence from overflights was convincing enough. It showed prisoners, and even signals laid out in a pattern with prisoners' laundry. Other resources allowed intelligence analysts to determine the number of American prisoners in the camp and even to identify forty-five of them by name and rank. How this was done has never been revealed. But it is known that when the chairman of the JCS briefed the President on the raid, he was able to provide him with the names of the prisoners being held in Sontay.

The decision had been made early on not to use "HUMINT"* resources; that is, not to use Vietnamese or American agents on the ground to check on conditions at Sontay. President Johnson had banned any new missions into North Vietnam, and President Nixon had continued this policy for two years prior to the Sontay raid. Because Vietnamese agents had not been used for almost two years, there was no way of knowing if these agents could still be trusted, if any of them had been "turned around," had become double agents. Any attempt to confirm on the ground the information obtained by technical means ran a high risk of compromising the entire mission. Accordingly, the planners relied exclusively on SR-71 flights, RF-4 Phantom overflights, satellites, and Buffalo Hunter drones. As it turned out, none of the Buffalo Hunter mis-

---

* HUMINT is a technical term in the intelligence business which designates data collected by field agents. It is distinguished from communications intelligence (COMINT), signals intelligence (SIGINT), electronics intelligence (ELINT), etc.

sions was successful. Six drones were shot down, and a seventh went astray and produced no photos of its target.

In late July 1970, DIA photo analysts began to suspect that the Sontay camp had been abandoned. The prisoners had probably been moved as a result of the heavy rains in the area, which had caused the river outside the compound walls to flood the camp and the surrounding countryside. Paradoxically, the prisoners had probably been moved for their own safety. Almost all the overflights after July indicated that the camp was empty (a number showed nothing, because the area was covered with clouds). This information was routinely passed along to the planners of the raid and to the JCS. But the planning went on. In early November, shortly before the raid, a DIA HUMINT source in Hanoi passed word that the prisoners at Sontay had indeed been moved to a new camp at Donghoi. With the earlier photo analysis now buttressed by evidence from an agent on the ground, this report was passed along to the planners of the raid and the JCS command group.

The head of DIA personally called on Admiral Moorer to tell him that the Sontay camp was empty. DIA's earlier reports had indicated the same thing, and the new information from the agent in Hanoi seemed to confirm the fact beyond any doubt. By that time, however, the raiders were in Thailand. But there was still time to call off the raid. The rescue team itself, of course, had no knowledge of these events. And although the information from the agent was rated B-3—as a usually reliable source with direct access to the information[8]—Blackburn and Moorer decided to allow the raid to proceed. In short, Sontay was not an intelligence failure. DIA did in fact predict that the camp would be empty. Rather, it was a command failure; it was the high-level commanders who decided to ignore the intelligence reports and proceed. Here again is the same pattern of command failure—the refusal of commanders to acknowledge new or existing information that runs contrary to a course of action to which they are already committed.

Military operations are usually judged on two grounds. First, whether or not the application of military technique was adequate; and second, whether or not the mission was accomplished. By far the more important of these two criteria, over the long run, is the

second. A perfect application of military technique is pointless unless it accomplishes the objective for which the mission was mounted. In the case of Sontay, the application of military technique must be rated at least very good, if not flawless. The planning of the raid was bold in concept, the training realistic, and the execution acceptable.

But the nagging fact remains that the mission did not accomplish its objective. Equally troubling is the fact that the ninety-one raids mounted before Sontay accomplished nothing, and neither did the twenty-nine mounted after. In each instance, something went wrong. Successful military operations require that all elements of a plan be implemented successfully and on schedule. If one is left out or executed badly, then the military operation fails. To be sure, the Sontay mission came close, but that is not good enough.

3

THE *MAYAGUEZ*

O N May 12, 1975, the SS *Mayaguez*, an American merchant container ship belonging to the Sealand Service Corporation of Menlo Park, New Jersey, plowed through the calm waters sixty miles off the coast of Cambodia. She was bound for the port of Sattahip, Thailand, with a cargo of mail, alcohol, and ammunition. As Captain Miller peered out from the ship's bridge, he saw three armed patrol boats close in on his right beam. As the first patrol boat neared, it fired a rocket across the bow of the *Mayaguez* and signaled it to stop. Obeying international law, the captain brought his vessel to a dead stop. The attacking patrol boat, clearly identified by the Cambodian flag flying from her mast, pulled alongside and began to board. When the Cambodians' intentions became clear, Captain Miller sent a radio Mayday message on the international distress frequency. With the Cambodians boarding the ship, Miller told his radio operator to send another message: "Have been fired upon and boarded by Cambodian armed forces at nine degrees forty-eight minutes north, one hundred and two degrees fifty-three minutes east. Ship is being towed to unknown Cambodian port."[1] Seven Cambodian soldiers armed with AK-47 rifles and, curiously, carrying a U.S. Army field radio, climbed aboard the vessel, rushed the bridge, and directed the captain to follow their instructions. The SS *Mayaguez*, an American merchant marine ship, had been seized in an act of piracy on the high seas.

The Mayday message reached the Sealand office in Jakarta, Indonesia, and was relayed through the U.S. embassy in Jakarta

61

to the National Command Center in Washington. At 7:40 in the morning, Washington time, Major General Brent Scowcroft, deputy director of the National Security Council, informed President Gerald Ford that an American ship had been fired upon and taken hostage. Scowcroft told the President that the present location of the ship was unknown. The President immediately directed that a meeting of the National Security Council be called for noon that day and further directed that U.S. aircraft based in U Taphao, Thailand, begin immediate search-and-reconnaissance missions to locate the *Mayaguez*.

Aboard the *Mayaguez*, the captain was complying with his captor's instructions to follow their patrol boats to the mainland port of Sihanoukville. Captain Miller, an old sea hand, was betting that before he arrived in Sihanoukville, his Mayday message would be picked up by U.S. forces and that American jets from Thailand would come to his rescue. Although he followed the Cambodian patrol boats, he did so at half speed, to give U.S. forces as much time as possible to react. By eight that evening, as darkness was falling, Captain Miller dropped anchor and brought his ship to a complete stop. His captors pressed him to go on, but Miller said his radar was inoperative and he could not safely navigate so close to shore. The ship remained at anchor until first light the next morning.

At six in the morning, the Cambodians indicated to Captain Miller by pointing at his charts (the Cambodians spoke no English) that they now wanted him to change course and proceed to Koh Tang island, a spit of land thirty-five miles off the Cambodian coast. After stalling for a few hours, the *Mayaguez* again got under way and headed for Koh Tang. Once again, Miller directed that his ship proceed at half speed, as he continued to play for time in the hope that U.S. aircraft would come to his rescue on the second day. At two that afternoon, the *Mayaguez* arrived at its destination off Koh Tang and dropped anchor. It had been almost twenty-four hours since the *Mayaguez* had radioed on the international distress frequency that it was being captured. And although U.S. reconnaissance planes had been launched almost immediately after the seizure and had been informed of the ship's last position, twenty-four

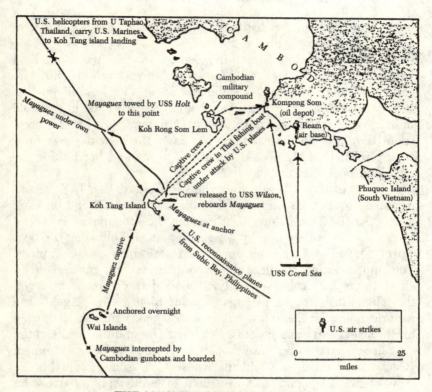

The following labels appear on the map:

U.S. helicopters from U Taphao, Thailand, carry U.S. Marines to Koh Tang island landing

C A M B O D I A

Cambodian military compound

Mayaguez towed by USS *Holt* to this point

Kompong Som (oil depot)

Ream (air base)

Koh Rong Som Lem

Mayaguez under own power

Captive crew in Thai fishing boat under attack by U.S. planes

Crew released to USS *Wilson*, reboards *Mayaguez*

Koh Tang Island

Phuquoc Island (South Vietnam)

Mayaguez at anchor

Mayaguez captive

U.S. reconnaissance planes from Subic Bay, Philippines

USS *Coral Sea*

Anchored overnight

Wai Islands

Mayaguez intercepted by Cambodian gunboats and boarded

U.S. air strikes

0   25
miles

THE *MAYAGUEZ* RESCUE MISSION

hours later U.S. planes had still failed to locate the *Mayaguez* at anchor one mile off Koh Tang island.

Captain Miller and his thirty-eight-man crew were removed from the ship to a Thai fishing vessel and taken to the island. The captain recalled later, in a public interview, that he noticed that the main cove on the island was heavily fortified, with a sizable military garrison armed with 20mm antiaircraft guns.[2] The crew spent the night on the island and at dawn the next day were put aboard a Thai fishing boat that put out to sea and headed for the mainland port of Sihanoukville.

It was at this time, dawn of the second day, that U.S. reconnaissance aircraft first sighted the *Mayaguez* at anchor off Koh Tang island. As the Thai fishing boat bearing the *Mayaguez*'s crew got under way, it was spotted by American planes. Following the boat closely, USAF A-7s staging from the American base in U Taphao, Thailand, overflew the boat and even made several gun runs in an effort to get her to heave to. The Cambodian commander forced the Thai fishing captain at pistol point to press on. Again, the American aircraft made low passes at the boat, and this time they fired rockets and cannon across her bow. The pilot of the attacking aircraft reported to his base that there seemed to be a number of "Caucasians" on deck. Told that these Caucasians might be the crew of the *Mayaguez*, the President ordered that the attack be broken off and the boat be allowed to proceed. U.S. aircraft had already fired on and sunk three Cambodian patrol boats that morning. No further attacks on the Thai boat were made, but the American planes followed it all the way to Sihanoukville. Once the fishing boat was inside the harbor, American planes loitered overhead for forty-five minutes, sending situation reports back to their base. After about twenty minutes, the boat carrying the *Mayaguez*'s crew moved across the harbor to another wharf. American aircraft were still overhead when the crew was transferred, inside the harbor cove, to Koh Rong Som Lem island in the bay of Kompong Som.[3] Thus, as far as the Americans knew, the crew of the *Mayaguez* were in the port of Sihanoukville.

Back in Washington, events were moving quickly. At the National Security Council meeting, Secretary of State Kissinger ar-

gued that the U.S. should take a very strong position. The American government ought to define the seizure of the *Mayaguez* as an act of piracy requiring a military response. His position was readily accepted by the other members of the Council. The President agreed. Later that day, the United States government announced that it regarded the seizure of an American merchant ship as an act of international piracy and demanded its immediate return. If the ship was not returned quickly, Cambodia would suffer "the most serious consequences."[4] The military was ordered to begin preparing to rescue the *Mayaguez* and to be ready for any military contingency.

The seizure of the *Mayaguez* came just two weeks after the end of Operation Frequent Wind, the evacuation of Saigon. Almost all the task-force elements used in that operation—which had been in and around the Cambodian coast—had begun to return to their normal duties. When the order came from the White House requiring the military to formulate contingency plans for military action, a quick review by the Pentagon revealed that they had few resources in the area with which to execute any operation. Only two Navy ships were anywhere near the scene, and both were at least twenty-four hours away from Koh Tang. The Navy ordered the attack carrier *Coral Sea*, then on her way to Australia, to change course and make all speed for the Cambodian coast. At the same time, the USS *Holt*, a destroyer escort, and the USS *Wilson*, a guided-missile frigate, were ordered to break off their exercises in the Philippines and proceed to Koh Tang. They would not arrive for twenty-four hours.

The United States still had at least two squadrons of aircraft deployed at U Taphao. But U Taphao was 195 miles from Koh Tang. The real problem was that the military had no ground forces in Thailand or anywhere nearby that could be quickly activated. The closest ground units that could be used were attached to the 3rd Marine Amphibious Force (MAF) deployed on Okinawa,[5] at least ten hours' flying time from Koh Tang.

On the evening of May 13, Major General Carl Hoffman, commander of the 3rd MAF on Okinawa, was directed by the Pentagon to provide a command group to begin planning an op-

eration to rescue the crew of the *Mayaguez*. He was also ordered to form a contingency battalion landing team (BLT) and to provide all other support needed by the commander of the 7th Air Force, located at U Taphao. As the senior commander in the area, the 7th Air Force commander would be in overall charge of the operation. It was clear from the beginning that any operation mounted against the *Mayaguez* or Koh Tang island would have to be staged from U Taphao, as there were no other facilities closer to the target. Command of the ground operations fell to Marine Colonel John M. Johnson, who led a command group formed from the 3rd MAF.[6]

Once it was decided to use U Taphao as the staging area for the rescue operation, the next problem was to position sufficient combat forces at the base to undertake the rescue. The Air Force had sufficient aircraft to support the operation (about two squadrons of A-7s, some helicopters, reconnaissance aircraft, and AC-130 gunships), but there were no combat troops closer than Okinawa. So the decision was made very early to airlift almost 1,100 combat Marines from Okinawa to U Taphao. The unit chosen was the Marine Battalion Landing Team 2/9.[7]

When the order came to deploy the Marines, they were out on a training exercise in the central training area on Okinawa. All four of the battalion's infantry companies had been in the field for almost two days, and their equipment was hardly ready for combat. Within three hours of receiving the warning order, however, all companies had returned to their main base at Camp Shaw, and in the next few hours the Marines cleaned their equipment and prepared to move to Kadena airfield, their normal deployment staging point. Other units on the island attached to the battalion were also preparing to deploy. By morning, all elements had been assembled at Kadena, and at 5:30 the command element boarded a C-141 aircraft and launched for U Taphao. One hour later, they were followed by the rest of Battalion Landing Team 2/9.[8] Within ten hours, the Marine assault force would be in place at U Taphao, ready to go into action.

The decision to use U Taphao, 195 miles from Koh Tang, as a staging base was forced largely by events and by the lack of a realistic alternative. The problem of the rescue force resolved itself

into how to get the combat Marines onto the *Mayaguez* and to Koh Tang. There was only one way to ferry troops quickly to a ship at sea or to a small island, and that was by helicopter. The Air Force was ordered to redeploy all its heavy-lift helicopters in Thailand to U Taphao. The 56th Special Operations Wing was ordered to U Taphao, along with the 21st Special Operations Squadron, flying CH-53 Sea Stallions. Along with these units, the 40th Aerospace Rescue and Recovery Squadron, flying HH-53s, also deployed to U Taphao.[9] En route to the base, however, one helicopter crashed. As a consequence, only thirteen heavy-lift helicopters were available to move the rescue force. Of these thirteen, two were assigned search-and-rescue missions and thus would have no direct role in deploying the combat assault force. This left the planners with only eleven heavy-lift helicopters, six HH-53 Jolly Green Giants and five CH-53 Sea Stallions. Clearly, the amount of lift was insufficient to move a large combat force. This meant, of course, that only a limited number of Marines could be deployed to the battle area. And this factor, perhaps more than any other, affected the choice of tactics in the *Mayaguez* operation. It also meant that a small force of Marines would be deployed against an enemy force of unknown size, disposition, and armament on board the *Mayaguez* and on Koh Tang island. The decision to use the available lift and go with a relatively small assault force rather than wait until more helicopters could be moved into place was the result of the need to execute the President's order for a quick military operation. Obviously, in Washington's view, time was of the essence. This placed the operation to rescue the *Mayaguez* at high risk.

Upon arriving at U Taphao, the commander of Task Group 79.9 was assigned the specific mission of recovering the *Mayaguez*. But, as time went on, the original recovery mission ordered by Washington was expanded by further instructions from the President and the Pentagon. The mission as finally defined was "to seize, occupy, and defend the island of Koh Tang, hold the island indefinitely [for a minimum of forty-eight hours] and to rescue any of the crew members of the *Mayaguez* found on the island and to simultaneously seize the *Mayaguez* and remove the ship from its current location."[10] (The ship was still anchored off the island of

Koh Tang.) All this was to be done with eleven helicopters available for lift and a small number of combat Marines which almost everyone recognized from the outset would be insufficient in most instances to execute an operation of this kind. Last, there was very little in the way of naval or air support that could effectively be brought to bear on the target. In short, the political pressure to do something immediately had overridden military common sense.

THE PLAN

The plan involved two different elements. The first was to airlift and put a sufficiently large combat force of Marines aboard the *Mayaguez* to recapture it from the Cambodians, who, it was presumed, were still aboard. The second component of the plan was to helilift a Marine combat assault force to Koh Tang to seize and hold that island. Unfortunately, there were not enough helicopters to do both at the same time. Indeed, there were not enough helicopters to lift a sufficiently large combat force even to subdue the island. Nonetheless, the decision was made by the military commanders at U Taphao to execute the mission.

The eleven available helicopters were to launch from U Taphao at the same time. Three of the helicopters, HH-53 Jolly Green Giants, would land directly on the deck of the *Mayaguez*. Since the *Mayaguez* was a container ship, however, there was almost no deck space on which to land a large helicopter. The ship's containers took up most of the deck, and they were made of aluminum and could not support the weight of the large HH-53s. Fortunately, someone on the planning staff realized that a landing aboard a container ship was not feasible. As an alternative, the planners ordered special ladders and rappeling gear which would allow the Marines to assault the ship directly from the helicopters. The helicopters would hover over the *Mayaguez* as the Marines rappeled aboard. Once on deck, the Marines would use the special platforms and ladders to move from container to container, until they had cleared the ship of the enemy force.

Fortunately, when this plan was brought forward for review

by the "murder board," a panel of officers outside the planning process who are routinely used to examine prospective military operational plans, it was pointed out that the plan was nothing less than suicidal. It required three heavy-lift helicopters to hover above the merchant ship, in a highly vulnerable position for the enemy on board the ship to direct heavy small-arms fire against them. They would be knocked out of the sky and crash onto the deck. The proposed plan almost guaranteed that at least one helicopter and perhaps more would be lost. This plan was rejected and a new one devised.

The plan completed just hours before the assault began was radically different. It called for the helicopters to ferry a force of forty-eight Marines, six Navy explosives experts, six civilian seamen of the Military Sealift Command, and a U.S. Army captain who spoke Cambodian. This combined force would not be directly heli-lifted to the *Mayaguez* but would be positioned aboard the destroyer USS *Holt*, which would be standing by, some two miles off the *Mayaguez*. The helicopters would come in and hover above the fantail of the *Holt* and the force transferred to her. Once the assault force was aboard, the *Holt* would close with the *Mayaguez*, pull alongside, and the Marines would storm aboard in true Barbary Coast fashion. If necessary, they would clear the ship with hostile fire. Seconds prior to the assault, Air Force A-7s would attack the ship, dropping riot-control agents, in this case CS vomiting and incapacitating gas, to disable and confuse the defenders. The Marines would go over the rail wearing gas masks and fight the enemy hand to hand.[11]

The remaining eight helicopters of the assault force would fly on past the *Mayaguez* and land 180 Marines onto Koh Tang island. The island is three miles long and has only two landing zones, both thin slivers of beach on opposite sides of a narrow land spit jutting into the water. The plan was to land two Marine contingents, one at each beach. The first element, about one reinforced platoon, would land on the western zone, while the rest of the assault force, about two platoons, would land on the larger eastern zone. A mortar section would deploy into the eastern zone to provide fire support with its 81mm mortars to the smaller Marine force deployed in the

west. Once the Marines were on the ground, the helicopters would fly back to U Taphao. There they would refuel and take aboard "a second wave of Marines" and return to the island with Marine reinforcements.[12]

The ability to reinforce the Marines placed on the beaches was questionable from the start. In the first place, the round trip from Koh Tang to U Taphao would take at least four and a half hours under optimal weather conditions. Second, the ability to move any sizable reinforcement unit to the island after the first wave landed depended completely on all eleven helicopters being available for the second round trip. This assumed that no machines would be lost to hostile fire, accident, or normal maintenance problems. Given the history of helicopter operations, this assumption was more than questionable; it was outrageously naïve. Yet the lives of over one hundred Marines hung on this faulty assumption. If the Marines were trapped on the beach, they would become easy targets for the Cambodian defenders. Further, the Marine assault was to be supported by naval gunfire from the *Holt* and the *Wilson*, while air strikes could be called in at the discretion of the ground commander. Air strikes would be mounted by USAF aircraft deploying from U Taphao and, later in the day, by aircraft from the carrier *Coral Sea*, which was steaming toward Koh Tang.

THINGS GO WRONG

At 2:30 in the morning of May 15, the combat Marines of the assault force assembled near their helicopters at U Taphao. Overall command of the operation was vested in the airborne mission commander, who would control the operation from his C-130, orbiting ninety miles away. Seats on the available helicopters were so scarce that Colonel Johnson, the commander of the ground assault group, decided to remain at U Taphao in order to give his seat to a combat Marine. Johnson and his staff planned to remain in Thailand while the first wave hit the island and then to go in with the reinforcements.[13] With the ground commander stranded in U Taphao, direct operational command of the assault passed to the airborne mission

commander orbiting in his command ship. The command and control links were, to say the least, awkward and unclear. Instead of a clear line of command running from the field units to a combat staff deployed on the island and then to a nearby command post on board ship (the normal operational relationship for Marine operations), these crucial control links ran from the commander on the ground to the mission commander orbiting in the air some ninety miles from the target. If anything happened to disrupt communications between the ground commander and the airborne commander, the Marines on the ground would be isolated. At 4:30 in the morning, the helicopters carrying the assault forces to the USS *Holt*, two miles from the *Mayaguez*, and to Koh Tang island lifted off and took up a heading for their respective targets. The mission was under way.

The assault on the *Mayaguez* went as planned, helped along by the fact that there was no resistance. The Cambodians had abandoned it.

The three HH-53s rendezvoused on schedule with the USS *Holt*, each helicopter in turn hovering over the *Holt*'s fantail and discharging its troops. Once the assault force was aboard, the *Holt* pulled alongside the *Mayaguez* and prepared to board and seize. At this time, the A-7s showed up on schedule and dropped incapacitating gas. As the Marines rushed the ship, they realized that it was empty. The Navy explosives experts began a systematic clearing search for demolition charges and booby traps; none was found. At the same time, the team of civilian seamen from the Military Sealift Command took over the bridge, started the engines, and made ready to move.

The assault on the ship began at 7:30, and by 8:30 the ship was secured and an American flag had been run up her mast. Before the assault, the Cambodians on the mainland had freed the *Mayaguez*'s crew, who were aboard a Thai fishing boat flying a white flag, making their way toward their ship. Interestingly, despite the many combat and reconnaissance aircraft in the area, no U.S. aircraft sighted the fishing boat carrying the crew toward the *Mayaguez*. The boat, flying its white flag, cautiously approached the USS *Wilson*, and when the *Wilson* recognized who was on the

71

fishing boat, they took the crew aboard. Word was flashed to Washington that the thirty-nine men were safe.[14]

It is important to emphasize that the crew of the *Mayaguez* was not rescued by U.S. military action. They were released by the Cambodians before the *Mayaguez* had come under combat assault by the Marines. Indeed, the crew's captors did not even know that the Marines had seized the ship. The crew's release had been secured by diplomatic means, through the intervention of third parties. But the military operation had gathered a momentum of its own. After the crew was aboard the *Wilson*, one would think that someone in the Pentagon or in the operational command in Thailand would have considered calling off the assault on Koh Tang island, since there was no longer any point to it. Equally, one would think that some thought would have been given to calling off the planned air raids against the mainland airport and oil-storage facilities in Sihanoukville, since the raids no longer served any military purpose. With the boat and crew recovered, there was no point in further military action. And even though the operation against Koh Tang was under way before the crew was discovered to be safe (the helicopters were still in the air on the way to the island), it could have been stopped. Even if the Marines were already on the beach, they could have been evacuated immediately. Instead, the plan proceeded, and no attempt was made to evacuate the Marines. In fact, as the assault began to go wrong, a concerted effort was mounted to reinforce the Marines, who, as it turned out, had landed in the wrong place.

As incredible as it seems, the Marines were put ashore on Koh Tang island in the belief that the American crew was being held there even though there had never been any evidence to that effect. U.S. reconnaissance aircraft did not discover the *Mayaguez* near Koh Tang until the crew was being moved to Sihanoukville. Since the *Mayaguez* was found anchored near the island, U.S. intelligence assumed that the crew was being held there. This turned out to be a classic intelligence failure.

On Tuesday morning, after searching for almost twenty-four hours, U.S. reconnaissance planes finally located the *Mayaguez* off Koh Tang island. At 8:00 in the morning, Cambodian time, these

aircraft reported that the Cambodians were moving the Americans to the mainland. U.S. combat aircraft even sank three fishing boats in the immediate area to get the Cambodians to return to the island. The American captives were placed on the open deck, in clear view, for reconnaissance aircraft to see; the crew was even allowed to signal to the aircraft. And although the A-7s made repeated passes at the fishing boat, often laying bombs and cannon fire off her beam and bow, the fishing boat pressed on for Sihanoukville. At one point, the A-7s dropped incapacitating gas on the boat. The overflights were so numerous that when Captain Miller was asked later how many times American planes had overflown the vessel, he estimated "about one hundred times."[15]

The various accounts of the incident make clear that the A-7 pilots dutifully reported their sighting back to headquarters in U Taphao, specifically passing on the information that "Caucasians" were seen on deck. These reports were relayed to the President and his advisors, who ordered the aircraft to break off the attacks and follow the fishing boat to Sihanoukville. The aircraft followed the boat carrying the crew and watched it enter the harbor. For forty-five minutes the aircraft remained overhead, until they witnessed the crew being moved to Koh Rong, a small island within the harbor itself.

Thus, the evidence pointed to the crew being detained on Koh Rong in the harbor. There was no evidence at all, except the fact that the *Mayaguez* was still anchored off Koh Tang, to suggest that the crew was being detained on Koh Tang island. Although this information was in the hands of the relevant commanders, including the President, for some unknown reason the assault on Koh Tang island was ordered to proceed anyway. Perhaps the point was to "teach the Cambodians a lesson." The assault on Koh Tang was an assault on the wrong island, and it was an assault entirely without a military point.

The original failure to determine the location of the crew was compounded by additional errors. Despite the fact that the United States had been involved in Vietnam for a decade and in Cambodia on and off for years, and despite the fact that American aircraft had overflown the area for years and that the islands had been used as

rescue points for downed pilots, when military commanders requested tactical maps of Koh Tang island they discovered that none existed in the intelligence inventory.[16] In order to obtain information about conditions on the island, intelligence operatives in Thailand resorted to Cambodians and Thais living in the U Taphao area who might have knowledge of the island. Fishermen and former sea captains were rounded up and interviewed. Even a former Cambodian naval captain who had defected to the Thais was located and interviewed. In the meantime, at least six reconnaissance overflights of Koh Tang were conducted and their reports forwarded to the planning commanders. In the end, the intelligence experts chose to believe the description of the island given them by the Cambodian naval captain. Relying on his description, the intelligence planners determined that there were no military fortifications or even permanent houses on the island. They expected to find no more than twenty people, most of them elderly.[17] It did not seem to have dawned on anyone that there was a paradox in maintaining that the crew of the *Mayaguez* was being held on Koh Tang island and at the same time maintaining that there were no enemy forces on the island.

In fact, there were between a hundred fifty and, more probably, three hundred well-trained Cambodian regulars on the island, deployed in fortified positions. And the enemy positions were located beneath a triple-thick jungle canopy, which hid them from detection from the air. The jungle canopy also provided a thick umbrella against air attack, and much of the weaponry normally used could not penetrate it.* As later events proved, the Cambodian force was well armed with AK-47 rifles, twin Soviet 12.7mm machine guns, 20mm antiaircraft guns, and shoulder-fired rocket-propelled grenades of both the RPG-50 and the 106mm variety, which the Vietcong had used to such great effect in the Vietnam war.

---

* Jungle canopy often grows twenty to fifty feet thick, making it impossible to penetrate with bombs and rockets. In Vietnam, the problem was partially but by no means successfully solved by using a Daisycutter, a 15,000-pound bomb dropped from a C-130 transport plane. It is so powerful that it kills earthworms in the ground as far away as one hundred yards from the crater.

Because of faulty intelligence, therefore, the Marine assault force was totally unprepared for the enemy they met. Moreover, they had scant knowledge of the terrain in which they would fight, and no maps. All the intelligence people could tell the Marine commanders was that the island was shaped like a C and was about three miles long and one mile wide. The island had a narrow sliver of beach, on which the Marines would land, and this was bordered by thick jungle and high grass. In the high grass, and just off the beach itself, were a number of small hills, or mounds, where the enemy had set up its defensive positions, thus commanding the tactical high ground. Once on the beach, the landing force would be unable to maneuver inland against the heavy enemy fire. Worse, the landing force would be unable to extract itself, because its back was to the sea.

The Marine assault force went in blind, and in insufficient numbers, with almost no advance air and naval gunfire support. The 180 Marines who would land in the first assault group were clearly outnumbered. The 127 Marines planned as reinforcements in the second group could not arrive for four and a half hours, and even then would add little to the punch of the attacking force. Normally, an assault force landing on an island beach requires at least a three-to-one numerical advantage to subdue an enemy in prepared defensive positions. Under the best conditions on Koh Tang, the Marines would have only a 1.5-to-one numerical advantage, assuming the smallest Cambodian force against the largest possible Marine force. In fact, the balance of forces favored the Cambodians by almost three to two. The Marines would face a numerically superior enemy who could expose them to hostile fire from at least two directions. And, given the terrain, the Marines would not be able to see the enemy positions that were firing at them.

The first flight of helicopters approached the island at 6:15, at dawn. The expectation was that no fighting would be necessary, as no enemy forces would be found on the island. The lead helicopters carried Cambodian-speaking language specialists armed with bullhorns. The plan was to have the helicopters land in force and the linguists announce that if the crew was released unharmed,

the Marines would leave peacefully.[18] Because there were supposedly no hostile forces on the island, no suppressive air or naval gunfire was used. That would have been pointless anyway, since the thick jungle canopy prevented observation of enemy strongpoints.

The first two helicopters approaching the eastern landing zone of the beach were shot out of the sky by a hail of small-arms and rocket fire. One helicopter was hit by a rocket-propelled grenade directly in the cockpit. The cockpit was blown off and the pilot killed instantly. The machine whirled wildly in the air and crashed into the surf. Nine men were killed in the crash. As survivors crawled from the wreck, three more Marines were cut down by machine-gun fire while struggling in the surf. The remaining thirteen occupants of the first helicopter, ten Marines and three Air Force crewmen, swam out to sea and waited three and a half hours before being picked up by the USS *Wilson*.[19] As the second helicopter approached the beach, it too came under intense fire and crashed. No one was killed, but the Marines were pinned down and unable to deploy. Their position was continually subject to intense fire. The helicopter itself was picked to pieces by gunfire, and one Marine and one Air Force crewman were wounded.[20] The Marines took fire all day from the heavy jungle and thick grass; their casualties began to mount. The landing in the eastern zone had gone so badly that it was decided to call off any further attempts to put troops in the area. As a result, twenty Marines and their officers of the 3rd Marine Platoon were trapped on the beach for almost two and a half days, continually exposed to hostile fire.

In the western zone, things went only marginally better. As the first helicopter approached the landing zone, it too came under withering fire. It had one engine shot out and its external fuel tanks riddled with small-arms and machine-gun bullets. The helicopter pulled up and headed back to Thailand. Although it was able to reach the mainland, it had to make an emergency landing fifty miles from its base at U Taphao, when its leaking fuel tanks ran dry.[21] The assault company commander, the officer who was to command the troops on the ground, was aboard this helicopter.[22] The Marines on the ground were left under the command of their platoon leaders, with no overall commander on the ground.

The second group of helicopters did manage to unload their troops in the western zone. In some instances, however, sergeants had to force their men to leave the machines and deploy. There were other instances of panic, as the rate of fire against the helicopters increased.[23] Once it had discharged its troops on the ground, a second helicopter lifted off, only to be hit again and again by enemy fire. It wobbled wildly, headed out to sea, and crashed, with the loss of one crewman, who drowned.

The remaining helicopters, three carrying combat assault elements, were able to put down in the western landing zone. However, only one was able to reach its intended landing position, and only after six attempts. The fire was so intense that the fourth helicopter, carrying the heavy-mortar team to provide heavy-weapons support, was forced to land almost a mile away from its intended position on the shore southwest of the island.[24] In fifteen minutes, the Marine landing had turned into a disaster. All positions were cut off from one another, either by thick foliage or the high jungle grass, and all were coming under heavy fire from concealed enemy positions. The Marines could do nothing but construct a perimeter defense and wait. As time passed, the number of casualties increased. Of the 180 combat Marines in the original helicopter landing force, only 109 were deployed, and these were largely ineffective as a combat force because they were separated from one another.[25] The Marines had lost almost 40 percent of their combat force in the initial assault on Koh Tang island. Worse, almost all the helicopters in the first assault wave had been shot down or severely damaged. Of the eight original helicopters that took part in the combat assault, all but one were destroyed or damaged.

The loss of the helicopters meant that the Marines no longer had sufficient airlift to move the second group of Marines from U Taphao to Koh Tang to relieve the pressure on the trapped men. Even if all had gone well, the Marines would still have had to hold out for four and a half hours until the helicopters reached U Taphao, refueled, and returned with the second assault group of Marines. Now there was no chance that a sufficiently large force of Marines could be brought to the island to help. The Marines had planned on having at least twelve helicopters to transport the relief force,

but now they had only five, and only one of these came from the original landing force as planned. Two more helicopters were now available, having discharged their troops aboard the *Holt*. Another helicopter had arrived at U Taphao too late to assist in lifting the first assault group, but was now available to lift the second. A fifth helicopter was also available, after having undergone repairs. Although it had mechanical problems, the machine was declared "up" for the mission.[26] But the five helicopters could only carry 127 men to reinforce the original 109 deployed on the Koh Tang beach. The Marines boarded the helicopters and left U Taphao by 9:30 that morning, headed for Koh Tang island to help their trapped comrades.

Long before, however, while the second assault group was en route to the island, the crew of the *Mayaguez* was picked up by the destroyer *Wilson*. While the flight was under way, higher headquarters at U Taphao, now informed that the crew was safe, ordered the helicopters to return to U Taphao, since the objectives of rescuing the crew and recapturing the ship had been accomplished. The commander of the Marine force en route to Koh Tang, however, was possibly not told that the *Mayaguez* crew was safe, or else decided to disregard the information. His mission was to capture the island and hold it for forty-eight hours. The fact that the crew and ship had been returned made no difference. He had been given a mission and was determined to execute it even if the mission no longer made any sense. Although the capture of the island was now pointless, no one in higher headquarters forbade the second assault group to proceed with its mission.[27] The second assault force approached Koh Tang island determined to accomplish a mission that was no longer necessary.

As the helicopters of the second assault group approached the western landing zone, they came under intense small-arms fire. After repeated attempts to land, four of the five helicopters were able to put down on the landing zone and unload their troops. The fifth machine was hit badly on its approach, pulled up and away, and limped back to its base in Thailand, taking its contingent of Marines with it.[28] Of the 127 men in the second assault team, a hundred were actually placed on the island. The wounded men

from the first group of Marines were quickly put aboard the helicopters and medevacked to U Taphao for treatment. With the second assault group ashore, the combined force now totaled 225 men, separated in three pockets and pinned down by an enemy concealed in defensive positions.

To the men on the beach it was no longer clear what their mission was. What was clear was that they had no possibility of securing the island or of rescuing anyone. To the ground commanders it was clear that they had to break out of their separate pockets and link up, to consolidate their defensive positions. Failure to do so would make it impossible to extract the force when the time came. Under the present circumstances, if they remained where they were, they would die one by one. The fighting was heavy and, at times, at close range. Some Marines performed great acts of individual heroism.[29] Near the end of the second day, the western-zone forces were able to link up and consolidate their positions, although the Marines in that zone remained separated from their comrades in the eastern zone by a corridor of enemy fire.

In the initial assault on the island, neither air strikes nor naval gunfire was used. Once ashore, however, the Marines realized that they needed as much air and naval gunfire support as they could muster to suppress enemy fire. But there was great difficulty directing this fire so that it had any effect on the enemy positions. The Marines had lost their tactical air-control radio in the surf when the first helicopter was shot down.[30] As a result, there was no way for the ground commanders to communicate with the aircraft that could deliver the air strikes. They were also unable to direct naval gunfire. The Marines adjusted to these circumstances as best they could by using the "wing-over technique" for directing air strikes.[31] An aircraft would make a run against a suspected target without dropping its bombs. As the aircraft came in over the general vicinity of the target, a Marine spotter on the ground would adjust the flight path of the aircraft to the left or right, until the aircraft flew a path sufficiently far from the Marines but close enough to the enemy positions to allow an attack. Once the flight path was established, the aircraft would make another pass, this time drop-

ping its bombs, it was hoped, on the enemy positions. But the lines of contact were too close to risk much air support, lest it strike Marine positions. The Marines called for no naval gunfire; in the past, too many men had been hit by their own gunfire in such circumstances. It was only near the end of the mission, as the Marines huddled on the beach during the helicopter evacuation, that it was possible to put enough distance between them and the enemy to permit effective air support.

As the Marines waited on the beach for the helicopters to pick them up, the Air Force threw everything they had at the enemy, including the 15,000-pound Daisycutter bomb developed in Vietnam for blasting out landing zones from thick jungle. Despite the heavy rain of fire, when the helicopters tried to land they were twice driven off by enemy fire. Naval gunfire and air attacks had not been planned in advance but had been placed at the direction of the Marine ground commander on an "on-call" basis. In any event, neither was used to any great effect or played a significant role in the battle for Koh Tang island.

While the Marines were pinned down on the beach, the Navy and Air Force conducted air strikes against the Cambodian air base at Ream. The official justification for attacking the base was "to protect the Marine operations" taking place on Koh Tang, thirty miles offshore.[32] In the initial wave, the fighter-bombers came from the carrier *Coral Sea*. Twenty-five attack aircraft flew fifteen sorties against the airport, using "smart bombs" against hard targets and cratering bombs against the runway. They also struck at the dozen or so T-28 propeller-driven aircraft on the rampways.[33] The attack came four hours after the Marine assault on Koh Tang had begun. If it was truly meant to protect the Marines from Cambodian air strikes, it came four hours too late. Moreover, since the Cambodians had made no effort to launch their aircraft against the island, there was no reason to believe they would launch them at all. The T-28s are American-built antiques, and no match for modern jets. Since Navy and Air Force aircraft had been orbiting and overflying Sihanoukville for almost two days and had already sunk three fishing boats, the Cambodians had gotten the message that the U.S. military was deployed in considerable strength and would be serious

about suppressing any attempt to use air strikes against Koh Tang. The U.S. aircraft could just as easily have continued to orbit the Ream airfield and to have struck the T-28s if they began to move. As if to underline the fact that the air strikes against Ream had no military point, almost an hour after the first strike a second attack was conducted, this time against the port and oil-refinery facilities located nearby.

At mid-morning on May 15, the President gave the order to stop all military activity and ordered the Marine force withdrawn from Koh Tang. The ground commander decided that the larger Marine contingent in the western zone could continue to hold out throughout the night if enough naval and air support were provided. But the small twenty-man element trapped in the eastern zone was in clear danger of being overrun once darkness fell. The decision was made in mid-afternoon to remove the entire Marine force that day, with priority given to the contingent in the eastern zone. Curiously, the first attempt to pull out the Marines in the eastern zone was made at 4:15 p.m., unbeknownst to the senior commanders at U Taphao. The details remain unclear. Someone seems to have ordered two helicopters, probably deploying from the *Coral Sea*, into the eastern landing zone, probably to deliver supplies or pick up wounded. As the helicopters approached the landing zone, they came under heavy small-arms fire. One machine was hit and had to limp back to the carrier, while the other broke off and aborted its attempt to set down. The twenty Marines remained trapped on the beach as darkness approached.[34]

At 6:10 in the evening, just twelve minutes before darkness fell, a single HH-53 managed to fly into the eastern zone, land, and successfully evacuate the Marines. This left 172 Marines in the western zone to be evacuated when circumstances allowed. Darkness was falling rapidly now, and the operation would have to be carried out in total darkness. This gave the enemy an advantage, since they could see the engine exhausts of the helicopters and could bring them under fire as they put down on the exposed beach. And in the dark, it was very difficult for the Marines to determine the source of enemy fire.

The helicopters made no fewer than five attempts to rescue

the Marines in the western zone.[35] In four tries, the helicopters were driven off by heavy fire. The Marines used OV-10 tactical air-control aircraft now on station (orbiting overhead) to spot muzzle flashes in the dark and direct AC-130 gunship fire down on the enemy. For two hours, the helicopters tried to land on the beach and get the Marines out. At each attempt, a small number of Marines made it to the helicopters. Finally, at 8:10, the helicopters went in for the last time to pick up the two remaining Marines, a captain and a gunnery sergeant who had stayed to search the beach and ensure that no one was left behind.[36] Within an hour, the Marines were aboard the helicopters and heading back to U Taphao. The battle for Koh Tang, a battle that should never have been fought, was finally over.

The decision to invade Koh Tang was costly in both men and machines. No fewer than twelve heavy-lift helicopters were destroyed or severely damaged. More important, the lives of eighteen men were lost: eleven Marines, two Navy corpsmen, two Air Force crewmen, and three Marines who have never been found and are presumed dead. Fifty men were wounded: forty-one Marines, two sailors, and seven airmen.[37] Of the 250-man combined force committed to the operation, sixty-eight had been killed or wounded; 26.5 percent of the force had been rendered ineffective. Normally, when a force suffers 30 percent casualties, it is carried on the rolls as "no longer combat-effective." In the case of the Marine force on Koh Tang, it had never been combat-effective from the minute it landed. It was separated, pinned down, and under continuous attack for two days. And it failed to accomplish a single mission it had been assigned.

WHY THINGS WENT WRONG

The rescue of the *Mayaguez* went well largely because it was unopposed. Had the government waited another hour, there would have been no need to attack Koh Tang at all. Even as the attack was under way, it became clear that the crew of the *Mayaguez* was safe, having been picked up by the destroyer *Wilson*. Despite this,

the senior commanders at U Taphao allowed the attack to proceed. Worse, the commanders committed a second group of Marines against the island after they knew that the crew of the *Mayaguez* was safe. Instead of expending their efforts to evacuate those Marines already committed to a pointless task, the commanders decided to throw more men into combat. The reinforcements that were finally placed on the island had no appreciable effect on the military situation except to complicate it and make the eventual task of evacuation even more difficult.

There is also no doubt that the intelligence community failed to support the operation effectively. They failed to discern that there was no reason to attack the island in the first place, since the crew was in Sihanoukville harbor. Further, they failed to provide accurate combat intelligence as to the nature and disposition of enemy forces on the island. Worse, they told the combat force that the island was undefended, when the island was garrisoned by a very well equipped force at least as large as and probably larger than the invading force. Finally, despite ten years of involvement in Southeast Asia, much of it in Cambodia, the intelligence people could not even provide a tactical map of Koh Tang island.

The commanders risked the lives of 250 Marines in a pointless venture to rescue a crew that was already safe. Even the original plan to land and reinforce the Marines depended on assumptions about the survivability and dependability of helicopters that ten years of experience in Vietnam should have immediately brought into question. Nonetheless, the plan was executed. Men died needlessly, and nothing was accomplished. From the perspective of military planning and execution, the *Mayaguez* incident, while it may have been some sort of political success, was a military failure.

OPERATION "EAGLE CLAW"
(THE IRAN RAID)

4

THE IRAN RESCUE MISSION

OF the military operations attempted by the United States between 1970 and 1984, none so clearly marked the decline of American military prestige and competence as the unsuccessful mission to rescue the fifty-three American hostages held in the U.S. embassy in Teheran. The regime of the Ayatollah Khomeini, before the world media, poked and prodded the bodies of eight American servicemen killed in the operation. The world wondered how a nation that could put a man on the moon and was among the most technologically advanced in history could fail to fly eight helicopters 540 miles, with no enemy opposition, and suffer equipment failures that prevented three of them from reaching their destination. Further, having only five helicopters at Desert 1, the U.S. could not even get them out undetected. The crash of an RH-53D helicopter into a C-130 while refueling on the ground at the landing site killed eight men and wounded several others. When it was all over, the impact of the failed raid surely contributed to driving President Jimmy Carter from office.

The disaster of the Iran raid dramatized the inability of U.S. military planners to conceive and execute a military operation even though they had almost six months to organize it. In the days immediately following the failure of the Iran raid, both the press and the American people, carefully briefed by the government and the Pentagon, tended to blame the failure on bad luck, the kind of thing that could happen in any military operation. Five years later, as much classified information has come into the public do-

main, it became clear that the failure of the raid had little to do with bad luck. It was an operation so poorly planned and executed that failure was almost guaranteed.

In November 1979, the American embassy in Teheran was attacked and captured by a contingent of Iranian Revolutionary Guards, the most radical of the Ayatollah Khomeini's adherents. Whether the captors intended to hold the Americans as long as they did—more than a year—remains uncertain. However, as the first days and then weeks dragged by and the United States took no direct action to change the course of events, the Ayatollah began to see great domestic and international propaganda value in holding on to the hostages. In the early days of the Iranian revolution there were still vestiges of moderation within the government, and these elements continued to assure U.S. officials in private that the hostages would not be harmed and that their release could be achieved by diplomatic means. Having allowed the first days to pass without any action, the U.S. played into the hands of the Iranian regime by continuing its diplomatic efforts and openly renouncing the use of military force to rescue the hostages or punish the new regime in Teheran. President Carter was committed to a peaceful solution.

From the beginning, however, there were voices within the Administration that pressed for some kind of military action. The truth is that the seizure of the hostages came as such a surprise that no military contingency plan existed to deal with the situation. Indeed, the Pentagon did not even have a staff element within the office of the Joint Chiefs of Staff whose job it was to anticipate and plan rescue commando operations if the need arose. Once the decision was made to develop a military option, an entire staff structure had to be created from scratch within the JCS.

Planning began in November 1979 with instructions from the White House to the JCS to assemble a staff and develop contingency plans. By December, the selection of a rescue force was completed and several training exercises were under way. From the outset, the decision was made to develop components of the force in different places rather than bring them together at a single location. At least two components trained at their normal assignment bases, so as not to raise suspicion. By the end of March 1980,

the last training exercises were held, and on April 16 the JCS met for final review and approval of the plan to rescue the hostages.

The JCS approved the plan and recommended it to the President, who on the same day, April 16, gave the order to execute it. Between April 19 and 23, the elements of the force deployed to their staging positions. The C-130s flew from Wadi Kena in Egypt, and then on to the island of Masirah in the Persian Gulf. The assault force and helicopter elements were deployed aboard the carrier *Nimitz* in the Persian Gulf. At dusk on April 24, six C-130 aircraft lifted off from their staging base on Masirah, headed south, and then refueled over Oman and turned north to head into the Iranian desert. A few hours later, at 7:30 that evening, eight RH-53D Sea Stallion heavy-lift helicopters took off from the deck of the *Nimitz* and headed north into Iran. Less than eight hours later, at a small airstrip deep in Iran's Dasht-e-Kavir (Great Salt Lake) desert, the assault force would keep its rendezvous with disaster.

THE PLAN

The rescue plan was as audacious as it was impractical. In the first phase of the operation six C-130 aircraft staging from Masirah were to proceed to a spot in the Iranian desert 265 miles southeast of the capital of Teheran. Three C-130s carried the 120-man assault team and a smaller force, the road-watch team, who were to provide security at the Desert 1 landing site. The three other C-130s carried fuel for the helicopters which they were to refuel at Desert 1. Desert 1, the first landing point in the desert, was located near the small village of Posht-e-Badam in the middle of the Dasht-e-Kavir desert, about five hundred miles inland from the Persian Gulf. The second element of the plan involved flying eight RH-53D Sea Stallion helicopters to Desert 1 from the carrier *Nimitz*, deployed in the Persian Gulf. The helicopters were to fly under the Iranian radar screen, using only night-vision devices and dead reckoning, and join the C-130s at Desert 1. The flight time for the helicopters was approximately five and a half hours.

The Desert 1 site left much to be desired. It was bisected by a fairly well traveled paved highway, and there was fear from the beginning that the normal traffic on the road might spot the raiders after they landed. One of the ironies of the operation was that the Iranians knew about the site and feared that one day it might be used to stage an attack against them. According to *Time* magazine, a map of the site had been discovered among the papers of Mohamed Jaffarian, a pro-Shah counter-insurgency specialist, who was executed after the revolution. Jaffarian was reportedly caught trying to burn the map when he was seized by Revolutionary Guards. Under interrogation, he told his captors that the staging site had been secretly built by the CIA, with the Shah's knowledge, for possible use in evacuating him should it become necessary.[1] The Iranian Air Force had even proposed destroying the site, suspecting that it might contain hidden navigational equipment (which it did not) that could guide incoming American planes. The situation in Iran was so confused during the early days of the revolution, however, that despite the fact that the Iranian security forces, themselves in disarray because of the purges against them, had knowledge of the CIA-built landing site, they took no steps to dismantle it or even to keep it under observation. Official reports suggest that, when the United States needed a site from which to stage the rescue, an exhaustive review of all possible landing sites indicated that only the one at Posht-e-Badam was acceptable.

Once the C-130s and the helicopters had rendezvoused at Desert 1, the plan called for the helicopters to refuel and take the assault team aboard. Then, still in darkness, the helicopters were to ferry the assault team to a commando "mountain hideaway" called Desert 2, located about fifty air miles from Teheran, in the mountains southeast of the city, in the area known as Garmsar. Desert 1 had been given the code name Watchband, and Desert 2 was Fig Bar. Also identified on the plan was another site, Helo Hide, near the town of Manzariyeh, about thirty miles south of Teheran. Once the assault team had been dropped at Desert 2, their helicopters would deploy to Helo Hide, fifteen miles east of Desert 2, land, and await the call to enter Teheran and pick up the Delta raiders and the hostages. The assault party would remain

in hiding at Desert 2 throughout the next day, resting and preparing its equipment. As darkness fell, the men of the assault force would board six 2.5-ton Mercedes trucks supplied by the advance team, a group of Army Special Forces agents who had entered Iran ten days earlier to aid the assault force.

The advance team, code-named Esquire, was commanded by Dick Meadows, an Army Special Forces major. Meadows was a close friend of the assault-force commander, Colonel Charles Beckwith, and had commanded the prisoner-rescue element in the Sontay raid in 1970. The advance team would be able to enter Iran and move about because of long-standing intelligence connections of the United States with Iran under the Shah. A number of safe houses and "rat lines" were readily available, as were former Iranian agents who had worked for the U.S. Despite the fervor of the new regime, many of these resources ("assets," in the intelligence lexicon) had not been neutralized or even disrupted. Moreover, the counter-intelligence capability of the Iranians, once centered in the dreaded but often incompetent SAVAK, had been almost destroyed by the purges and executions carried out by the Khomeini regime. At the height of the regime's revolutionary fervor, therefore, movement in and out of Iran by American agents was relatively easy.

The advance team had been gradually infiltrated into the country, with the first men arriving some ten days in advance of the rescue attempt. Some came overland by bus from Turkey and Pakistan, others by commercial aircraft, and some came in as civilian businessmen and tourists. Their mission was to provide the trucks and vehicles necessary to move the assault team from Desert 2 to the embassy. They would also guide the assault force to the embassy and the Foreign Ministry, through the maze of streets in Teheran. The plan called for the four-man advance team to be evacuated on the same helicopters that would airlift the hostages and the combat team out of the country.

In addition, there is some evidence that there were other American forces positioned in the country to assist the raiders. While it is impossible even now to pin down the exact size and mission of these forces,[2] it appears that they were located around

the town of Manzariyeh, near the Desert 2 site. There was both a Ranger force of at least platoon strength and a combat control team. The Ranger force was code-named Shoulder, and the combat control team was Waist Coat. Their job was to prepare the way for a larger Ranger force of company strength to attack and seize the small airstrip outside Manzariyeh, from which the hostages and the rescue force from the helicopters would be evacuated by two C-141s.

Once night fell, the assault force at Desert 2 would load into the vehicles, which would slip one by one into the city and rendezvous at a "warehouse" that had been acquired by an American agent. The ground assault team was the super-secret and highly trained Delta Force, a special counter-terrorist group. Once inside the city, the commandos would divide into three teams. A small, thirteen-man party would leave for the Foreign Ministry building, where U.S. chargé d'affaires Bruce Langdon and two other diplomats were being held captive. The majority of the force, now split into two assault teams, would drive to the embassy compound, where the fifty hostages were held, and take the embassy itself.

The assault on the embassy had been very well rehearsed and should have been among the easiest to execute, because the men guarding the hostages were getting sloppy in their security precautions. Further, their numbers had been reduced. The original guard force had numbered about 160 men, but by the time of the raid, that number had dropped to twenty.[3] Moreover, in the Foreign Ministry there were two guards watching three people. The time when the guards were changed and the exact positions of the guards were known to U.S. intelligence and had been verified. Intelligence had been extensive and productive. Using satellites, communications intelligence, signal intelligence, and human agents, the Americans had been able to keep close tabs on events in Iran. Moreover, the Americans had an agent within the embassy. An Iranian cook had stayed behind and regularly relayed information from inside the embassy to U.S. agents in Iran. Thus, U.S. intelligence services knew the location of the guards, the size of the guard force, the guards' regular schedules, when they slept, what they ate, the quality of their weapons and ammunition, etc.

Since the 1970s, it is standard U.S. practice to test the security of its embassies in mock attacks. The Iranian embassy had been tested by an Army Special Forces team in 1974. Four attempts were made at that time to breach the security of the embassy compound, and in each case the assault force succeeded. However, the recommendations made by the security team in 1974 had gone unimplemented, so that weaknesses uncovered in 1974 still existed to be exploited in 1980.[4]

The U.S. government, to deceive the Iranians, stated publicly that no military action was contemplated; that it had never been considered because it was certain to fail and result in very high casualties among the hostages. Interviews with individuals who had tested the embassy's security in 1974 and who helped plan the operation indicate that the planners regarded the actual assault on the embassy compound as probably the easiest part of the operation. The assault force was armed with satchel charges and silenced machine guns and pistols. Despite press reports that special knockout gas was to be used (probably a confusion with flash-and-stun grenades), no such plan existed, for the simple reason that knockout gas would incapacitate the hostages as well as their guards, and it would be difficult to drag unconscious hostages to the waiting helicopters. Delta Force intended to assault the embassy with rapidity, stealth, and overwhelming violence.

The overall operation was not without risk. The CIA had estimated that as many as 60 percent, or thirty-two, of the hostages might be killed or wounded. Although the Pentagon has denied that any such estimate was made, it has been learned, and reported by *Time*, that the Pentagon planners themselves believed the number of casualties among hostages and rescuers might run as high as one hundred.[5] Even the final plan envisioned the possibility of losing from fifteen to twenty hostages.

The assault on the embassy was to begin at 8:40 in the evening and was to be completed by 9:30 at the latest. As soon as Delta Force began its assault, the five helicopters at Helo Hide, code-named Bluebeard Involved, would launch from their hiding places for separate landing zones within the city of Teheran.[6] The sixth helicopter, code-named Honeydew, would remain behind because

it was not needed. At exactly 9:30, each helicopter would set down at its assigned "bus stop" and take aboard a "packet" of hostages and members of the assault force that had run across the street from the embassy to Amjadiyeh Stadium. It is unclear how many "bus stops" there were. The original plans captured by the Iranians at Desert 1 show that at least one helicopter would deploy to the "construction-site bus stop" a little over two miles from the embassy, while two others were to land at the soccer stadium across the street from the embassy. One additional helicopter would hover over the stadium while the other orbited over the construction site, both serving as emergency backups in case a helicopter was shot down or unable to fly because of mechanical failure. Three helicopters were all that was needed to lift out the hostages and the rescue team. The handwritten notes of the helicopter pilot on the plan indicate that each "bus stop" would be covered from the air by AC-130 Spectre gunship fire, which was on call over a special frequency. Further, the helicopters could call in naval air support simply by transmitting the code word "Thunder" over a designated frequency.

By 10:00, the helicopters carrying the hostages and the assault force were to be clear of the city, and by 11:00 they were to deploy to the airfield outside Manzariyeh, which, by this time, was to have been seized by a company of Rangers in a daring air assault that evening. Once on the ground, the American contingent would be airlifted out by two C-141 aircraft that had flown in from Masirah, guided by specially equipped navigation aircraft called Combat Talons.

After the helicopters had lifted off from Teheran and the C-141s had been moved into place for the rescue, a large number of Navy fighter and fighter-bomber aircraft would cover the escape. During the rescue attempt, Navy aircraft staging from the carriers *Coral Sea* and *Nimitz* in the Persian Gulf would fly along the Iranian border, ready to speed toward Teheran if the assault force got into trouble. The exact number of aircraft involved has not been revealed, but two aircraft carriers can easily launch fifty aircraft against enemy targets. These aircraft would be used to suppress any Iranian air or ground reaction. Moreover, the Pentagon had targeted all

the airfields in and around Teheran from which Iranian fighters could rise to strike at the rescue force. Apparently, the United States was prepared to destroy those forces on the ground if radio communications, routinely intercepted by the Americans, indicated that the Iranians were going to launch their aircraft against the rescue force. Although the Iranian Air Force was once the most powerful in the Middle East, by the time of the rescue mission that force had been severely depleted in both strength and ability. Of Iran's seventy-six advanced F-14 fighters, because of a lack of spare parts and pilot training, only seven could be put into the air. Iran's Phoenix missile, a devastatingly accurate weapon, was no longer operational, for lack of maintenance. Iran had some 187 operational F-4 fighters, at least fifty of which were deployed near Teheran,[7] but none of these was equipped for night combat. The American contingency plan to have aircraft standing by to intercept and destroy any Iranian force that attempted to stop the rescue was a good one and could probably have been executed with great effect.

THINGS GO WRONG

The public has probably never fully appreciated how important timing was to the success of the mission. On the day of the raid, military meteorologists predicted that there would be only nine hours and sixteen minutes of darkness for the C-130s and the helicopters to rendezvous at Desert 1, and for the helicopters to refuel and fly on to Desert 2.[8] The plan called for the complete operation to take eight hours. There was only one hour and sixteen minutes of darkness, at the maximum, for delays. If anything went wrong, especially if the helicopters arrived late or the refueling took longer than scheduled because of mechanical difficulties, the mission would have to be aborted, or it would helicopter into Desert 2 in broad daylight. By dawn, the Iranian Air Force would be fully alert, its radars manned and operating, and the sky full of aircraft on routine border patrols and on training flights. The chances that they would

come across the rescue force were good. Thus, from the beginning, the plan was time-sensitive.

Things went wrong almost from the beginning. Two hours into the flight from the *Nimitz*, helicopter #6, carrying the leader of the helicopter flight, had a warning light on its instrument panel go on. The warning light (BIM) indicated that the main rotor blade had a cracked spar. The commander of the aircraft landed in the desert, and another helicopter followed him down. The crew inspected the main rotor spar and could find no crack. They did find, however, that the sending unit of the indicator light was working normally. At this point, the commander of the helicopter decided to abandon the machine in the desert and fly on to Desert 1 with the other helicopter.[9]

The decision to abandon helicopter #6 turned out to be crucial. And it seems the type of decision that was based on the crews' unfamiliarity with the performance of their RH-53D aircraft on long flights. In fact, the BIM light on the RH-53D has a tendency to go on, warning of a cracked spar, when there is nothing wrong at all. The Pentagon noted in its report that in a check with the Sikorsky Company, the manufacturers of the aircraft, it was found that in five years 210 instances of the BIM indicator light coming on had been recorded. In each instance, close inspection revealed not a single crack in the main spar. Moreover, the technical manuals for the machine make clear that even if a crack develops in the spar, the RH-53D can still fly for seventy-nine hours without endangering the integrity of the main rotor—enough time for the helicopter pilots to have completed their mission.[10] Most interesting, in the rehearsals of the mission, there had been a number of instances in which the BIM light had come on. In each case, when the rotors were checked, not a single cracked spar was found. Had the crews been more proficient, they would have known that the tendency for the BIM light to come on was almost a normal condition of the RH-53D. Thus, the decision to abandon the helicopter should never have been made. The decision to abandon a perfectly good helicopter in the desert was one major factor in the mission's failure.

With one helicopter down and abandoned, the rest of the flight

continued toward Desert 1. It is important to remember that the decision to abandon the helicopter was made two hours into the flight. Three hours after lifting off from the *Nimitz*, the rest of the helicopters ran into large clouds of suspended dust which reduced visibility to almost zero. Not only were the pilots unable to see the ground, they were not able to see the helicopters flying with them. And in the dust cloud, their ability to navigate by dead reckoning was severely restricted. The formation integrity of the flight was lost and the helicopters became scattered all over the sky. Moreover, no method had been devised for the commander to communicate with the rest of his flight. The reason for failing to permit communications was to preserve communications security (COMSEC) in the belief that Iranian listening posts might pick up any transmission and be alerted to the flight's presence. Worse, there was no contingency plan if communications became impossible.

As the flight separated and each helicopter continued on its way to Desert 1 unsure of its own position, the leader of the helicopter squadron became disoriented while making a turn and decided to land in the desert to try to regain his bearings. Another helicopter followed him down. Once on the ground, the commander became even more confused. Using a low-frequency radio transmitter so as to reduce the risk of detection, he contacted the Joint Task Force commander, airborne in his C-130 command post over the Persian Gulf. The helicopter commander was instructed that the sky was clear over Desert 1 and was told to proceed to the landing site.[11] The helicopter rose up, plunging back into the dust storm. But by this time the integrity of the flight was completely lost and each helicopter was proceeding on its own, unable to communicate either with the flight leader or with the other helicopters that were somewhere out there in the darkness. The visibility within the dust cloud was marginal. The plan had not anticipated a dust cloud, and in fact, "the minimum visibility conditions for the operational requirements of the mission were not defined or tested in practice."[12] This was a complete surprise.

Four hours into the mission, while the helicopters were still in the dust clouds, the instrument panel on helicopter #5 indicated

that its navigational system had failed. Unable to find his true position or to communicate with either the flight commander or the mission commander, the pilot of #5 decided to abort.[13] Worse, he had no way of informing anyone that he was doing so. Number 5 turned around and flew four hours back to the carrier *Nimitz*, where it landed with its fuel tanks almost empty. At this time, the commander of the helicopter flight had no idea that any machines were not operational and not proceeding toward Desert 1. And the decision to abort came only twenty-five minutes away from the end of the dust cloud. Had helicopter #5 pressed on, it would have broken out of the clouds less than fifty-five minutes away from Desert 1.[14]

But there was no contingency plan for communicating with the flight leader, the mission commander, or Desert 1, and the pilot of helicopter #5 feared that any transmission might compromise the mission. Had he been able to communicate, he would have been told that the sky over Desert 1 was clear and that the C-130s had already landed and were in position to refuel his helicopter. When the pilot was debriefed, he was asked if he would have pressed on had he known that he was only twenty-five minutes from exiting the dust cloud and that the sky over Desert 1 was clear. He answered yes.[15] Had he arrived at Desert 1, the equipment that had failed could easily have been replaced with parts from helicopter #2, which had had to abort after reaching the landing site.

The commander of helicopter #2 had noticed a warning light on his instrument panel indicating hydraulic pump failure and that its fluid tanks were dry. Although the danger was much greater than the problems that faced #5, the commander had pressed on to Desert 1, where he landed safely. Once on the ground, the pilot and the on-site commander inspected the helicopter, and confirmed that it had lost its hydraulic fluid, due to a cracked B-nut; the loss of fluid had caused the pump to fail.[16] And things got worse. As the helicopters began to settle in at Desert 1, it became evident that, of the original eight helicopters launched from the *Nimitz*, only five had made it in serviceable condition. One had turned back, one had been abandoned, and one had arrived in an unusable condition.

Even if all eight machines had made it to Desert 1, it is unlikely that the mission could have continued except at very grave risk. After the helicopters became separated in the dust storm, they flew individually erratic courses and had to search around continually to establish their positions. As a result, four of the five helicopters arrived late, some as much as an hour late. And #2 arrived eighty-five minutes late.[17] This delay would probably have meant canceling the mission, or flying into Desert 2 in broad daylight. One of the major causes of the failure of the Iran raid, then, was the inability of the helicopter pilots to navigate in marginal visibility and to do so over a long period of time. This situation was brought about by the decision to use the wrong helicopter pilots for the mission.

It is clear that when the pilots encountered the dust cloud, they were "surprised and unprepared to accurately assess its impact on their flight."[18] The pilots had never been briefed about the possibility of encountering dust clouds. Neither had the C-130 pilots. The obvious question is why no one was prepared. The fault was not with the weather-forecasting team. The official investigation report indicates clearly that the weather team did its job relatively well in predicting the weather conditions over Desert 1 and Desert 2. In fact, the weather team did anticipate the possibility of suspended dust clouds and prepared a report in which they included an explanation of the· phenomenon—even a table indicating the location, month, and frequency of dust-cloud suspensions that might be expected along the route to Desert 2.[19]

If the meteorologists raised the possibility that dust clouds might be encountered, why were the pilots not informed and trained for it? The answer seems to be that the Joint Task Force planning staff was so concerned with maintaining operational security that it severed the direct link between the weather forecasters and the pilots.[20] Normally, weather forecasters brief pilots in detail and in person. Such a meeting not only informs pilots about conditions but, more important, gives them the opportunity to raise questions. But this practice was suspended during the preparations for the Iran raid. The weather team never briefed the pilots directly. Instead, a special intelligence officer was assigned to act as liaison between the weather team and the pilots.[21] This officer would be

briefed by the weather team, and he would condense the information and brief the pilots.

Anyone who has ever been a briefing officer understands that the time available is always too short. Accordingly, the briefing officer must select and present material which he feels is most important to the mission. This is exactly what happened here. The intelligence officer ignored the warning about dust storms, either because he did not think it was particularly important or because he did not understand. Incredibly, the crews were never briefed on the problem and, thus, did not train to overcome it.

At Desert 1, other things began to go wrong. The first plane to arrive, a C-130, carried the on-site commander, the combat control team, and the road-watch team. On its approach to landing, this aircraft had to abort because it almost hit an Iranian truck on the highway that bisected the landing zone. The aircraft made another pass at the landing zone but overshot its approach in the dark and had to go around again. On the third attempt, the C-130 managed to land.[22] The near-miss with the truck probably compromised the security of the landing site at Desert 1.

Upon landing, the road-watch team took up positions at either end of the road that bisected the landing zone. Almost immediately, the team had to deal with civilian traffic coming down the road. In one case, a bus carrying forty-three Iranians was stopped and the passengers herded toward the C-130. The on-site commander, not knowing what to do with them, made the decision to take them out of the country when the C-130s left. Within ten minutes two vehicles, a fuel truck and a pickup truck, approached from the opposite direction. The road team tried to block their way. The driver of the fuel truck attempted to run the roadblock, and in a hail of gunfire his truck exploded. The driver abandoned the vehicle and ran back to the pickup truck, clambered in, and escaped down the road, probably to the nearest village to sound the alarm.[23] The American force had been discovered in the middle of the Iranian desert, and the news would reach the Iranian government probably within hours.

As the on-site commander and other element leaders arrived aboard the C-130s, they found that the helicopters were late. But

there was no way to contact the helicopters that were still in flight. The commanders on the ground could not know that one helicopter had been abandoned in the desert, that another had aborted and turned back, and that a third was limping its way to Desert 1 with its hydraulic pump broken. Nor had they anticipated the effect of the dust storms on the formation integrity of the helicopter flight. As they waited on the desert floor, the separated helicopters were desperately trying to find the landing zone. Moreover, the communications sets that would have allowed the on-site commander to reach the task-force commander were not aboard the first C-130 to land. For some reason, they had been placed in the third airplane.[24] The men at Desert 1 sat on the ground for almost eighty minutes waiting for the helicopters while the engines of the C-130 were kept running, consuming precious fuel that would be needed to refuel the helicopters.

No preparations had been made for establishing command and control procedures at Desert 1, or for establishing clear lines of authority. Apparently, no thought had been given to the command structure or staff support that would be needed to carry out the loading of men and equipment and the refueling of helicopters. The scene on the desert floor was one of confusion. One has only to imagine the roar of the sixteen C-130 engines. And, once the helicopters landed, the noise of twelve RH-53D turbofan engines added to the din. The blades of the helicopters churned up small tornadoes of dust, while the force of the C-130 engines pushed the dust laterally across the landing site. There was no way to determine in the darkness, and with the noise and the swirling sands, who was in charge or where the central command points were located. No provisions had been made for determining the location of a central command post in advance and ensuring that all the members of the mission knew where to find it.[25] Originally, some thought had been given to staff organization, but the idea had been dropped as the planners became convinced that the operation could be executed more efficiently if staff were kept to a minimum. Accordingly, individuals were to be drafted on the spot to perform tasks for which they had not been trained. The ability of the on-site commander to communicate with the key element commanders

was almost non-existent. It had been decided in advance that, to maintain security, radio communication would not be used, but no one had thought of assigning runners to the command post to transmit orders to element commanders.[26] Things were so confused at Desert 1 that not all the key people in the operation even knew who was in command. Amazingly, when the helicopter pilots were debriefed after the raid, a large number of them did not even recognize the name of the on-site commander![27]

As a result of the unclear lines of command and control, orders were routinely questioned and frequently had to be given twice. Often, the individuals who gave the order had to go directly to the individual who was to execute it and explain. These conditions persisted right up until the crash of an RH-53D helicopter into a C-130 tanker which was refueling it. Even then, when the order was given to evacuate, some element commanders, especially the helicopter pilots, questioned the order.

As time passed, it became clear to the on-site commander that at least two of the helicopters were not going to arrive. The plan required that at least six helicopters be available for staging to Desert 2. Since only five were operational, the assault commander, Colonel Charles Beckwith, had to make the decision to abort the mission or continue with five machines. Beckwith decided that the mission should be aborted. He informed the on-site commander, who radioed the recommendation back to the Joint Task Force commander, who passed it on to the Pentagon. The Pentagon sent it along to the White House, where the decision to accept Colonel Beckwith's recommendation was made. Just before dawn, Beckwith ordered the raiders to board their C-130s and their helicopters and prepare to evacuate Desert 1.

While the determination was being made, the helicopters conducted their planned refueling, since the pilots still believed that the mission would continue. Desert 1 had been divided into north and south refueling zones. Since all aircraft and helicopters at Desert 1 kept their engines running, the engines of the C-130s which had arrived on time had been running on the ground for almost an hour and a half. It had been decided to keep the aircraft engines running to eliminate any risk of not being able to restart them.

Thus, refueling was done with all engines running, in the dark and with no lights, and with a great deal of dust and turbulence within a very small area. As helicopter #3 lifted away from its tanker to make room for another helicopter to take on fuel, it wobbled and went into an extreme bank. Its main rotor blades struck the C-130 tanker behind the cockpit, and both helicopter and tanker exploded. The five-man crew of the C-130 perished in the cockpit, as did the three Marines aboard the helicopter. The munitions aboard the C-130 began to explode, and projectiles struck some of the helicopters waiting to take on fuel. Amid ear-shattering noise, fire, and confusion, the on-site commander decided to abandon Desert 1 as rapidly as possible. He also decided not to destroy the remaining helicopters or to sanitize them of the classified material left on board. Leaving the helicopters on the ground, the party boarded the remaining three C-130s, loaded the wounded aboard, and took off for Masirah. The problems which had plagued the mission in practice—on-time navigation and refueling—had turned Desert 1 into a disaster.

The evacuation of Desert 1 left behind five RH-53D helicopters intact, with all classified material on board. During the planning for the Iran raid, the suggestion had been made to follow the procedure used in the Sontay raid, where explosive charges had been placed aboard the helicopters in advance. Wires to the explosives were taped along the floor of the helicopters and left unconnected to a timing detonator. If the machine had to be abandoned, all the crew would have to do is connect the wires to the detonator, set the timer, press the clock button, and leave the machine. A few minutes later, the helicopter would be destroyed. This plan, although strongly advocated by Colonel Beckwith and the Army elements in the force, was vetoed by the Marine crews, who felt it was too dangerous. They refused to fly the mission if their helicopters were wired to explode.[28] In order to compensate for this fact, a special helicopter-destruction team was on board one of the C-130s. Their job would be to destroy the helicopters on the ground by throwing thermite grenades into the cockpits. However, when the first helicopter went down in the desert with a suspected rotor-blade failure, the destruct team was in the air

aboard the C-130s. And the helicopter crews had no ability to destroy their own machines if the need arose.

The confusion caused by the crash at Desert 1 was so great that the destruct teams never attempted to destroy the helicopters. The rush to board the airplanes precluded any attempt to carry out that mission, even though more than twenty minutes elapsed between the time of the crash and the lift-off of the C-130s. In addition, because the helicopters were loaded with fuel and munitions, the explosions caused by thermite grenades tossed into the aircraft would be very dangerous to the destruct teams. The helicopters were parked so closely together that if one exploded, the odds were good that it would injure other members of the team trying to blow up another helicopter. In short, the helicopter-destruct plan was more a bureaucratic compromise between the Army and the Marines than a feasible plan. It had never been rehearsed and was unworkable. In any event, no attempt was made at Desert 1 to destroy the helicopters.

The crews of the helicopters were supposed to sanitize their machines of classified material. The crews of the two helicopters in the southern refueling zone did in fact remove the classified material, but the three machines in the northern refueling zone were not searched.[29] The crews were ordered not to by the on-site commander; they were ordered aboard the evacuation plane. Incredibly, the on-site commander did not know what classified material was being left behind![30] He had not been informed what classified material the machines carried, so as to minimize the chances of a security leak. What was left behind was the complete plan for the landing at Desert 2 as well as the operations within Teheran. (Why the classified material was brought along to begin with remains a mystery; why there were several copies is even more puzzling.) In one of the great ironies of the Iran raid, the only people outside of the Joint Chiefs of Staff, including the members of the rescue team, who were treated to the entire plan were the Iranians who captured it intact.

Once airborne, the C-130s turned west, and at 7:30 a.m. the word reached the President that the force was safely out of Desert 1 and heading back to a secure airfield in Masirah. Although two

DC-9 Nightingale medical aircraft were standing by with full medical staffs, there were no specialists or equipment to treat the badly burned. Once again, the planning process had failed to anticipate an event.

The mission to rescue the hostages came a cropper in the first stages of its execution, with the loss of eight dead U.S. servicemen and a terrible loss to American military prestige. For the next six months, the Ayatollah Khomeini taunted the United States through the world media. The Republican candidate for President, Ronald Reagan, made the Iran debacle a major campaign issue, which eventually contributed to the defeat of Jimmy Carter for a second term. The highest-level planners of the American military establishment had assembled the best military minds to organize the operation. They had been given a blank check to obtain whatever equipment they needed, and, contrary to popular belief, the political leadership in the White House placed no restrictions on the plan. The President reserved the right to reject or approve the final plan, but he did not interfere in its formulation. The plan was developed entirely by the military.

WHY THINGS WENT WRONG

To understand the failure of the Iran raid, we must focus on four factors. First, the planning staff had no experience in operations of this sort, and the planning structure was so confused and bureaucratic as to make communication among its members difficult and, in some cases, almost impossible. Second, each component of the force was so compartmentalized, in order to prevent security leaks, that no one had overall authority to check the components to ensure that they were capable of performing their missions. Third, there was an overemphasis on operational security. The planners seemed so concerned with the possibility that the plan might be discovered that they even blocked communications within the planning staff and the rescue force itself, making a detailed overview of the plan impossible. Fourth, a number of key decisions seem to have been made on the basis of interservice

rivalry, bureaucratic consensus, and political criteria rather than on operational requirements. There seems to have been a bureaucratic imperative to give each service a role, regardless of whether it could best contribute to the success of the mission. In some instances, this imperative ruled even when a course of action seemed to work against the chances of success.

In the beginning, when the President ordered the JCS to prepare a contingency plan to rescue the hostages, the JCS discovered that it had no staff planning element with expertise on missions of this type. A staff element had to be created within the JCS from whole cloth and assembled a bit at a time. It was an ad hoc, inexperienced group which finally devised the plan, and it took almost two months to assemble the complete staff. Even then, some responsibilities were unclear. The staff structure left much to be desired. It had unclear lines of responsibility and authority. For example, an Air Force officer was put in charge of helicopter training. The Marines, who had originally not been included as part of the force, felt left out. Accordingly, they sent a Marine colonel and pressured the JCS to have him assigned as a consultant. As planning progressed, he pressed harder and harder for a Marine role in the mission. With the support of his superiors, he finally obtained for the Marines the task of flying the helicopters. Once the Marines were assigned that mission, a continuous tension developed between the Marines and the Air Force officers over how to train the pilots. There was continuous bureaucratic infighting. The Marines felt that they were being slighted by the Air Force, who did not understand Marine aviation procedures. The Air Force, for its part, felt that the Marines should never have been given the mission to fly the helicopters because they had no experience in long-range overground flying or in-flight refueling. The Marine colonel did end up supervising the flight training, although, incredibly, he was not placed in the chain of command. In order to smooth the ruffled bureaucratic feathers of the Air Force, the officer who had originally been assigned to train the helicopter pilots but who had lost out to the Marine colonel was relieved of his original assignment and made the on-site commander at Desert 1. The Marine colonel, originally assigned as a consultant to the staff, ended up commanding the helicopter flight.

Assignments often seemed tailored to relieve interservice pressures and to sustain peace in the bureaucracy, rather than on the basis of operational requirements. For example, at Desert 1, there were no fewer than three senior colonels on the ground, in charge of separate components. There was the helicopter flight commander, who was a Marine; the C-130 flight commander, who was an Air Force colonel and who also doubled as on-site commander; and the combat assault commander, an Army colonel. Despite the plethora of senior officers at Desert 1, however, no one had full operational authority. When a decision had to be made as to whether to abort the mission, no one on the ground had the authority to implement the decision. Instead, it had to be radioed back as a recommendation to the Joint Task Force commander, who bucked it to the Pentagon, who bucked it to the White House. The planning was confused in its formulation, and so too was the training. The result: a confused command structure. With three senior officers at Desert 1, the exact authority that each exercised was highly compartmentalized and unclear to others.

The factor that seems to have mesmerized the planning staff is concern for operational security (OPSEC).[31] The staff seemed totally preoccupied with the fear that the operation might be compromised before the raid. Certainly, a concern for operational security was justified. What seems to have happened, however, is that the planning process turned a legitimate concern into a caricature of bureaucracy. It not only twisted the planning and skewed the formulation of the plan itself; it undermined its execution as well.

The report of the Holloway Commission, appointed by the military to determine the causes of failure and chaired by Admiral Holloway, noted: "The great emphasis on OPSEC, although vital to mission success, severely limited the communications necessary among the staff to coordinate the operation, particularly in handling unforeseen contingencies . . . Because of the stringent OPSEC requirements compartmentalization was considered necessary. The rigid compartmentalization during the early stages is considered to have been a deterrent to training and readiness progress. Clearly during the final stages of preparation all element leaders should have been thoroughly familiar with the overall plan. This could

have enhanced greater integration of all elements of the force."[32] Paradoxically, the staff was kept small to enhance its efficiency. The Holloway Report found that staff planning procedures were completely inadequate, in that they were too complex and displayed unclear lines of authority.[33] Its finding that the JCS should have used the existing contingency planning structure (CONPLN) rather than create a special ad hoc planning element is eloquent testimony to the inability of the American military to plan military operations.

Another failure of the planning process also resulted from an excessive concern for security. When a military operation is planned in the office of the JCS, it is normally subjected to review by "murder boards" before final acceptance. These boards are staffed by officers completely outside the planning process whose job is to review the plan for feasibility. Their object is to prevent "staff blindness," a condition in which officers who formulated a plan develop a vested interest in seeing it executed and, because they are so close to the process, cannot see its flaws. The planning process in the military is, among other things, fraught with bureaucratic considerations. The military clearly understands this, and the normal contingency planning process contains provisions for external review.

In the Iran raid planning, concern for operational security was so extreme that the normal review process was bypassed. Only the officers who had formulated the plan reviewed its performance in rehearsal.[34] Early on, consideration had been given to creating a special panel of officers to review the plan. But this proposal was rejected by the JCS itself as a possible violation of security requirements! According to the Holloway Report, "the JCS were acting in essence as their own staff action officers and were denying themselves the staffing support they normally enjoy when reviewing plans of a less sensitive nature. In sum this meant that the hostage rescue plan was never subjected to rigorous testing and evaluation by qualified independent observers and monitors short of the JCS themselves."[35] The failure to have an independent review was disastrous.

The Holloway Commission, upon reviewing the planning pro-

cess after the operation had failed, was almost immediately able to pinpoint a number of conceptual flaws in the plan. Had the normal review process been allowed, these flaws would very likely have been discovered and a more feasible plan adopted. Certainly, it would have been a less complex one. Moreover, the concern for OPSEC forbade any final overall written plan to be produced.[36] All examinations by planning officers and the JCS were done orally. This meant that the members of the JCS never had an opportunity to retire to their offices to examine the plan in detail. The obsession with operational security so distorted the planning process that security took precedence over feasibility.

The rescue force did not train together as a complete unit. Instead, each component trained separately, at dispersed training centers, some at their home bases. Moreover, each component trained under the direction of its own commander and its own service officers, so that, in the end, none of the components was ever evaluated by officers from the other services. Some components were brought together from time to time, and some partial rehearsals were undertaken at a "remote western training site in the U.S." The training was planned and conducted in a highly decentralized manner within an informal component command structure that does not appear to have been adequate for assessing the quality of training and for certifying that the components were prepared to accomplish their assigned tasks. What rehearsals were held were piecemeal, with each unit trained in its own phase of the operation. There was not even one rehearsal that combined all the mission elements: "a thoroughly integrated training exercise of the entire joint task force for the final plan was never conducted."[37] Each component commander certified to the other commanders that his unit was ready. But this certification was free from review by other commanders, the planning commanders, the Joint Task Force commander, and even the JCS. In addition, because each component was drawn from a separate service, it had its own manner of doing things, its own standard operating procedures (SOP). In a number of instances, these procedures did not dovetail with those of the other services. In communications, for example, the Marine helicopter pilots used their own SOP, with

the result that they were unable to communicate with each other, the ground forces, or even the aircraft that had landed at Desert 1.

It is difficult to overestimate the impact of the decision to train the components separately rather than as a unit. As it turned out, the very problems that plagued the operation had emerged time and again in training. The Marine helicopter pilots who had to fly long distances overland, for example, encountered the same problems in training as during the actual mission. In a number of training missions, the BIM indicator light warning of a cracked rotor spar had come on. In addition, one helicopter suffered a hydraulic-pump failure of the kind which crippled the helicopter at Desert 1. Yet these things either were ignored or their implications were not realized. The Marines had great problems learning to navigate long distances overland. They often got lost and had difficulty finding landing zones. And the Marine helicopter pilots had problems refueling with the C-130s. Marines, it must be remembered, have almost no experience flying helicopters long distances overland or refueling either in flight or from tankers on the ground. The pilots had to learn new skills, among them how to refuel from a C-130 on the ground with its engines running, a standard Vietnam practice. In fact, at one point in the training, consideration was given to dropping fuel bladders on the desert floor, so the Marine pilots could land and simply refuel with hoses![38] Another proposal was to reconfigure the C-130s with special hoses and pumps so that the helicopters could pump fuel from the aircraft while at rest on the ground. In the end, neither proposal was adopted, either for security reasons or because they would have taken too much time to put into effect.

Clearly, the training for the mission was inadequate. Had things been done correctly, with an external review—or even if component commanders had had an opportunity to examine the performance of the other components with which they would have to work—perhaps some of the major problems would have surfaced and been dealt with.

In deciding on the number of helicopters, the planning staff seems also to have made an error in judgment. The planners con-

sidered a number of long-range heavy-lift helicopters for use in the mission, including the CH-46, CH-47, CH-53, RH-53D and HH-53. The CH-46 and CH-47 were immediately dismissed because they lacked the necessary range. The HH-53, which was just entering the inventory, was also dismissed because it did not have a proven track record. It also was too big and could not fit below any carrier deck with its rotors in place. Thus, the choice was the CH-53 or the RH-53D. The RH-53D Sea Stallion was picked largely because it could be dismantled and could easily be reassembled at a point from which it could fly to the carrier *Nimitz*. In fact, six of the eight helicopters were positioned aboard the *Nimitz* two weeks after the hostages were taken. The other two were deployed about a month later.

While the RH-53D was the only helicopter that could realistically have been used in the operation, the planners seem to have given insufficient attention to the mechanical problems this helicopter had encountered while in service with the fleet. Though its military capabilities are good, the RH-53D has a poor operational record marred by a history of mechanical breakdowns. The RH-53D, in its normal operations with the fleet, has been "mission capable" only 47 percent of the time.[39] The designation "mission capable" indicates that the machine can fly but does so with one or more of its operational systems—anything from navigational gear to radar equipment—inoperative. If the standard is "fully mission capable" (the helicopter flies with all its main systems operative), the RH-53D achieved this standard only 17 percent of the time over the last five years of its service with the fleet.[40]

Given the RH-53D's poor record and the necessity of a normal backup in operations of this type, it is evident that the planners failed to allot an adequate number of helicopters. Once again, this can be traced to a concern with OPSEC. The fear that too large a force would be discovered by Soviet satellites caused the planning staff to keep the number of men and machines in the assault force to the lowest possible level. The Holloway Report concluded that, under normal circumstances, at least ten helicopters, and more probably eleven, would have been used. The report also notes that if the planners had examined the "historical data" concerning the

RH-53D's breakdown rate, they would have recommended at least twelve helicopters, to allow for breakdowns and accidents.[41] There is no doubt that the decision to reduce the force to eight helicopters, with a minimum of six required for mission success, was a serious mistake that a more experienced and better organized staff would not have made.

When the question came up as to who would fly the helicopters, the Air Force produced a computer listing of its available pilots; 114 of its pilots were qualified for long-range helicopter flights. Of these, ninety-six were rated long-range pilots and had had extensive experience with in-flight refueling. Of these, eighty-six also had recent experience with special operations forces (SOF).[42] In the initial planning stages, the Air Force had assumed that these pilots would be used in the rescue operation. They were currently rated on the RH-53D, and, more important, they had the particular experience needed. They were experienced in the use of long-range navigational devices as well as with terrain-following radar (TFR) and forward-looking infrared (FLIR) systems. This was precisely the kind of long-range close-to-the-ground helicopter flying that was called for.

But the decision was made not to use Air Force pilots. Instead, Marine helicopter pilots who had flown naval missions with the RH-53D were to be used. This meant that the rescue force would have to rely on aviators trained only in short-range flight. Such missions consist of flying no more than thirty to fifty miles from the ship. So the pilots had little experience in long-range, overland flying, and no experience in low-level terrain-contour flying. Why, then, were they chosen?

The official explanation was that it was easier to take an existing unit and train it in additional skills, because the "unit structure would facilitate training and cohesion," than it would be to assemble a group of pilots who had the skills but who did not belong to the same unit.[43] At best, this reasoning is rather thin. In all likelihood, the decision was dictated more by bureaucratic considerations and interservice rivalry. As the plan took shape, the Air Force was given the role of flying the C-130s to the Desert 1 site and of evacuating the hostages from Manzariyeh once they were rescued.

The Army had the primary role of conducting the assault on the embassy. That the Army was given this assignment seemed particularly to anger the Marines, who feel they are the best quick-assault force available to the American military. The Navy, of course, was guaranteed a role because the *Nimitz* was the launch point for the entire operation. And in the later stages of the mission it was the Navy that would provide the all-important air cover for the evacuation of the hostages from the country. Thus, every service had a role in the mission except the Marines. The Marines had not even been included in the early planning. They had sent a liaison officer to the planning staff and he managed to edge his way into becoming responsible for training the helicopter pilots. The decision to use the Marine pilots although they did not have the skills required seems to have been made on bureaucratic grounds, to ensure that every service had some role in the operation. It was the Marine pilots who became lost, had difficulty in navigating, and who failed to reach Desert 1 on time and with the required number of helicopters. The choice of these pilots may have been the single greatest mistake of the planning staff.

Another problem was that the pilots were given limited training in long-range over-ground flying. Moreover, the Marine helicopters were not equipped with either FLIR or TFR.[44] And the Marine helicopters carried no navigators aboard; navigators would have been aboard if Air Force pilots had been used. Thus, the Marines launched into the mission without a thorough grounding in the navigational techniques and equipment needed to fly in minimum visibility over the Iranian desert. The helicopters did have both PINS and Omega navigational systems on board, the normal navigational aids used in large helicopters. But since Marine crews do not normally use these systems in their missions, they had had only marginal instruction in their use. The pilots themselves expressed very low confidence in their equipment as well as in their ability to use it.[45] It was decided therefore, that the primary method of navigating the helicopters would be by dead reckoning, using night-vision devices to follow the terrain. In short, they would fly a simple compass heading while looking out the window!

Signal intelligence security had been stressed from the beginning. There was considerable apprehension that any transmissions made during the mission might be picked up by enemy listening posts. With regard to the helicopter crews, this presented a particular problem. The Marines devised a system in which communication between helicopters while in flight was to be accomplished by signal lights, with no use of radio. Moroever, the basic premise in training was that if there was no communication between helicopters at all, then the assumption was that everything was going right and everyone was to proceed as planned.[46] This procedure rested on the ability of the helicopters to see one another. When the helicopters flew into the dust clouds and had to fly through them for almost three hours, they became separated. And it was impossible to see the signal lights while in the dust clouds. Thus, there was no effective way for the helicopter flight leader to communicate with his helicopters while en route to Desert 1.

Some attention was given to the difficulty the helicopters would have in navigating overground for such a long distance. One plan was to guide the helicopters to Desert 1. This plan was proposed by the Air Force and was based on a procedure commonly used by Air Force helicopters.[47] The Air Force suggested the possibility of having the helicopters rendezvous with at least one C-130 as soon as they made landfall over Iran. The C-130 would then lead the helicopters on to Desert 1. But this proposal was not accepted by the planners, for reasons that remain unclear. In the official report, no explanation is given for the refusal to accept the use of pathfinders to guide the helicopters to Desert 1. The report does point out that "in retrospect pathfinders would most likely have enabled helicopter #5 to reach Desert 1 and the mission to proceed."[48] It might be added that pathfinders would have made it possible for the helicopters to reach Desert 1 on time, since they would not have become lost in the dust clouds.

A major question remains: Why did the planners choose to land at Desert 1 in the first place? It is clear that the planners were aware of the high risk of being discovered at Desert 1 by the traffic routinely traveling the road that bisects the landing zone. It was

noted that, even if all went well at Desert 1, the wheel ruts left by the C-130s and the general disturbance of the land patterns would almost certainly be discovered.[49] If a helicopter or other equipment had to be abandoned at Desert 1, it would most certainly be quickly discovered. Thus, landing at Desert 1 under any conditions involved a serious risk of disclosure. The official reason for picking Desert 1 is that, according to JCS determinations, there was no alternative landing site available, and although there was a high risk that the operation would be compromised by the landing, the risk simply had to be taken.

The further question is why a stop at Desert 1 was required at all. Since the aircraft had to fly almost six hundred miles from the *Nimitz* to Desert 2 within eight hours, and since there were only nine hours and sixteen minutes of darkness, the stop at Desert 1 should have been avoided. The official report notes, however, that "early in the hostage rescue planning it became clear that a desert rendezvous in Iran to refuel helicopters and onload the assault force had many advantages."[50] It seems reasonable to conclude that the reason for stopping at Desert 1 was to refuel the helicopters for movement to Desert 2. And there was a need to refuel the helicopters on the ground because the helicopter pilots had no experience in in-flight refueling. A simpler plan would have used Air Force pilots experienced in long-range navigation and in-flight refueling. The C-130s could have rendezvoused with the helicopters off the coast of Iran and easily guided them to a point either over Desert 1 or beyond. There they could have refueled in the air, a procedure which the Air Force handles almost daily. This would have eliminated the need to stop on the ground and would have reduced the time required to reach Desert 2. And no helicopters would have gotten lost. If one had to abort, the commanders would have known it immediately. Once the C-130s had refueled the helicopters, they could have broken off and returned to their base, with no greater risk and probably less risk of being detected than in a landing at Desert 1. An alternative plan to use in-flight refueling was never considered, since that would have required a reversal of the original decision to include each of the services in the operation. The bureaucratic consensus underlying

the plan had to be maintained at all costs. As things turned out, the costs were very heavy indeed.

The mission was aborted because only five helicopters arrived in operational condition when the plan required six. There has never been an official explanation why six helicopters were required. In fact, in an earlier plan it had been determined that five were sufficient. How many helicopters *were* needed to execute the mission? A critical factor was the lift capacity of the RH-53D. The RH-53D can carry fifty-five passengers. How many people had to be airlifted out of Teheran? The available data suggest that no more than 177 had to be airlifted to Manzariyeh for evacuation. This included the 120-man assault team, the fifty-three hostages, and the four-member advance team. Five helicopters could easily have lifted this many people out of the city. Further, there was no need to take the advance team out at all. This team had been put into Iran by various means ten days before the rescue attempt and had developed an escape and evasion plan, complete with routes for leaving Iran in case something went wrong. The advance team had already made plans to get out of Iran if the mission failed or they were detected. They would leave the way they came in, by bus and truck and overland routes through Kurdistan and Pakistan. Indeed, when the mission failed, the advance team was left behind, and the entire team got out without incident, although it took them almost sixty days to do it.

The Delta commander, Colonel Beckwith, has maintained that five helicopters were insufficient to lift the 120-man Delta Force and its equipment into Desert 2. The argument is not convincing. The RH-53D, empty, has a weight of 32,077 pounds. When fully loaded with cargo and fuel, it can fly at a gross weight of 69,813 pounds. With 5,400 pounds of fuel in its regular fuel and long-range ferry tanks, the RH-53D can still lift 32,336 pounds of cargo. With five flyable helicopters, the total lift capacity of the helicopters at Desert 1 was approximately 161,000 pounds.[51] If each Delta commando weighed 200 pounds and carried a 60-pound pack and a 10-pound rifle, each soldier would weigh 270 pounds. This meant that the Delta Force weighed 32,400 pounds in all, leaving a lift capacity for equipment of approximately 130,000 pounds. The main

equipment Delta had to lift to Desert 2 was a thousand pounds of Flex-X explosives and enough camouflage netting to cover the five helicopters at Helo Hide. Even assuming that camouflage netting weighed ten tons—an outrageous assumption—this still left a flight lift capacity of 100,000 pounds. Moreover, the helicopter flight would have taken place during the night, so that temperature and humidity would not have been serious factors in reducing the RH-53D lift capacity. It would appear, then, that the five helicopters that arrived at Desert 1 in operational condition had sufficient lift to execute the mission. Shortly after the ground commander made the decision to abort, the fiery crash occurred that made his decision academic.

CONCLUSIONS

The Iranian rescue mission is a classic example of an operation planned and executed by a bureaucracy. The planners, in a number of instances, subordinated operational requirements to other considerations, such as interservice rivalry and the need to sustain the bureaucratic consensus underpinning the plan. The mission was over-officered, but command responsibility was not fixed; rehearsals were carried out in a systems component fashion to the point of inflexibility. No major dissent from within the military was possible, as a consequence of the planners' rigid cloak of secrecy. No one was allowed to review the plan except those who formulated it. The plan relied far too much on technology and at the same time ignored information that clearly indicated that the technology could not be relied on. Finally, the plan rested heavily on a previously established consensus—a consensus that removed responsibility for failure.

The planning and execution of the Iran mission is an example of the propensity to substitute management of systems for military planning. This is part of a larger trend in that direction and away from the individual officer's taking responsibility and exercising judgment. Even the language of the plan reflects a tendency to avoid decisions and to "revalidate prior agreements" made by the

planners. There is a tendency, too, toward overstaffing any project while at the same time limiting the ability of individual officers to make judgments.

To many, the failure of the Iran raid was simply bad luck. The truth is that it was almost predestined to fail. The Iran raid reveals in microcosm many widespread pathologies, and its failure was a logical result of a process that needs serious reform.

5

DEATH IN BEIRUT

THE most recent United States military involvement in Lebanon began during the Israeli–PLO war of June 1982. On June 6, Israel attacked PLO bases in Lebanon with six and a half divisions, with the objective of destroying the PLO and securing its northern border. Although the Israelis had given assurances that this would be a limited incursion, the attack went much farther than expected. In six days, the Israelis reached the gates of Beirut and trapped fourteen thousand PLO fighters inside the city. Although the Israelis had disavowed any intention of engaging the Syrian Army, they delivered it a stinging defeat. By mid-June 1982, the Israelis had surrounded Beirut and were deployed opposite Syrian forces in the Bekaa Valley.

From the beginning, the United States tried to restrain Israel from attacking. Once the war had begun, however, the U.S. shifted its policy and tried to limit the war. When that failed as well, the U.S. tried to bring about a quick cease-fire. By August, the U.S. had worked out an agreement between the Israelis and the PLO trapped in Beirut. The agreement permitted the PLO to withdraw with their weapons and retire to Syria and to positions in the Bekaa Valley. The PLO feared that if it retreated and abandoned its defensive positions it would be decimated by Israeli air strikes. A great concern of the PLO was that it had to leave behind thousands of supporters and family members in the urban neighborhoods of Burj el-Barajneh, Sabra, and Shatilla. The PLO had been involved for almost six years in the Lebanese civil war, along with other

117

rival confessional factions. Its leaders were convinced that, once their families were left defenseless, some attempt would be made by either the Christians or the Israelis to massacre them. Accordingly, one of the primary concerns of the PLO in the negotiations to effect its withdrawal from Beirut was to obtain some sort of guarantee of protection for their families left behind.

In order to break the deadlock and bring about the withdrawal of the PLO from Beirut, the U.S. agreed to guarantee the safety of the PLO fighters during the disengagement process. More important, it guaranteed the safety of the civilians who remained. By the end of August, the U.S. had worked out an accord between the PLO and the Israelis. The U.S. agreed to three major points. First, it would guarantee the safety of the PLO, who would withdraw in trucks from Beirut and move along the Beirut–Damascus Highway and redeploy to Syria and in the Bekaa Valley. American guarantees were vital because the PLO understood that once it was strung out on the narrow highway it would be very vulnerable to air attack. Second, the U.S. would guarantee the safety of the families of the PLO and other civilians left in West Beirut. Finally, the Americans agreed to stop any attempt by the Christian militia or the Israelis to enter West Beirut, where most PLO civilians and families lived. The camps of Burj el-Barajneh, Sabra, and Shatilla were to be off-limits to both Christian and Israeli forces. In addition, the Americans promised to keep a protective force in Beirut for at least thirty days. There also seems to have been an oral agreement that the U.S. would stay longer if the threat to PLO civilians persisted.

On August 25, 1982, eight hundred men of the American 32nd Marine Amphibious Unit (MAU) landed in Beirut and took up positions between the Israelis and the PLO. For seven days, the PLO gradually withdrew, and at week's end the withdrawal was completed without incident. The local population openly welcomed the Marines as protectors and treated them well. The Shiites and the PLO civilians of West Beirut saw the Marines as the only shield against Christian revenge or intimidation by the Israelis. All went well for the next fourteen days. By then, the PLO withdrawal was completed, and life in West Beirut had settled into a rough routine.

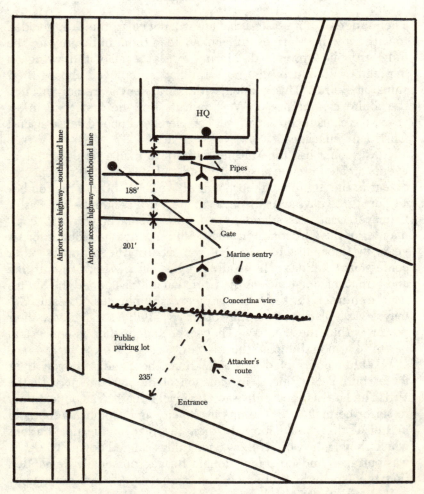

MARINE COMPOUND AT BEIRUT AIRPORT

Then suddenly, for reasons that are still not clear, the U.S. decided to withdraw the Marines rather than keep them in the city for the full thirty days promised. Marine forces began withdrawing on September 10 and by the next day had redeployed aboard their ships off Beirut. This sudden withdrawal sent a tremor through the Shiite community of West Beirut. For the first time in six years, the civilian population was completely without defense against Christian vengeance.

No sooner had the Marines withdrawn than a series of violent events created greater instability and violence, raising the specter of fear in the Shiite neighborhoods of West Beirut. On September 14, just three days after the last Marine left, President-elect Bashir Gemayel was assassinated by a bomb. Gemayel was also commander of the Christian Phalange militia, which had fought for six years in Lebanon's bloody civil war against the country's other confessional militias. His death touched off a week of mourning and threats of vengeance as the Christian militia blamed the Shiites for the murder. In the Christian view, the murder of Bashir Gemayel was a blatant attempt by other rival militias to increase their power within the country. They expected further violence and began to arm and deploy their forces.

Within hours of the assassination, the Israelis moved their forces into West Beirut, in violation of the agreement with the U.S. The Israelis apparently saw Gemayel's death as an opportunity to seize the major PLO camps in the city and establish a foothold in Beirut that would increase their leverage in the negotiations which they knew would follow once things calmed down. The U.S. was outraged and President Ronald Reagan personally demanded that the Israelis withdraw. Within three days, the Israeli Army pulled back to its earlier positions on the outskirts of the city.

Within days, Amin Gemayel, Bashir's brother, assumed leadership of the Christian army and replaced his brother as candidate for president of Lebanon. He ordered his troops into West Beirut, and they surrounded the Shiite camps of Burj el-Barajneh, Sabra, and Shatilla. From Saturday, September 18, through Monday, September 20, Christian militia forces entered the camps of Sabra and Shatilla in a blood lust of revenge, killing at least seven hundred

men, women, and children. The world and the U.S. were outraged.

The U.S. reacted to the massacre at Sabra and Shatilla with resolve, and the decision was made to have the Marines reenter Beirut. This time, American Marines would be put ashore under the cover of a multinational force which comprised contingents of French, British, and Italian troops. A week later, on September 26, the first French and Italian contingents entered Beirut. On September 29, the 32nd MAU went ashore with a force of twelve hundred men. Once again, the Marines were welcomed by the residents of West Beirut as protectors.

THE PLAN

It remains unclear to this day why the United States reentered the Lebanese quagmire after Sabra and Shatilla. Certainly, there was some element of guilt behind U.S. policy. The American President had pledged that if the PLO abided by its agreement the U.S. would insure the safety of the civilians left behind. Those pledges had not been honored. It is also probable that the United States saw an opportunity to play a larger role than originally anticipated. There was some thought that the U.S. might be able to aid the Israelis in reaching a final peace treaty with Lebanon, as the U.S. had helped with Egypt at Camp David. If the U.S. was able to bring about a peace treaty on the Camp David model, it would be a major foreign-policy coup. There was also the belief on the part of some American policy-makers that since the PLO had been driven out, Lebanon could be reconstituted under a new Christian pro-U.S. government. Some American policy-makers appeared to believe that the civil war had been caused by the PLO. Now that they were gone, the Americans felt that they could help the Lebanese work out their problems.

Not much attention was given to the Syrians, largely because Syria had been dealt a defeat by the Israelis less than two months before. Perhaps no one could have foreseen the degree of support which the Soviets would provide to allow the Syrians to rebuild their military might within a matter of six months. Nor did anyone

foresee that the political astuteness of President Assad of Syria would allow him to play a decisive role in Lebanon. American policy, then, was based on a number of factors, some of them naïve conceptions. At the time, however, these goals seemed to many to be attainable, including the Israelis. Moreover, they seemed attainable at only minimal risk.

From the beginning, the mission of the Marines was unclear. Officially, they were to provide a "presence" and to act as "peace-keepers" by staying neutral in any factional strife that developed. How this was actually to be achieved was unclear and unstated. It was almost as if the U.S. military presence itself became the policy. Moreover, the goals of U.S. policy were unclear to the Israelis as well as to rival Lebanese factions. Nor was it clear how long the U.S. was prepared to stay in Lebanon. One thing was evident, however, and that was that U.S. policy could succeed only as long as the major parties to the dispute continued to perceive the Marines as a neutral force. But from the outset, the various parties in Lebanon came to see the Marine presence as meaning different things.

The Moslems and Shiites saw the Marines as a device for protecting them from the vengeance of the Christians, who were clearly bent on revenge after the assassination of Bashir Gemayel. The Shiites were under no illusions but that the Christians intended to regain control of the Lebanese state by force of arms if necessary. From the Israeli perspective, the Marine presence signaled strong U.S. support for the Israeli goal of forcing the Lebanese to sign a peace treaty with Israel, thus securing its northern border. For the Christian Phalange, the Marines were seen as supporting the Christian objective of reestablishing themselves as the primary political and military power in Lebanon, as they had been before the outbreak of the civil war in 1975. Thus, each major participant in the Lebanese drama ascribed a different role to the Marines. To the U.S., the Marines may have been a symbol of the desire to see peace in Lebanon, but the specifics of that commitment were unclear to the other participants. Further, the Marine commitment had been made without a specified time limit, and all the major parties in Lebanon wondered from the beginning whether Amer-

ican resolve would be strong enough to stay the course, whatever that course turned out to be.

The political mission of the Marines and the military requirements to secure the force from hostile attack come into conflict almost immediately. The commander of the 32nd MAU, Colonel James Mead, was ordered to take control of the Beirut airport. Why the airport was chosen as the site for the Marine presence remains a mystery. Perhaps, as one Lebanese has suggested, the airport is the single symbol of the authority of the national government. The Marines were ordered to garrison the airport, but it is less clear whether they were also ordered to keep the airport open. There was certainly some disagreement on this point in the military chain of command. The report of the Long Commission (a committee established by the military to investigate the events in Beirut) indicated that it was unclear whether the Marines were assigned the mission of keeping the airport open and, if necessary, were expected to use force to do so.[1] It appears that the ground commanders felt that part of their peacekeeping mission was indeed to keep the airport open, although their superiors seem to have disagreed.

When Colonel Mead was ordered to occupy the airport, he decided, in excellent military fashion, to deploy his troops not at the airport itself but on the high ground several miles to the east. He proposed to station only a small force within the airport grounds. Mead recognized that the airport, positioned as it was on a small flat plain overlooked on two sides by mountains rising three thousand feet and with its back to the sea, represented a bull's-eye that could not be defended.[2] Without command of the heights and without effective artillery support, to deploy his troops on the airport itself was to put them in a death trap. Although Mead is on record as having made these recommendations to his superiors, his advice was ignored by the White House, and the Marines were ordered to occupy only the flat ground of the airport compound itself. Thus, the initial military decision was overruled on political grounds. The Marine commander knew that if hostilities broke out, his men, without control of the surrounding mountains, would be defenseless.

On November 3, the 32nd MAU was replaced at the airport by the 24th MAU. Once again, the local Marines were welcomed as protectors in the Shiite neighborhoods which abutted their positions. The Marines did what they have always done in foreign countries when there is no war. They dated local girls, romances sprang up, and even a marriage proposal or two were made. They purchased goods from local stores and, following the Vietnam practice, began to send their laundry out to be done by local merchants.[3] There were no threats, and the Shiites in Burj el-Barajneh, Sabra, and Shatilla were friendly, since they saw the Marines as their protectors. But in order for the Marine presence to be effective, especially in the eyes of the Shiites, all the Lebanese factions had to perceive the U.S. force as neutral in the factional and religious strife that smoldered just beneath the surface of Lebanese society. If the Marines appeared to be taking sides—especially if they began to appear to be in an alliance with the Christians—the Moslems, Shiites, and Druse of Lebanon would regard the Marines as enemies.

The first step in eroding the perception of neutrality came in November, when a Defense Department team completed an assessment of the Lebanese Army, by now commanded almost entirely by Christians, although it also comprised some Druse and Shiite troops. The DOD study was ordered to address the requirements for arming and training the new Lebanese Army. In Washington and in the Pentagon, the idea seems to have taken root that a national Lebanese Army could be formed that would displace and overcome the power of rival militias and contribute to the formation of a stable, pro-Western state under the leadership of Amin Gemayel. Washington policy-makers had forgotten the history of Lebanon and were underestimating the force of confessional hatreds in a society that has for most of its history been marked by civil war. The United States would reap the whirlwind in less than a year.

With the DOD study completed on December 21, the U.S. began shipping military equipment to the Lebanese Army. It also provided American Special Forces advisors to train it. To the rival militias, this looked suspiciously as if the U.S. was casting its lot

with the Gemayel regime. Inviting Gemayel to Washington only furthered this impression. The Christians, in their negotiations for the formation of a new constitution, continually flaunted to their rivals the fact that the U.S. was committed to a Christian government with Amin Gemayel at its head. Worse, American support for the Lebanese Army, perceived by the rival militias as a Christian Phalange army, was used by Gemayel to avoid making any concessions in restructuring the political and constitutional order, to which the other militias felt they had a right as a consequence of their victory in the civil war. Slowly, the U.S. was being drawn into a morass while American policy-makers appeared not to realize what was happening. On December 28, 1982, the U.S. aggravated the situation by announcing that the talks between the Lebanese and the Israelis would begin shortly. The purpose of these negotiations was to arrive at a new political settlement between Israel and Lebanon which would guarantee the security of Israel's northern border. To many in Lebanon—Christians and non-Christians—the U.S. appeared to be furthering Israeli policies at the expense of Lebanese interests.

Despite these circumstances, the Shiite population near the airport continued to display no overt hostility toward the Marines. Beneath the surface, however, the view among the leadership of the militias was changing. In January, the Israeli Army began conducting reconnaissance patrols in force along the Sidon road near U.S. positions. A short time later, they began to conduct reconnaissance by fire. In at least five instances, rounds fell within the Marine compound. Despite a number of attempts to work out some coordination between the Marines and the Israeli Defense Force, the provocations continued, and on January 5 another attempt was made by the IDF to penetrate Marine positions. It seems probable that the IDF was trying to signal the Lebanese that, regardless of the Marine presence, the Israelis would not be stopped if the necessity arose. Perhaps the object was to pressure the negotiations in the Israelis' favor. The IDF may have been trying to indicate that it would move militarily if the Lebanese were not more forthcoming in the talks. On February 2, Marine Captain Charles Johnson leaped on an Israeli tank that had tried to penetrate the Marine

perimeter. He drew his pistol and pointed it at the tank commander, ordering him to withdraw. At the same time, Marine helicopter gunships orbited overhead, their TOW missiles armed and trained on the Israeli tanks.[4] The Israelis withdrew. This public display of Marine resolve to deal with Israeli provocations was greeted in the neighborhoods of West Beirut with great delight, and for a while it seemed to reestablish the Americans as neutral protectors. Within a month, however, as the negotiations revealed the harsh demands made by Israel on the Lebanese (with American support), the last vestige of public support for the Marine presence in Lebanon vanished.

On February 15, 1983, the 24th MAU was relieved in place by the 22nd MAU. The peace-treaty negotiations dragged on, and Gemayel's Christian government continued to increase its strength as a result of American arms and training. During this time, over a thousand Moslems and Shiites were kidnapped and interrogated by the Lebanese Army. Most of them were killed or simply disappeared. The rival militias began to fear that, if something was not done soon, they would lose the game by default. On March 15, they sent the first signal to the multinational force that they no longer saw it as neutral but considered it a supporter of the Christians in their attempt to dominate Lebanese politics. On that day, an Italian patrol was ambushed in a West Beirut neighborhood. On the next day, March 16, 1983, the Marines took their first casualties from hostile fire. In the Shiite neighborhood of Ouzai, bordering the airport, a hand grenade wounded five Marines. The confrontation had begun, and during the next month, open warfare broke out in Lebanon among the rival militias. The Marines responded by increasing the number and frequency of their patrols along the airport perimeter.

THINGS GO WRONG

If the U.S. had not gotten the message, delivered on March 16, that it was no longer regarded as neutral, that message was

driven home with a vengeance on April 18, when the U.S. embassy in Beirut was hit by a truck bomb attack. According to the Long Commission, seventeen U.S. citizens and forty other personnel working at the embassy were killed.[5] In the Shouf Mountains, rival artillery duels increased in intensity, and the number of dead began to mount. Lebanon was once again inching its way toward civil war.

On May 17, the U.S.-supported accord between the Israelis and the Lebanese was signed. The Lebanese government made it clear that it opposed the agreement and had signed it only because of U.S. pressure. Once again, artillery duels broke out between the rival militias in the Shouf. Any vestige of neutralism that was left to the U.S. was rapidly being eroded. On May 30, the 22nd MAU was replaced by the 24th MAU in positions around the airport. The Marines found a much different environment from the one they had left. The Shiites around the airport were now openly hostile. The fighting in the mountains escalated as the militias continued to arm themselves for an eventual military showdown. By this time, the Druse were receiving open military support from Syria, and the Shiites, mostly in Beirut, became more aggressive.

The decision on June 25 to have the Marines conduct joint patrols with the Lebanese Army in West Beirut was a major turning point. It openly demonstrated that close cooperation with the Christians had become official American policy. In West Beirut's Shiite neighborhoods, things turned ugly, and shortly thereafter, the Marine commander began reporting in intelligence channels that his men were becoming the targets of rocks and insults whenever they approached West Beirut.

On July 14, a Lebanese Army patrol was ambushed in West Beirut by members of the Shiite Amal militia, and fighting spread rapidly through the neighborhoods of Burj el-Barajneh, Sabra, and Shatilla. It lasted for three days. The Christian army was able to establish its presence there, but the Amal militia more than held its own in the fighting and took a heavy toll of the Christian forces. At the same time, fighting in the Shouf between Druse and Christian forces increased sharply, and on July 22 the airport was shelled from the mountains by Druse artillery, which closed the airport.

For the first time, three Marines were wounded by artillery fire. The shelling made clear that the rival militias no longer regarded the Marines as neutral, but rather considered them allies of the hated Christian army and, thus, fair game in the incipient civil war. As if to confirm this perception, Gemayel in July received public promises from the Reagan Administration to expedite the delivery of more military equipment to the Lebanese Army. Shortly thereafter, the Druse leadership, joined by other rival militias, announced that they did not accept the May 17 pact with the Israelis but regarded it as an unfair treaty forced on the Lebanese by the Americans.

By August 1983, the Israelis decided that they could no longer influence political events in Beirut. They were taking heavy casualties almost every day in the Shouf Mountains. Rumors began to circulate that the IDF would withdraw from the Shouf, setting up a line at the Auwali River near Sidon. In anticipation of this withdrawal, the militias in the Shouf increased the tempo of fighting and began maneuvering for military advantage. A full-scale civil war was raging in the Shouf, with the Israelis acting as referees. From August 10 to August 16, the airport was closed because of shelling from Druse artillery in the mountains, and once again the Lebanese Army clashed with the Shiite militia in Beirut. Thirty rounds of artillery fire landed on the Marine positions during the six-day period, wounding one Marine.

On August 28, the Marines again came under artillery fire from Druse positions above the airport. Using Firefinder counter-battery radar, the marines returned fire and silenced the Druse battery. Two Marines were killed in the attack. Two days later, the IDF officially announced that it would withdraw from the Shouf. A day later, the Lebanese Army moved in force into West Beirut and began a running firefight with the Amal militia in its own neighborhoods. Prior to its withdrawal from the Shouf, the IDF allowed almost two thousand Lebanese Army troops to pass through its lines and seize the town of Bhamdun. The Druse were outraged at what they regarded as Israel's betrayal, and fighting for the town broke out. On September 4, the IDF withdrew from the Shouf, removing the last restraint against military action between Christian and Druse forces in the area. On the same day, Druse artillery

shelled the airport, killing two Marines and wounding two others. On the next day, the Druse forces, with support from returning PLO, drove the Christians from Bhamdun and pressed them back against the suburbs of Beirut. The Druse now controlled the Shouf Mountains, and the gateway to Beirut was open, except for the Christian-controlled town of Souk el Gharb.

The Christian army reinforced Souk el Gharb in panic and, in so doing, had to redeploy its forces in such a way as to abandon the high ground overlooking the airport to the Druse. Once the Druse occupied this area and deployed their artillery, the Marines were left exposed to hostile fire at almost point-blank range. The Druse no longer regarded the Marines as anything but allies of the Christians, and the Marines came under frequent shelling as the Druse moved into position for the battle for Souk el Gharb. The Marines fired back with their 155mm guns, using target-acquisition radar. When this counter-battery fire failed to stop the shelling, on September 7 the Navy flew its first airborne recon-naissance missions to aid Marine gunners in locating targets. A day later, naval gunfire was called in for the first time as American destroyers directed their fire against Druse artillery positions in the hills overlooking the airport.

One of the most disastrous decisions for the Marines in Beirut was made by the White House on September 12, 1983. Deluged by reports from Special Envoy Robert McFarlane and the ambassador in Beirut, the White House began to believe that the fall of Souk el Gharb would spell the end of the Lebanese government. Washington declared publicly that the successful defense of Souk el Gharb was essential to the "safety of the Marines" at the airport.[6] In truth, the fall of Souk el Gharb would not endanger the Marines any more than they already were, since all the high ground around the airport was already occupied by the Druse and their artillery; they could have obliterated the Marine position at any time. The decision to bring American forces to the defense of the Christian army at Souk el Gharb was a political move designed to avoid the appearance of political defeat. If it had any military consequences at all for the Marines, it was to increase their danger from the Druse artillery, not lessen it.

Colonel Timothy J. Geraghty, the Marine commander at the

Beirut airport, saw the decision to have U.S. forces fire in support of Christian troops at Souk el Gharb as a serious military mistake that would endanger his troops. He protested vigorously in a number of messages, noting that if American gunfire was used in support of the Christians "we'll get slaughtered down here."[7] The Lebanese continued to press for naval gunfire support and air strikes against the Druse around the town. On September 12, the White House approved the request for air strikes and naval gunfire and transmitted the order down the chain of command to the appropriate commanders. The order came down until it reached Colonel Geraghty. Authority to call in naval gunfire rested with him for almost a week. He refused to execute the order, on the grounds that it would touch off a chain of events that would end in the massacre of his men. But circumstances were moving beyond his control.

On September 14, an emergency shipment of arms and ammunition from the U.S. was delivered to the Lebanese Army as the battle raged around Souk el Gharb. The battleship *New Jersey* was ordered to deploy off the Lebanese coast and would arrive on September 29. Pressure was increasing on the military chain of command as McFarlane pressed the field commanders to force Geraghty to call in gunfire to support Christian forces. Offshore, a twelve-ship and 13,000-man naval task force was in place. Finally, on September 29, as the U.S. ambassador's residence came under fire, Geraghty relented and called for limited gunfire support, knowing that it risked his troops and provided nothing in the way of significant help for the Christian army around Souk el Gharb. That decision sent a clear message to the Druse that the American military had openly chosen sides in the civil war and was now fully engaged.

At 10:04 a.m., the nuclear-powered missile cruiser USS *Virginia*, with support from the frigate *John Rogers*, began shelling Druse positions around Souk el Gharb. F-14 Tomcat aircraft were in the air to conduct reconnaissance missions in support of A-6 and A-7 fighter-bomber air strikes. The naval air strikes were never carried out. The shelling by the Navy lasted on and off for almost six days. The situation at Souk el Gharb stabilized, and in the middle of the fighting the *New Jersey* arrived off the coast. An

uneasy cease-fire settled over the town. Ten days before, on September 19, the Marines had become open targets for snipers firing from the Shiite neighborhoods which abutted the Marine positions around the airport.

In response to the fighting, the Marines organized counter-sniper "hit teams" and began to fire back whenever they were attacked. Unfortunately, they began to announce their "confirmed kills," which further outraged the Shiites. On October 1, the Christians received a huge shipment of equipment, including armored personnel carriers, M-48 tanks, ammunition, and long-range artillery pieces. In addition, the U.S. publicly announced that it would increase its training efforts. The U.S. seemed deliberately to be telling the other militias that it would not allow the defeat of the Christian army under Gemayel's leadership.

At this time, the Marines began to receive intelligence reports indicating the possibility of direct terrorist action against their positions. On October 18, four Marines were wounded when a Marine convoy was attacked with a car bomb. On Sunday, October 23, 1983, the Marines at the airport were hit by a terrorist attack which, according to FBI experts quoted by the Long Commission, delivered "the largest non-nuclear explosion that we had ever seen."[8] When the dust settled, 240 Marines were dead, and over one hundred wounded. The Lebanese civil war had come home to the U.S. Marines.

On that Sunday morning, at 6:22 a.m., a contingent of three hundred Marines lay sleeping in their headquarters building. A single Mercedes flatbed truck loaded with 12,000 pounds of explosives wrapped around butane-gas canisters accelerated through the parking lot south of the headquarters building. It crashed through a single strand of concertina wire fence and headed directly for the Marine billets. The truck drove over the wire, passed between two Marine guard posts without being fired upon, plowed through an open iron gate, passed between two pipe barriers, crushed the guardhouse at the entrance, and drove into the lobby of the building. There the driver detonated the explosives. The force of the explosion was so great that it ripped the building from its foundation, sending the thrust of the blast through the roof.[9] The force

of the explosives was increased by the gas canisters that had been placed on a marble slab in the truck to send the explosive blast upward. The blast was so great that it drove the floor of the building, itself eight inches thick, eight feet into the earth.[10]

The massacre of the Marines at the airport touched off a fire storm of criticism in the United States. The military moved immediately to protect itself by leaking reports that it had opposed the positioning of Marines in so vulnerable a spot to begin with. Reports filtered out of the Pentagon that those in the chain of command directly responsible for the Marine contingent had gone on record prior to the attack as noting that the Marines were in grave danger and suggesting alternatives to their deployment. Particularly interesting is the memo of General Bernard Rogers, the NATO commander directly responsible for the Marine contingent, which proposed a number of alternatives to the Marine deployment almost a week before the attack.[11] The military's advice was ignored as the hard-liners in the White House, led by McFarlane, convinced the President that any redeployment of the Marines would appear as weakness and suggest a lack of American commitment to the Gemayel government. The decision was made to keep the Marines in place, where they made a tempting target.

The Marine massacre increased public and congressional pressure on the U.S. to withdraw from Lebanon, but the President held fast and, incredibly, even seemed to deepen the American involvement. On October 27, President Reagan gave a speech, widely quoted in the press, in which he defined the American presence in Lebanon as a "vital interest" and equated a withdrawal or even a redeployment of the Marines with "walking away" and "turning our backs," which could only further encourage terrorism, lessen the chances for a peaceful settlement, and raise doubts as to our willingness to support Israel.[12] As if to demonstrate his resolve, on December 4, in response to the firing by Druse gunners on American reconnaissance aircraft, naval aircraft staging from an aircraft carrier off the coast attacked Druse artillery positions in the Shouf and along the Beirut–Damascus Highway. The result was something less than a spectacular success. The U.S. put twenty-eight aircraft over the target and had two shot down and one dam-

aged. Two pilots were killed, and an American navigator was taken prisoner as he parachuted over Druse lines.[13] (He was returned three weeks later, when his release was obtained by the Reverend Jesse Jackson.)

The civil war was flaring up as control of Lebanon slipped from the hands of Gemayel and his Christian army. Druse and Shiite militia, with Syrian support, continued to deliver a series of stinging defeats to the Christian forces. Gemayel's reputation sank so low that he became known, derisively, as the "mayor of Beirut." On December 14, in response to repeated shelling in and around the airport, the battleship *New Jersey* entered the fray by firing its sixteen-inch guns, and continued firing at enemy positions from time to time. But there is no evidence that its firepower had any effect on the ability of the militia armies to conduct attacks at the time and place of their choosing.

Opposition to U.S. policy was mounting within the Pentagon and among members of the multinational force. The French publicly expressed fear that the U.S. would become even more deeply involved in the Lebanese quagmire and eventually draw them into the conflict. Within the White House, Secretary of Defense Weinberger and the Pentagon chiefs argued strongly to remove the Marines from Lebanon. Secretary of State Shultz, committed to the May 17 peace treaty as his major accomplishment in office, wanted the Marines to remain, as proof of the U.S. commitment to enforce the accords. The President finessed the issue by asking that plans be drawn for redeploying the Marines to safer positions near the airport. One contingency called for removing the Marines entirely from the airport and placing them aboard ships deployed offshore.

McFarlane and the Secretary of State pressed for a policy that would avoid the appearance of defeat and settled on a program of naval shelling, justified on the grounds that it would protect the Marines. The Pentagon opposed the policy, arguing that it would prompt further attacks against the Marines. In the end, however, the Pentagon could not produce an alternative for redeployment, and the White House adopted the policy of firing on targets regardless of the threat they posed to the Marines. The attacks were

regarded as a symbol of American will, a show of gunboat diplomacy, but were of no real military significance and had no effect on the ability of the enemy to continue operations. On January 26, President Reagan approved a plan to redeploy the Marines offshore, a gradual process that was supposed to last until June 1984.

In early February, the Druse pressed their attack on Souk el Gharb once more, and on February 8 the Navy unleashed a barrage of three hundred shells, including some fired from the *New Jersey*. The effect on the battle was negligible, and the fighting went on. Although the President continued to make strong public statements about American resolve, one of which charged the Speaker of the House with cowardice, the U.S. presence in Lebanon was almost at an end. The political damage to the Administration was growing, and it was now clear that the original assumptions on which U.S. policy had been based were no longer valid, if, indeed, they had ever been. On February 26, 1984, the Marines began deploying to their ships, and although naval gunfire continued to be directed at enemy targets on the mainland—apparently hitting few of them— the American military presence in Lebanon ended by the end of the month. On March 30, the President announced unilaterally that the U.S. was ending its participation in the multinational force. U.S. forces had spent 533 days in Lebanon and had suffered 241 dead and 131 wounded. The Lebanon adventure had failed to achieve even a single objective.

WHY THINGS WENT WRONG

When Colonel James Mead, commander of the first Marines to enter Beirut, was given the task of deploying Marines around the airport, he pointed out in strong terms that the airport was militarily indefensible. He wanted to occupy the high ground to the east of the airport and made it clear that if the mountains overlooking the field were not in friendly hands the U.S. Marines would become sitting ducks if fighting ever broke out. Colonel Mead was overruled by the White House and the Pentagon chiefs, who concurred in the decision to position the Marines at the air-

port. From the very start, the Marines were sent into a situation that was militarily untenable.

Further, the mission of the Marines was unclear. To the commanders on the ground, their mission was to provide a "presence" and to be "peacekeepers." The commanders took this to mean that the physical presence of the Marines would be sufficient to demonstrate the resolve of the United States and to help achieve policy objectives in Lebanon. Although their superiors did not anticipate combat, the ground commanders realized that their position was militarily indefensible. The Long Commission, investigating the disaster at the Beirut airport, concluded that "perceptions of the basic mission varied at different levels of the chain of command."[14] The report went further in blaming the military, noting that lack of clarity had led to very practical difficulties as to what the Marine commanders on the ground could or could not do to achieve their mission. According to the Long Commission, these problems "should have been recognized and corrected by the chain of command."[15] As it turned out, the difficulty was never recognized by the chain of command and was never corrected.

Seemingly, it was never intended for the Marines to engage in combat even if attacked. Moreover, the ability of the Marines to sustain a presence depended on the environment within the country remaining "benign," non-hostile. Yet, six months before the attack against the Marines, the environment had changed to overtly hostile as rival militias began shooting at one another, the Israelis withdrew from the Shouf, and a civil war began in earnest. Before the Marines came under fire, it should have been evident to the military that the original assumption of a benign environment so necessary to the mission's success was no longer valid. But, apparently, this situation was not understood until after the bombing of the U.S. embassy in April. At least by then, someone should have assessed the increased danger. Yet no one did, and no command guidance was issued to local Marine commanders to adjust to changing circumstances. The Long Commission concluded in this regard that "appropriate guidance and modification of tasking should have been provided to the US Marine national force to enable it to cope effectively with the increasing hostile environ-

ment. The commission could find no evidence that such guidance was in fact provided."[16]

The Marines at the airport continued to operate under the rules of engagement (ROE) originally adopted when they first deployed. Each Marine was given a "white card," which he had to memorize and obey in the performance of his duties. The ROE forbade the Marines to load their weapons or to put their weapons on ready. All weapons were allowed to have a loaded magazine in place, but no rounds could be chambered so the weapons could be fired immediately. No Marine could fire a weapon in self-defense unless he was authorized to do so by a commissioned officer. Crew-served weapons were permitted to have ammunition nearby, but no crew-served weapon was to be loaded. Release authority to fire a crew-served weapon was to come from an officer only. In case of attack, the Marines were ordered not to respond but to inform local Lebanese authorities—namely, the Christian army, which was supposed to come to their aid. Under extreme circumstances, the rules of engagement allowed a minimum use of force to protect lives.[17] Even the MAU commander had no authority to return fire if fired upon. Instead, the ROE required him to "seek guidance from higher headquarters prior to using armed force if time and the situation allowed."[18]

This set of engagement rules was in effect for the Marine guards at the embassy when they were attacked. After the attack, a "blue card" set of rules of engagement was issued which allowed the Marines more latitude to protect themselves and to increase the security of their positions around the embassy compound.[19] Yet, even after the embassy was attacked, there was no change in the rules of engagement for the Marines around the airport, despite the fact that they were clearly under the same kind of threat and to the same degree. In any case, at the embassy there was no real threat of snipers and none of the artillery conditions faced daily by the Marines at the airport.

The contrast between security at the embassy and at the airport is striking. The Marines at the embassy always carried loaded weapons, whereas those at the airport were not allowed to. Those at the embassy were permitted to return fire immediately, whereas

the Marines at the airport had to obtain permission of an officer first. The area around the embassy looked like a fortress, and traffic approaching it was closely watched and restricted. At the airport garrison, there were no significant fortifications in place, and traffic was allowed free access, even to the battalion landing-team head-quarters area. At the embassy, assault vehicles with machine guns at the ready were in place to block traffic and return fire; at the airport, no armed vehicles were deployed. Armored vehicles had been in place at one time to restrict traffic, but after the embassy attack they were removed by order of the local commander! Finally, the Marine guards at the embassy were equipped with anti-tank weapons specifically designed to destroy any approaching vehicle suspected of being driven by a terrorist. At the airport, no such weapons were deployed.[20]

Perhaps most appallingly, after the attack on the embassy neither the chain of command nor the local commander took any action to reassess the vulnerability of the Marines to a terrorist attack. The intelligence assessment report on the embassy attack went into great detail concerning the nature and methodology of the attack and indicated a high probability of other attacks. But the report, according to the Long Commission, was not made available to the Marine commander or to the task-force commander, nor did they request to see it.[21] After the attack, a special team was sent to the embassy to advise the embassy defense force on how to protect itself against future attacks. But this team was not assigned the task of evaluating the Marine defenses at the airport.[22] The Long Commission found "a lack of systematic and aggressive chain of command attention to the anti-terrorist security measures in use by the US Marine National Force (USMNF) on the ground at the Beirut airport."[23] The report further charged that the chain of command was guilty of a "lack of effective command supervision" and concluded that the failure of the commanders to pay appropriate attention to the ineffective defenses at the airport "constituted tacit approval" of that ineffectiveness.[24] In strong language, the commission recommended that disciplinary action be taken against those in the chain of command, including the commander of the Marine garrison at the airport.

The failure to appreciate the threat of a terrorist attack was compounded by the failure of the intelligence community to deal effectively with a number of reports it had received since April indicating that the Marines would be the target of a similar attack. The structure of the combat intelligence community is such, however, that while it is able to deliver intelligence support to ground-force commanders, that support is primarily geared to deploy air and naval forces. Little in the way of intelligence reporting and assessment is targeted at helping the small-unit commander determine what threats he is facing and how to cope with them, a weakness the Long Commission documented.[25] A sub-committee of the House Armed Services Committee investigating the Beirut massacre concluded that "the MAU in Lebanon did not receive adequate intelligence support in dealing with terrorism. Serious intelligence inadequacy had a direct effect on the capability of the unit to defend itself against a full spectrum of threat. The Marines did not possess adequate capability to analyze the massive amount of data provided them. The chain of command should have provided a special intelligence officer with expertise in terrorism capable of assembling all-source intelligence in a usable form for the ground commander."[26]

Inadequate intelligence capability contributed to the failure to appreciate and anticipate the threat facing the Marines. Paradoxically, General Rogers, the NATO commander responsible for the Marine forces, apparently did give some consideration to the possibility of a terrorist attack. In November 1982, almost eleven months before the Marines were attacked and five months before the embassy in Beirut was attacked, General Rogers had offered the Marines anti-terrorist training under Army auspices. According to the Armed Services Committee, the offer was rejected by the Marines, "in view of the training the Marines are provided before they are deployed, plus the training they get while there plus their coordination with the Lebanese."[27] A more probable explanation for the refusal is interservice rivalry. The Marines simply were not going to have any shortcomings pointed out by an Army general.

Yet, as the Long Commission noted, Marine training for dealing with terrorist attacks was limited and wholly inadequate.[28] The

only instruction Marine units were given in the nature and methodology of terrorist attacks consisted of a one-hour class conducted for the members of the infantry battalions by the attached counterintelligence NCO.[29] Segments of the command briefing did address the threat, but only in passing and not in detail. According to the Long Commission, "the US Marine National Force was not trained, organized, staffed or supported to deal effectively with the terrorist threat in Lebanon."[30]

By October 1983, a terrorist attack was very probable. And the capability of the enemy to strike was "beyond the imagination of the local commanders as well as other members of the chain of command."[31] In addition, the local commander made a number of mistakes in military basics which increased the vulnerability of his men. In the first place, he ignored the elementary practice of always dispersing one's men in a combat area. Instead, he garrisoned almost three hundred men, one-fourth of his total force, in a single building. He also failed to provide sufficient security in and around the garrison area. There were, for example, no physical barriers to stop or slow an approaching vehicle. A single strand of concertina wire and a metal fence—with a gate left temptingly open all the time—was all that stood between the enemy and its target. No security precautions were taken to check or routinely observe the traffic in the airport parking lot, from which the terrorist vehicle staged its attack. It had to drive between two Marine checkpoints to reach its target, but the Marines had orders not to carry loaded weapons. Not a single Marine was able to bring the vehicle under fire as it hurtled toward its target.

When added to the other failures, the failure to take routine precautions that the commander of any deployed military force would have taken under normal circumstances borders on criminal negligence and gross incompetence. Both the congressional investigating committee and the Long Commission placed the blame for these failures on the Marine unit commander and other members of the military chain of command. It recommended strong disciplinary action as well against all officers involved in these decisions. While absolving the Marine commander of "neglect" and "dereliction of duty," the congressional report did conclude

that his actions constituted "a case of misjudgement with the most serious consequences."[32]

In the final analysis, the disaster at the Beirut airport was the result of incompetence, of officers, staffs, and military institutions failing to do what they are charged to do by law and public trust. The chain of command was unable to anticipate events, a common occurrence in Vietnam, and even when the situation changed radically, they failed to appreciate the changes and take action. Military leaders did not lead, and commanders did not command. They just followed orders and were overtaken by events.

Equally distressing is the fact that although the Long Commission recommended disciplinary action against a number of officers, the White House intervened. The President assumed the "blame" for the Marine tragedy and, in an unusual move, blocked further legal proceedings against the officers responsible. The Marine commander, his deputy, and General Rogers all received "letters of caution," to be placed in their files. No one in the military seems to have heard of a "letter of caution" before it was issued and defined by the White House as the most limited form of reprimand the Secretary of Defense can administer to a military subordinate. In the words of one officer, "the military was let off the hook."[33]

The death of the Marines at the airport was the most tragic and costly example of military failure and incompetence to emerge from the Lebanon adventure. But the incompetence and failure were overshadowed by the death of so many men, the most in a single day since Vietnam, as well as the "success" of the Grenada invasion three days later. There were at least three other military failures in Lebanon: the ineffectiveness of the air strikes against enemy gun positions; fleet security; and the impotence of naval gunfire, most particularly the ineffectiveness of the battleship *New Jersey*.

In the early daylight hours of December 4, twenty-eight naval fighter-bombers were launched from an aircraft carrier off Lebanon, with the mission to strike at Druse antiaircraft and artillery positions around Beirut. The purpose of the raid, the Pentagon announced, was to punish the enemy for firing on two unarmed

reconnaissance aircraft the day before. Neither of the F-14 Tomcat reconnaissance aircraft was hit; both returned safely to the carrier. The excuse for the fighter-bomber raid seems a bit thin, since these aircraft had been fired on a number of times before and no punitive action had been taken. The F-14s were attacked by conventional antiaircraft guns rather than SA-7 or SA-9 missiles. To many observers, the real point of the raid seems to have been political rather than military.

Since the terrorist attacks on the embassy and on the Marine barracks, the Reagan Administration had promised to punish those responsible, but, in fact, nothing had been done. Pressure for American withdrawal was building in Congress, and it was clear that the congressional and special investigating committees appointed to look into the tragedy would lay the blame at the feet of the military. Further, the Israelis retaliated almost daily with air strikes against enemy positions that fired on IDF troops or aircraft. Indeed, a day before the American raid, two pairs of Israeli aircraft had struck at militia and Syrian positions in retaliation for an attack on five Israeli soldiers. While an American air raid would have no appreciable effect on the military equation in Lebanon, the White House apparently felt that military action would relieve some of the political pressure that was building up in the United States.

What was troublesome about the raid from the perspective of military technique was that it failed to destroy any of its targets. No official list of targets destroyed was ever published, as is normally done when air raids are undertaken. The raid cost two aircraft, the lives of two pilots, left another aircraft damaged, and delivered a U.S. navigator alive into the hands of the Syrians. Moreover, the air raid only confirmed to the Lebanese the American unconcern for civilian casualties, which had increased dramatically as a consequence of naval shelling, which often hit civilian villages. In the air raid, one of the downed aircraft crashed into a village, killing several civilians. In the opinion of military experts, the air raid seemed to have been conducted in a manner that violated almost every principle of air-to-ground attack.

In the first place, the Navy sent twenty-eight aircraft over a target area so small that almost every one of them could be hit by

ground fire. This practice of saturating the target area creates a "target-rich stream" of aircraft, against which ground fire can be most effective.[34] The Israelis, who have been conducting such raids for years, almost never use more than two to four aircraft at a time. They attack in pairs, never staying above the battlefield more than a few seconds, thus minimizing exposure of the attacking aircraft to ground fire. Instead of following the Israeli practice, the U.S. placed far too many aircraft in a very small target area directly above the antiaircraft positions, thus making the aircraft easy targets. Experienced pilots who used this technique in Vietnam found it terribly dangerous. By flying single-file during the attack, the aircraft present a predictable line of approach for enemy gunners to fire at.[35] The first few aircraft may get through unscathed, but the remaining aircraft in the line make perfect targets. Knowing the line of approach, the battery gunner has only to fire in front of the approaching aircraft and let it fly into the exploding shells. The attack altitude was 20,000 feet, so the gunners had ample time to aim and track their targets. Although no information has been officially released concerning the number of guns in the target area, to experienced observers it seemed that there could not have been many, certainly fewer than ten, or far more aircraft would have been destroyed.[36]

In trying to explain the loss of its aircraft, the Navy claimed that the intensity of the ground fire "came as a surprise" to the pilots flying the attack missions.[37] Yet, since the U.S. had been flying reconnaissance missions for weeks over the area and also had access to satellite photographs, it is difficult to see how the Navy planners could fail to know the number and placement of the guns. These were in fact the very gun emplacements the planes were sent to attack. Very likely, then, the Navy tried to compensate for the large number of suspected gun emplacements by putting more aircraft in the sky, an error in basic military technique.

Equally puzzling is the failure of the Navy pilots to attack their targets from a low altitude. Again, the Israeli experience has taught us always to use low-altitude attacks. A low-altitude approach reduces the time over the target, during which an aircraft is exposed to ground fire, and preserves the element of surprise. Such attacks

by the Israelis are almost always accompanied by the dropping of parachutes carrying brightly burning magnesium flares. This is designed to draw away heat-seeking missiles fired at the aircraft. The temperature of the burning magnesium is higher than that of the exhaust gases from the jet engines, so the heat-seekers home in on the flares rather than on the aircraft. Not only were no flares used as decoys, but the attacking aircraft began their approach from 20,000 feet, thereby increasing the time they were exposed to ground fire.[38] Of course, from that altitude, surprise is not possible.

Although the A-6 and A-7 aircraft used in the raid are equipped with advanced electronics which permit them to fly both night and low-visibility missions, the Navy did not take advantage of this capability and launched the attack in broad daylight.[39] Moreover, they failed to take advantage of the early-morning fog that shrouded the target area. Instead, the aircraft waited until the fog had lifted and the daylight silhouetted them against the morning sky.[40]

After the bombing of the Marine compound, the Navy began to receive intelligence reports that its ships offshore might also come under terrorist attack. The reports indicated that the most likely method of attack would be high-speed boats or light civilian aircraft loaded with explosives which would be flown or driven kamikaze-style into American ships. The fact that the American embassy and the Marine compound at the airport had already been destroyed apparently led the Navy to take these threats seriously.

A study of the fleet's ability to defend itself came to the conclusion that the ships off Beirut had no credible defense against low-flying aircraft or high-speed boats crashing into a ship. The Navy's response was to order all ships to remain in motion at all times; under no conditions was a ship to stay at anchor and present a stationary target. The discovery that there was no defense against such simple modes of attack raised the larger question of fleet defense, since the fleet off Lebanon was supposedly protected by the Aegis radar missile defense system, called the "shield of the fleet" by the Secretary of the Navy.[41] This system, never adequately tested during its development and plagued by problems, was supposed to detect and track a number of aircraft and missile targets

at the same time, compute their courses, and launch defensive missiles against them in time to prevent them from reaching the ships. Unfortunately, the system is ineffective against low-flying cruise or rocket missiles of the Exocet variety, which showed such destructive power during the Falklands war and in the Gulf war.[42] Now it turned out that the Aegis could not stop low-flying civilian aircraft or high-speed boats! In fact, during its development tests, the Aegis never had to track more than two aircraft at a time and never had to prove itself against missiles flying lower than two hundred feet.[43]

The world's preeminent naval power, deployed in strength with the latest electronic weaponry and defensive gadgetry, found itself almost defenseless against power boats and civilian aircraft. Although not admitting that the fleet was vulnerable, the Navy sent out an emergency request to the Marines for help. The Marines were ordered to screen their ranks for all available Stinger missilemen and to deploy them immediately to the fleet off Lebanon. The Stinger is a shoulder-fired antiaircraft missile that has had its own problems during development and testing. Experienced military observers were treated to the spectacle of Marines standing deck watch, guarding the fleet with relatively primitive shoulder-fired missiles, while the multi-billion-dollar Aegis system went idle. Fortunately, no terrorist tried to attack the fleet. Military analysts indicate that the chances are slim such an attack could have been stopped by the Stingers deployed in a manner for which they were not designed.

During the Lebanon incursion, the Navy deployed twelve ships off the coast. Among these were an aircraft carrier and a number of missile frigates and cruisers capable of delivering naval gunfire against mainland targets. The most powerful of these ships was the battleship *New Jersey*, which had seen action during Vietnam and was recommissioned in 1982 and then deployed off Lebanon. Despite the massive array of naval gunfire support, once again the application of basic military technique was so poor that almost none of the shells fired against ground positions hit their targets.

The *New Jersey*'s sixteen-inch guns can hurl a shell weighing

1,900 pounds almost eighteen miles. The shell exits the barrel at a speed of 2,960 feet per second, faster than a bullet fired from an M-1 rifle.[44] The *New Jersey* is capable of firing two rounds a minute. Frigates and cruisers like the *Virginia* and the *Rogers* can fire five-inch guns. Although much smaller than the sixteen-inch guns, these "five-inchers" can fire between twenty and forty rounds per minute. Their shells can make a crater twenty feet wide and five feet deep, compared with the *New Jersey*'s guns, which carve out a crater fifty feet wide and twenty feet deep.[45]

Unless one is addicted to the sounds of these guns, a sound deeply beloved by the romantic Navy brass, the real question is: Can these guns really hit anything?

Although Secretary of the Navy John Lehman told the House Armed Services Committee in December 1983 that the guns were "very accurate" and that "great care is taken not to fire into civilian areas," the facts suggest not only that naval gunfire in Lebanon was inaccurate but that the firing from naval ships never destroyed a single military target.[46] There is, unfortunately, plenty of evidence that a large number of civilian villages were hit, resulting in a significant number of casualties.

Hitting a target with a shell fired from sixteen miles is very difficult. In the first salvo, which is always fired blind, the chances that a shell will come within two thousand yards of its target are relatively small. In order for large guns to be even relatively accurate, it is necessary to have a forward observer either on the ground in sight of the target or aloft in an aircraft to adjust fire. Even then the odds are that the round will not hit the target with any degree of accuracy. Even when the fire is directed by a forward observer, all that can reasonably be expected of large naval guns is that they will land within one hundred yards of the target fifty percent of the time![47] Under the best of conditions, then, the chances are greater that a naval gun round will miss its target than that it will hit it.

On December 3, 1983, the Navy unleashed a naval barrage against Druse artillery positions in the Shouf Mountains. It was the single largest concentration of naval gunfire delivered by the U.S. since the Vietnam war. In one morning, the *New Jersey* sent

290 sixteen-inch shells winging their way toward their targets. The frigates and destroyers chimed in with 450 five-inch rounds. Ten days later, the Pentagon issued a report on the effectiveness of the gunfire. The conclusion was that "virtually all of the more than 700 shells fired at Druse and Syrian positions in Lebanon ten days ago by US warships missed their targets by very large distances and had little or no military or political impact."[48] Without a forward observer, naval gunfire is next to useless. Paradoxically, the point of recommissioning a naval battleship rested on its assumed ability to hit targets without having to expose U.S. military personnel to hostile fire. The result is an almost totally useless multi-million-dollar military system that cannot function as planned.

Had the U.S. military some sense of history, it would have been able to predict the ineffectiveness of naval gunfire from the experiences of World War II, Korea, and Vietnam. In all three, naval analysts have noted that naval gunfire was useless in destroying specific military targets.[49] To be sure, naval gunfire can be used as a weapon of mass destruction, to hit towns and villages, but it is ineffective to hit precise military positions and not destroy the area around them. In Lebanon, artillery positions were often located in villages friendly to enemy militias. Firing on them meant destroying homes and causing high civilian casualties. Naval officials admit that the naval shelling had two main effects: "to put big holes in mountainsides"; and to kill civilians and damage property.[50] Even the Druse militiamen, the most frequent targets of naval gunfire, say that they had no fear of the big guns, because they never hit anything. "Had they actually hit something," one Druse commander said, "things might have been different."[51]

CONCLUSIONS

An examination of events in Lebanon during the 533 days of the U.S. presence reveals a degree of incompetence and failure in the application of military technique that suggests that the American military has great difficulty executing operations for which it has planned. It places in doubt the ability of the U.S. military

establishment to plan realistically. More important, it seems that once plans have been adopted and the orders to execute issued, the U.S. military has great difficulty adjusting those plans to changing circumstances. This seems to be a particular consequence of a military structure that is heavily bureaucratized and diffuses responsibility.

Even if a commander fails, he is not likely to be punished as long as he sticks to the plan, which, in most cases, he has had very little say in formulating but must execute nonetheless. This separation of the execution from the planning has proved fatal in a number of American military operations in the past and remains a puzzlement to foreign military observers, especially the Israelis and the Germans, who almost never expect an officer to execute a plan he has had no part in formulating. In the American military, there is safety in numbers. As long as one's superiors in the chain of command have a stake in the plan's formulation, when things go wrong a subordinate can rely with some degree of certainty on his superiors to protect the executor of the plan, as a way of protecting themselves. The real danger to an officer lies in changing the plan, because if things go wrong, then he has only himself to blame. More important, he has no powerful allies in the chain of command to protect him. And so, in Lebanon, despite the fact that local commanders and members of the chain of command were found guilty of serious misjudgment, no one was punished. And when incompetence is not punished, nothing is learned. And when nothing is learned, the same mistakes are likely to be made again in a different place and at a different time.

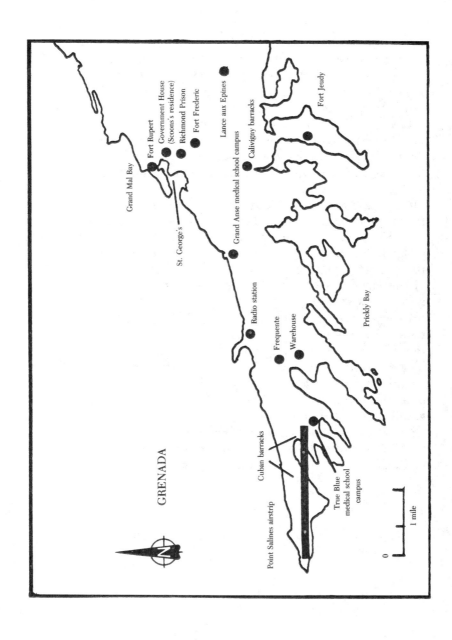

GRENADA

Point Salines airstrip

Cuban barracks

True Blue medical school campus

Frequente

Warehouse

Radio station

Grand Anse medical school campus

St. George's

Grand Mal Bay

Fort Rupert

Government House (Scoon's residence)

Richmond Prison

Fort Frederic

Lance aux Epines

Calivigny barracks

Fort Jeudy

Prickly Bay

N

0   1 mile

6

GRENADA

THE decision to launch Operation Urgent Fury and invade Grenada was based on a number of factors. The first was the U.S. desire not to allow the establishment of "another Cuba" in the Caribbean. The fear that Grenada would move closer to Cuba, and, by implication, to the Soviet bloc, grew on October 19, 1983, when Prime Minister Maurice Bishop was overthrown and executed by a group of leftist rivals on Grenada. The United States thought that this group, more radical than Bishop, and to his left, would move Grenada into the Cuban orbit. Paradoxically, Cuba had openly supported Bishop in the struggle with his more radical rivals.

A second factor influencing the American decision to move with force against Grenada was the fear of another hostage crisis. The published reports of the American decision-making process make clear that the President and his advisors feared that the almost eight hundred American students at the island's medical school would be held hostage by the new revolutionary regime. President Reagan, having criticized President Carter during the 1980 election campaign for failing to act against the Iranians, was acutely sensitive to another possible hostage situation. He leaned very strongly in the direction of a military solution to the problem.

The Reagan Administration was also concerned about the new 12,000-foot airstrip being built by Cuban workers with British technical help. The Administration seems to have convinced itself that the new regime would deploy Cuban and eventually even Soviet MIG or bomber aircraft on the new runway. Although assured

repeatedly by Bishop and the new leadership that the runway was merely for large jumbo jets to boost Grenada's tourist-based economy, the Reagan Administration persisted in seeing the new airport as a means of opening up Grenada to Cuban and Soviet military force.

Perhaps equally important, the Reagan Administration came to power believing that the U.S. had lost its credibility because of its failure to act successfully in the Iran crisis and to do anything forceful about the invasion of Afghanistan. The Reagan Administration felt that the world no longer believed that the U.S. would respond to a military challenge and that this perception alone tended to increase the probability that the Soviets or others would create such challenges. Thus, the need to reestablish U.S. credibility may well have been a major motive in U.S. action in Grenada. As one official noted privately, "this Administration came to power with the intention of punching someone in the nose."[1] When Alexander Haig was Secretary of State, the decision to respond to Soviet provocation had been focused on El Salvador. When that situation proved to be increasingly complex, the Reagan Administration determined that Grenada was the obvious place to "stand tall," to reestablish U.S. military credibility.

The initial discussions concerning Operation Urgent Fury began almost a week before the invasion. The military plans were completed seventy-two hours before the actual invasion. Naval units were put to sea and others redirected to assemble off the island. Army forces were assembled at Fort Bragg, North Carolina, and a Ranger battalion was moved to Fort Stewart, Georgia. After two days of meetings, the decision to move against Grenada was taken at 6 p.m. on Monday, October 24.[2]

It is interesting to note that the President placed full operational control of the mission in the hands of the office of the Joint Chiefs of Staff. The JCS had a free hand in both planning and execution. Overall responsibility for the mission's success rested with the chairman, General John Vessey. The President's action seems rooted in his belief that the Iran raid would have succeeded had it been left solely to the military. President Reagan believed, mistakenly, that there had been a considerable degree of interference from the White House throughout the planning of the Iran

raid. He knew that the decision to abort the raid was made in the White House after the aircraft collision in the Iranian desert. Reagan leaned toward the view that, had the military been given a free hand, events would have turned out differently in Iran. By placing responsibility for the invasion in the hands of the JCS, Reagan was showing his faith in the military. Politically, of course, if things went wrong, the JCS would have no one to blame but itself, which let the President off the hook. On the other hand, if things went well, the President was in a position to reap the political benefits. In any case, from the very outset, Operation Urgent Fury was a military show; there would be no political interference.

THE PLAN

The plan called for a number of military special operations before the actual invasion of the island by the main force. These missions, seven in all, were to go off at about the same time, about an hour before dawn. The main-force units were comprised of Marines, Rangers, and, later in the day, the 82nd Airborne Division. The object was to overwhelm the defenders of the island in a quick, massive "surgical" operation that would keep damage and loss of life to a minimum. The main military objectives were to rescue the students at the medical school, evacuate Governor General Scoons, and capture the new Grenadian leadership. The rescue operation would be used as the public rationale for the invasion, but in fact its objectives went considerably beyond. Enough forces were to be put on the island to destroy the Cuban defenders and the Grenadian army. What the U.S. planned was nothing less than taking over the island and installing a regime more friendly to American interests.

The Ranger landings just before light were to mark the official start of the invasion.* Two of the special operations missions were

---

* The Pentagon maintained that the Ranger airdrop marked the "official" start of the invasion, thus making it possible to deny that there were any other U.S. forces on the island before the Rangers. With increasing press scrutiny, however, it has since been admitted that some U.S. special operations forces were in fact on the island before the Rangers.

assigned to Delta Force, which was formed in the mid-1970s as a counter-terrorist and hostage-rescue force. Delta was to parachute onto the island's airstrip the night before the invasion. They were to reconnoiter the airstrip at Point Salines and make sure it was usable. At first light, just thirty minutes before the arrival of the Rangers in their C-130 aircraft, Delta was to assault the airstrip and clear it of the construction machinery the Cubans routinely left at the end of the day's work. With the airstrip cleared, the Rangers would be able to land their aircraft and seize control of the airport. Delta was given a second mission on the same morning. A second Delta group was to conduct a lightning assault against Richmond Prison to rescue what the U.S. termed "political pris-oners," who, according to the official explanation, might be used as hostages. Besides the Delta operations, there were a number of special operations by Seal teams, the Navy's equivalent of Delta Force. The Seals are basically sea-going commandos, whose job, essentially, is reconnaissance and counter-terrorism at sea. One Seal mission called for a twenty-two-man team to be landed by helicopter on the estate of Governor General Scoons.[3] They were to evacuate him to safety aboard the USS *Guam*. Additional Seal teams were to reconnoiter the Marine landing zone at Pearls air-port, seize the transmitter of Radio Free Grenada, and attack and take control of the island's main diesel generating plant near Grand Mal Bay.

These special-operations missions do not constitute what, in military parlance, is called a coup de main.[4] Properly understood, a coup de main implies the use of a military force to seize an enemy's defenses in depth, with a significant concentration of force in order to overwhelm enemy strongpoints. Once these points have been taken, large follow-up forces deploy and link up with the strike teams. None of the special operations missions in Grenada was really designed to seize anything of military significance, however. At least five of the special operations missions could have been omitted without any significant effect on the invasion's success. The Delta missions, while important, were in the end not vital. As for the Seal teams, their missions did nothing to reduce the ability of the enemy to resist the main body of the American forces.

Generally, the plan was to use special operations missions to carry out political tasks (rescue Governor Scoons and destroy the radio station), or else as show pieces to demonstrate U.S. special operations capability.

Command and control of all special operations missions was vested in the Joint Special Operations Command (JSOC). JSOC had been created after the disaster of the Iran raid, precisely to avoid the problems of command, control, and integration of mixed force units that resulted in the failure of the Iran mission. JSOC is a special planning group outside the normal channels of command. Ostensibly, it has supreme authority in controlling its own resources and those attached to it. In Grenada, JSOC was in charge of all special operations missions, including Delta Force operations, the Seal reconnaissance teams, and all the rescue and seizure missions. The initial Ranger deployment and the aircraft used to execute it were also controlled by JSOC. The JSOC command and control staff was deployed over the island in a C-130 command and control aircraft.

In addition to the special operations forces, there were the regular force missions that were to deliver the main blow against the island's defenders and to ensure adequate follow-on to the special operations themselves. These conventional operations included the Ranger deployment at the Point Salines airport as the initial strike force to secure the airport with a force adequate to permit reinforcement by the 82nd Airborne. Another conventional operation was the Marine heliborne assault from the carrier *Guam* to capture and secure the airport at Pearls on the other side of the island. The major source of military manpower would come from the 82nd Airborne Division, which would deploy a brigade of three thousand men airlifted in C-141s from Fort Bragg to Point Salines. A second brigade would be staged at Fort Bragg, to deploy as needed. Command of the regular force missions was in the hands of Admiral Joseph Metcalf and his deputy, Army General Norman Schwartzkopf. The invasion plan called for committing two Ranger battalions of about eight hundred men each. The 1st Ranger Battalion had been airlifted two days before the invasion from its home base at Fort Lewis, Washington, to its deployment station at Fort Stewart, Georgia. It was to deploy with the 2nd Ranger Battalion,

stationed at Fort Stewart. Elements of both battalions were combined into a strike force of about six hundred men. At the same time as the Rangers seized the airport at Point Salines, the Marines would put ashore a battalion landing team (BLT). A BLT normally mounts about eight hundred men, broken into three infantry companies and one weapons company, accompanied by five to seven tanks and their command element. If one includes the hundred and fifty men from the special operations teams that would be deployed prior to the main force, the plan was to put about 5,600 men on the ground. With reinforcements, the force would grow to eight thousand.

Arrayed against them were the Cuban and Grenadian forces. According to JCS estimates, the U.S. could expect to find between seven hundred and eleven hundred Cuban soldiers on the island, augmented by fifteen hundred People's Revolutionary Army soldiers (the Grenadian army), buttressed by another two thousand to five thousand Grenadian territorial militia.[5] As it turned out, fewer than fifty of the defenders were Cuban regular forces.[6] The remaining Cubans were construction workers. They were just that, workers and engineers. To be sure, they had had some military training, having served in the Cuban Army as conscripts. The workers were able to fight rather well. But actual Cuban military personnel did not exceed fifty. The People's Revolutionary Army never did engage U.S. forces in any significant way, although it did take a toll of some of the special operations forces. Many ran away once the invasion began. And many refused to fight, because they did not support the new regime, which had killed Prime Minister Bishop. The territorial militia was essentially unarmed. In terms of actual combat forces, the U.S. outnumbered the island's defenders approximately ten to one.

It is an interesting question whether the JCS took its own estimates of enemy forces seriously. If one assumes that they did, they must have expected to have to deal with almost 7,200 fighters on the island. Against this number they planned to throw some 5,600 men in the initial assault, which implies that U.S. forces would be outnumbered and too understrength to accomplish their mission with any speed. Even counting the reinforcing brigade of the 82nd, U.S. forces would total eight thousand men, far below

the three-to-one ratio traditionally required of a force attacking a deployed defense. Although official reports have made much of the fact that a large number of enemy troops were subdued by the American forces, in fact no one at the JCS level ever took these estimates seriously or expected more than a thousand Cuban and Grenadian soldiers to fight. Certainly, no one expected them to fight very well. The night before the invasion, the chairman of the JCS assured the President that American casualties would be light and the operation would go quickly, largely because of the number and quality of forces on the island, as well as their unsophisticated weapons.[7]

The estimate that the strength of the enemy force would be marginal proved to be correct. One gets the clear impression from an analysis of the weapons captured and the equipment destroyed that the Grenadian defenders were a small force armed with a hodgepodge of obsolete World War II equipment, some of it hand-me-downs from the Cuban Army. The defenders could mount only eighteen BTR-60 armored personnel carriers, most armed only with machine guns. Even these had been brought to the island less than a month before the invasion and, because the crews were not well trained, served essentially as military transport rather than as fighting vehicles. There were some twenty ZSU-23 antiaircraft guns, but most never got into battle. Of the twenty, twelve were captured intact and without any damage; the degree to which they were used with any effect was marginal. A significant amount of small arms were captured, including 290 machine guns, 6,330 AK-47 assault rifles, a handful of 81mm and 120mm mortars, and about six million rounds of small-arms ammunition. Most of this equipment was not captured from prisoners but was taken from a warehouse and other storage points at Frequente barracks. It was simply left behind as the defenders withdrew. Although there was clearly more equipment than men to use it, the Cubans were not deployed to defend the island. They had been sent to Grenada as advisors and only recently had begun constructing defensive positions. No hardened defensive positions were encountered by U.S. forces. By any reasonable standard, the enemy force was marginal in terms not only of its strength but also of its equipment and firepower. Despite this, the U.S. forces seem to have had a rela-

tively hard time subduing the Grenadian defenders. For example, it took a brigade of the 82nd Airborne almost three days to move the three miles from the airport to the capital of St George's.

THINGS GO WRONG

Shortly before midnight on Monday, October 24, a team of thirty-five or forty men (the numbers remain classified) chuted up in their quarters in a building near the airport on the island of Barbados.[8] They wore black jumpsuits equipped with web support vests, infrared night-vision goggles, flak vests, and black watch caps. The soldiers carried 9mm German-made Heckler–Koch silenced machine guns; each soldier also carried a 9mm sidearm. Just before midnight, they boarded a C-130 Hercules transport, with its insignia painted out, for the forty-five-minute flight to Grenada. The men of Delta Force would parachute onto the island in the early-morning darkness of Tuesday, October 25.

Their mission was to place themselves at the Point Salines airport before the main invasion began at dawn. They were to take up positions in a grassy ravine near some abandoned construction buildings at the far west end of the airstrip. Although the specific details of the mission remain secret, it seems certain that it was a twofold mission. The first objective was to reconnoiter the airstrip and determine its usability for the Ranger force that was to land on the runway at dawn. If the runway was unusable, as it was expected to be, Delta's mission was to assault the airstrip at first light and "hot-wire" the construction machinery left parked on the runway by the Cuban construction workers.

Sometime after 2 a.m., the Delta team was spotted by a member of the Cuban garrison. The circumstances remain unclear, but the alarm was sounded and the Cuban garrison came to life and began to deploy around the ravine, which was only a half mile from their barracks. Delta was quickly surrounded on three sides as the Cubans began to pour heavy small-arms fire into the ravine from the surrounding slopes. Some men of the Delta Force found their way into a wooden building on the edge of the ravine. As Cuban fire poured through the walls, the number of dead and wounded

began to mount. For almost four hours, until an AC-130 Spectre gunship finally arrived overhead (prior to the Rangers' arrival)[9] and began to spray the defenders with minigun and even automatic howitzer fire, Delta Force fought for its life.

When Delta was finally rescued at dawn by the Ranger landing, twenty-two of its men had been killed or wounded. Although the military has refused to acknowledge that there were any dead or wounded or even that Delta Force was on the island, sources close to and even inside Delta report that at least six men were killed and another sixteen wounded. Moreover, Delta's failure to execute its mission alerted the defenders to the larger invasion. The alarm was sounded throughout the island almost four hours before the main forces arrived. When the Rangers parachuted onto the airstrip later that morning, the enemy was waiting for them with their AK-47s and ZSU-23 machine guns.

A second Delta mission launched in the early daylight hours of the first day was to assault Richmond Hill Prison and rescue the "political prisoners" being held there.[10] This second team assaulted the prison in nine Blackhawk helicopters flown by the pilots of Task Force 160, the "Nightstalkers."[11] Task Force 160 is a secret helicopter battalion stationed at Fort Campbell, Kentucky. Flying both Blackhawks and OH-6 Cayuse helicopters, Task Force 160 is assigned to airlifting Delta on its missions. Its helicopters carry no identifying insignia and some of its OH-6s are painted black. The OH-6s mount chain guns and rockets and, in some configurations, carry out secret electronic missions. Some of the helicopters are also configured with special night-flying devices.

At 6:15 that morning, Delta Force flew over Prickly Bay near Point Salines on the way to assault Richmond Prison. As one Blackhawk helicopter, flown by Captain Keith Lucas, passed over Prickly Bay point, it was struck in the cockpit by a burst of small-arms fire from the ground. The helicopter crashed into a ridge, tumbling over the hill, and its rotor blades flew off and plunged into the surf. The machine began to burn. Immediately, another Blackhawk dropped from the assault formation and flew cover while awaiting the arrival of a Navy H-3 Seaking rescue helicopter.[12] The main assault group, now reduced to seven helicopters, flew on to Richmond Prison.

Richmond Prison is located atop a steep, sixty-degree promontory behind the town of St. George's. Built on the remains of an old eighteenth-century fort, the prison cannot be approached by foot from three sides except through dense jungle growing on the steep mountainside. The fourth side is approachable by a narrow neck of road with high trees running along it. The prison, located on an elevated mountain point, offers no place for a helicopter assault force to land. Richmond Hill forms one side of a steep valley. Across and above the valley, on a higher peak, is another old fort, Fort Frederic, which housed a large Grenadian garrison. From Fort Frederic, the garrison easily commanded the slopes and floor of the ravine below with small-arms and machine gun fire. It was into this valley and under the guns of the Grenadian garrison that the helicopters of Delta Force flew at 6:30 that morning.

The helicopters of Task Force 160 flew into the valley and turned their noses toward the prison. Unable to land, they began to rappel the Delta raiders down ropes dragging from the doors of the helicopters. Suddenly, as men swung wildly from the rappeling ropes, the helicopters were caught in a murderous cross fire from the front as forces from the prison opened fire, and more devastatingly, from behind, as enemy forces in Fort Frederic rained heavy small-arms and machine-gun fire down from above. According to eyewitness accounts by Grenadian civilians who were in houses and in the mental hospital situated above the ravine,* a number of helicopters were hit—some eyewitnesses say as many as five—and crash-landed on the valley floor. The raiders, many wounded or injured, scattered and hid, to avoid the hail of gunfire. The helicopters that could flew out of the valley. Delta Force's assault on Richmond Prison had been a failure. In at least one instance, a helicopter pilot of TF-160 turned back without orders and refused to fly into the assault. Charges of cowardice were filed against him by some members of the Delta Force but were later dropped. Later, air strikes were called in against Fort Frederic,

---

* I conducted interviews with a number of Grenadians who witnessed this action, including members of the hospital staff, and even Grenadian soldiers who were at Fort Frederic when the incident happened.

but they missed the fort and destroyed the mental hospital about three thousand feet away. The prison itself was taken the next day by the Marines, who found it abandoned.

At about the time that Delta Force was being pinned down at the end of the Point Salines runway, Navy Seal teams were put to sea to undertake a number of special operations. Two four-man teams in rubber whaleboats approached a small beach about a half mile from Point Salines. Their mission was to seize the transmitter building of Radio Free Grenada and knock it off the air. As they approached the beach in the early-morning hours, the Seals had no way of knowing that Delta's presence had been discovered at Point Salines and that the alarm had been sounded throughout the island. They did not know that enemy forces around the transmitter had been reinforced and were on alert. The Seals landed on the beach and moved inland down a narrow path bordered on both sides by thick jungle. The transmitter building was less than four hundred yards up the path, across a narrow paved road. At a point where the path takes a sharp turn, the Seals came under heavy small-arms fire. Almost immediately, the point man was shot and killed, followed quickly by another man. Two more Seals were wounded. The remaining men were able to extricate their wounded comrades from the jungle, gain the beach, and return to sea in their boats. The Seal team had failed to accomplish its mission, and Radio Free Grenada continued to broadcast appeals to resist the invaders, until it was silenced in mid-morning[13] by an AC-130 Spectre gunship whose miniguns and automatic cannon reduced the transmitter building to ruins.

Farther up the island's coast, near Pearls airport, other Seal teams also failed to accomplish their missions. Two four-man teams were dropped by C-130 aircraft in the sea near the end of the Pearls runway. They were to reconnoiter the airport to determine what fortifications there might be. The Marines intended to conduct a heliborne assault against the airport and had to know the nature and strength of its defenses. Although the method of bringing them in remains classified, it seems likely that the Seal teams were LAPESed into the water. LAPESing (low-altitude parachute extraction system) is a technique whereby men and equipment are pulled from the back of a low-flying C-130 aircraft by drogue par-

achute as the aircraft skims the water. What seems to have happened is that one four-man Seal team deploying from the aircraft in their rubber whaleboat were knocked unconscious by the impact on the water. Thrown from the boat as it hit the water, and weighed down with weapons and equipment, they were dragged under and drowned. The second team managed to hit the water safely, start the boat's engine, and proceed toward the beach. As they approached their landing point, a boat rounded a jut of land near them. In all probability, it was a civilian fishing boat putting out early in the morning to take the day's catch. The Seals spotted the boat and shut down their engine, apparently flooding it. The engine was probably also swamped by a wave. As the fishing boat passed, the Seals attempted to restart their engine but couldn't. The current began to drag them out to sea, and they were unable to overcome it. The boat and the Seals drifted away from the island. Eleven hours later, they were picked up by a Navy ship. As a result of the Seal team's failure, the Marine helicopter assault had to go in blind. The failure of the Seals to reconnoiter the proposed Marine landing zone almost caused a disaster. As the Marine helicopters approached the original landing zone—shown as an open field on their old maps—it turned out that the "field" was actually a grove of banana trees. Unable to land, the Marine pilots searched for another place and could not find one, so they had to land on the exposed runway of Pearls airport. As it turned out, the force was unopposed at the old Pearls airport, and within two hours of landing, the Marines deployed south and cut the main road at Grenville. Pearls airport had been secured.

Meanwhile, another Seal team of twenty-two men had been inserted into the grounds of Governor General Scoons's residence, with the priority mission of rescuing him and members of his staff.[14] The objective was to evacuate him by helicopter to the USS *Guam*. Unfortunately, the Seals were spotted while inside the compound and were quickly surrounded by a mixed force of Cubans and Grenadians. The size of the enemy force is in some doubt, but most observers put it at no larger than fifty men. A Cuban-manned BTR-60 armored personnel carrier was brought up near the gate, while other forces deployed to cut the one escape route from the estate, trapping the Seals and Governor Scoons. Shortly thereafter,

the Cubans tried to assault the main gate with their BTR-60; a heavy rain of small-arms fire poured into the house. Unable to match the volume of fire, the Seals called for AC-130 Spectre gunship support. The Spectre quickly appeared overhead and began pouring fire into the enemy positions. The attack from above halted any further attempts by the Cubans to assault the compound, and although sporadic exchanges of fire occurred throughout the morning and the next day, no serious effort was made by either side to change the situation. Nonetheless, the Seals had failed to execute what had been designated a priority mission; and they had been trapped by the enemy. It was not until twenty-six hours later, during the following day, that the Marine landing at Grand Mal Bay relieved the "siege" of the governor's house. There is some dispute about the number of Seals wounded in this operation. Reporters, press accounts, and eyewitnesses suggest that as many as ten of the twenty-two-man force were wounded.[15] The JCS continues to maintain that no Seals were wounded in the operation.

It must be kept in mind that JSOC had overall operational responsibility for the execution of all these special operations. In retrospect, it appears that some of the same problems of command, control, and communications which contributed to the failure of the Iran raid also surfaced in the special operations conducted in Grenada. Almost all the operations were a failure. The two Delta missions clearly went wrong. The attempt to reconnoiter the Marine landing zone resulted in one team dead and the other floating aimlessly at sea. The mission to seize and destroy Radio Free Grenada was a disaster, costing two dead and two wounded. And, finally, the attempt to rescue Governor Scoons also failed. In addition, JSOC lost control of the aircraft assigned to it to ensure that the Ranger landing was executed correctly and was properly reinforced.

It seems safe to suggest that the creation of JSOC after the Iran debacle has done little to improve the ability of U.S. forces to conduct commando operations, at least if the operations in Grenada are any test. JSOC was not able to control its operations and bring about a successful outcome. Indeed, most of the "black" (secret) operations that have come to light were failures. Only the seizure of the diesel generating plant seems to have gone off suc-

cessfully. Here a sixteen-man Seal team surprised and captured six civilian employees of the local power company on the morning of the first day of the invasion.[16] Four months after the invasion, the J-3 section of JSOC, the section responsible for plans and operations, was reorganized and a number of officers transferred.

The military, after its failures in Iran, had concluded that the problem was essentially organizational and had developed an "organizational fix"—namely, the creation of a new planning group—as a solution. As with many other organizational fixes, this one did not live up to expectations. The truth is that JSOC presided over an operational disaster which, while not of the same proportion as the Iran raid, from the technical perspective of planning and execution certainly came very close.

The first of the regular forces to arrive on Grenada were the Rangers. Two Ranger units had been targeted for deployment in Grenada. The Rangers were deployed directly from their staging base at Fort Stewart, Georgia, and refueled in flight over Florida, flying almost seven and a half hours in ten C-130s all the way to Grenada.[17] After the men were parachuted onto the island, the plan was for the aircraft to stop over in Barbados, refuel, and return to Fort Stewart, where they would pick up the remaining Rangers. But something went wrong, and of the total 1,600-man Ranger force, only about five hundred, or about one-third, ever made it to the war. Apparently, the decision to deploy the Ranger force was restricted by the availability of airlift. The Rangers used ten C-130s assigned to them as their airlift. Because airlift was at a premium, a decision had to be made as to which of the two Ranger battalions to deploy. In typical joint-operation planning, the decision was made to deploy neither at full strength. Rather, purely for political and bureaucratic reasons, elements of both battalions, together with their separate staffs, were assigned to the initial assault. Such a plan violated both simplicity and unity of command and created problems once the Rangers landed.

The aircraft assigned to the Rangers were normally detailed to the 82nd Airborne Division as part of its organic airlift capability. JSOC must have been given assurances by the 82nd and its parent command, 18th Airborne Corps, that these aircraft would remain at the disposal of JSOC until the Ranger airlift had been completed

in its entirety. Events on the ground changed this, and JSOC lost control over the airlift almost immediately after the first airdrop. As a consequence, two-thirds of the Ranger force never got into action.

What happened is that, after the Rangers parachuted onto the island, they came under unexpectedly heavy fire. Press reports note that Cuban positions engaged the Rangers from less than four hundred yards. As the attack proceeded, there was considerable confusion, since command of the Ranger force was split; there was no single commander for the entire force. Ranger radio transmissions began to "spike"; that is, to greatly exaggerate the firepower and strength of the enemy. These estimates from the ground forces engaged in battle were transmitted over the command net and reached the 18th Airborne Corps commander. Fearing that the 82nd would have to go into Grenada with more troops than expected, to relieve the pressure on the Rangers, and fearing that the available airlift would be insufficient, someone in the higher headquarters decided to overrule the JSOC commander and ordered the C-130s en route to Fort Stewart to divert to Fort Bragg. The aircraft diverted as instructed, leaving two-thirds of the Ranger force sitting on the tarmac at Fort Stewart listening to the war on their radios.

The initial Ranger deployment over Point Salines took the form of a parachute drop that was not planned but had to be improvised in the air on the way to the island.[18] Because of Delta's failure to clear the runway, and because Delta's presence had alerted the island's defenders to a possible follow-on assault, the Rangers could not land at Point Salines. The aircraft were rigged for landing, not for a parachute assault. (A C-130 rigged for parachute assault holds about 64 men and their equipment; when equipped for landing, it accommodates about eighty. The C-130s were all the more crowded as they also carried a number of OH-6 helicopters aboard.)[19] While en route to Grenada, the Rangers had to rig their aircraft for a parachute assault. The Rangers, delayed twenty-seven minutes, would have to parachute into Point Salines, knowing full well that they would be parachuting into the gunsights of an alerted enemy. Since the aircraft had been packed for an air-land assault, most of the reserve parachutes were stowed. As the Rangers exited

their aircraft at five hundred feet, many of them jumped without reserve parachutes.[20] Further, much of the heavy medical and communications equipment, including the heavier anti-tank weaponry, was not rigged for airdrop and consequently had to be left behind. All this may explain some of the initial confusion on the ground, as the Rangers had difficulty gathering and coordinating their forces for the assault. And it would explain why few anti-tank weapons were brought to bear in the early hours of the invasion.

The parachute assault did not go well. Once over the drop zone, the pilots of the two lead aircraft refused to follow the orders of the jump master and veered off at the last minute, to "avoid extremely heavy anti-aircraft fire." However, the ground fire was only small-arms rifle and machine-gun fire. An explanation offered by the Pentagon spokesman is that the first aircraft had trouble with its navigation equipment.[21] The enemy units that had Delta Force pinned down at the end of the runway began to bring fire to bear on the incoming aircraft. Since the first two planes tracked away from the drop zone, the first Rangers to jump were from the third aircraft, containing the command elements for the 2nd and 1st battalions. There were anxious minutes on the ground as the command element discovered that they were alone, that the two planeloads of Rangers had not preceded them. The next load of Rangers did not arrive for seven minutes.

The Gaylord film, made on the spot by an American living on Grenada, shows the Ranger aircraft being committed to the drop zone one at a time. The film shows an interval of from one to ten minutes between aircraft dropping their paratroopers on the runway.[22] The Pentagon spokesman, Michael Burch, appearing on ABC Nightline, noted that it took *two hours* for all the Rangers to complete their insertion on the island. This piecemeal deployment of the airborne force probably resulted from the different time it took each aircraft to rerig en route. Piecemeal deployment undoubtedly contributed to Ranger casualties and allowed the enemy to mount a more effective resistance. The refusal of the Air Force pilots to make their runs over the drop zone prompted some officers to consider pressing charges of cowardice against them. As in another instance where cowardice was charged in the Grenada operation, however, the Army "counseled" the officers out of pressing

charges. A year later, the Army stated that such charges had been investigated and found groundless.[23]

The Rangers floating to the ground were under small-arms and machine-gun fire. Upon landing, they appeared confused by the degree of resistance. They had dropped onto the alerted Cuban defenders, who shot some Rangers in their parachutes both in the air and on the ground. Other Rangers landed in the water, which surrounds the airstrip on two sides.[24] Cuban defensive positions were, in one case, as close as four hundred yards to the drop zone. One officer, who was wounded on the runway, was quoted as saying: "They were waiting for us. We could hear the shooting and the bombs but we could not see anything."[25] After about twenty minutes, as more Rangers hit on the airstrip, they began their assault, thus relieving the pressure on the exhausted Delta Force. By and large, the Cubans gave ground easily. The Rangers hotwired the construction machinery and drove it off the runway, opening it for use by incoming reinforcements.

The JCS report notes that the Ranger assault began at 5:27 Tuesday, October 25.[26] (Actually, it was twenty-seven minutes later.) In less than an hour, the JCS reports says, the "runway was cleared." At seven, according to the same report, the Rangers began the assault to clear the area near the end of the runway. They encountered some resistance, but gradually the Cubans withdrew from the airport, moving back up the access road to positions around Frequente. Air Force Spectre gunships were brought in to attack Frequente. Over one hundred and fifty Cuban engineers, workers, and soldiers surrendered. By 10 a.m., the Rangers declared the area safe and secure.[27] The Rangers dug in around the airport and held the area until the 82nd Airborne arrived to relieve them in place at about 2 p.m.

With the Rangers in command of the airfield, it was time to reinforce them with a full brigade of the 82nd Airborne Division, which arrived from Fort Bragg that afternoon in their C-141 Starlifters. According to the Pentagon, the 82nd arrived at 2 p.m., almost five hours after the Rangers had declared the landing zone secure. Upon arriving, however, they came under what the Pentagon called "heavy fire."[28] As *Time* reported, the Cuban barracks on the airfield had not been taken at all, and the Rangers controlled

only one end of the airstrip and did not press the attack.[29] Significantly, the True Blue medical school campus lies at the other end of the runway and apparently was still in Cuban hands by late afternoon of the first day. Just why the Rangers did not press the attack is unclear. One reason might be that the strength of the Ranger force was insufficient. When they jumped, they had been forced to leave much of their ammunition and heavy weapons behind. Although they cleared the west end of the runway (partly because the enemy withdrew), they were unable to attack and subdue the Cuban barracks less than a half mile away. They threw up a perimeter defense on their end of the runway and held on for the better part of four hours, until reinforced by the 82nd. When the lead elements of the 82nd arrived, the Cubans continued to direct machine-gun and small-arms fire at their aircraft; even an armored car was thrown into the fight, appearing sporadically at the end of the runway to direct fire at the landing paratroopers. As the paratroopers scrambled from their aircraft, two men, a company commander and a squad leader, were hit and wounded on the runway.

As the 82nd deployed more and more men on the runway, the fighting moved east, toward the Cuban barracks. It was heavy enough to stop the Americans. They called in air strikes, flown by A-7 Corsairs launched from the carrier *Independence*. AC-130 gunships were called in, and even combat assault helicopter gunships. It still took more than five hours to subdue the Cubans, and they were able to execute a tactical withdrawal and move gradually back as the 82nd, now combined with the Ranger forces, began to press the attack. By the end of the first day, about 170 Cubans and Grenadians had surrendered, some of them military men, but most of them construction workers and engineers. The 82nd and the Rangers began their sweep of the Cuban barracks area, meeting only sporadic resistance, and continued to advance up to the single road connecting the airport to St. George's. Once in command of both ends of the runway, Ranger and paratrooper units moved unopposed onto the True Blue campus of the St. George's Medical College, only yards away from the runway's eastern end. There the Americans threw up a perimeter defense. At 9:45 a.m. the next

morning, the students were moved to the runway and were evacuated from the island on C-141 Starlifters.

At daybreak on the first day, the Marines helilifted some 250
men of the I-84 Amphibious Readiness Group into the airport at
Pearls. The Seal team that was to reconnoiter the landing zone had
been killed in the attempt, and so the Marines had to go in blind,
covered by aircraft and Cobra gunships. The airstrip at Pearls was
secured with little resistance, and within two hours the Marines
had set up defensive positions, cut the road at Grenville, and
declared the airport secure. The Marines had executed their part
of the plan perfectly and now had little else to do.

However, far to the west, the Army assault by the combined
Ranger and airborne forces was meeting resistance in and around
the Cuban barracks. And as the day wore on, the 82nd met resistance at Frequente, where the enemy was delaying the paratrooper
advance on the road beyond the warehouse. Equally troublesome
was the fact that the Seal team sent to rescue Governor General
Scoons had been trapped for ten hours. Something had to be done
to rescue the Seal team and to break the resistance to the advance
along the road to St. George's. Despite overwhelming numbers
and firepower, as well as complete control of the air, the 82nd was
unable to break the back of the Cuban resistance. The Army advance had slowed to a crawl and was in danger of stalling. The
deputy commander of the operation, General Schwartzkopf, decided to call in the Marines to reestablish the momentum of the
Army advance and to lift the "siege" of Governor Scoons's house.

The Marines, safely ashore and in control of Pearls airport,
were just beginning to reinforce with their tanks and amphibious
vehicles when the call came for them to redeploy across the island
to St. George's. The deputy commander ordered the tanks to sail
around the island on their amphibious transporters and to put
ashore at Grand Mal Bay, below and to the west of the governor's
residence. The Marines obliged, and at approximately 7 p.m. that
evening, at dusk, they landed at Grand Mal, moved inland, and
took up positions on the soccer field in full view of the governor's
house.[30] They trained their guns on the Cuban and Grenadian
forces encircling the house. The Marines executed their operation

with flexibility and speed as they first deployed their tanks without infantry support. However, the tanks were without support and in exposed positions for almost five hours, until a Marine infantry company under the command of Captain Dick was helilifted from Pearls to join them.

Except for a company left behind to garrison Pearls airport, the rest of the Marine assault force was helilifted back to the USS *Guam*, which then began moving west to reinforce the landing party at Grand Mal Bay early the next morning. At daybreak, Wednesday, October 26, some two hundred Marines and thirteen amphibious vehicles, backed up by more tanks, put ashore at Grand Mal. This placed the Marines within four miles of the defenders on the St. George's road. The Marines were also in a position to aid in the attack on Fort Rupert and the Richmond Hill Prison, which would occur the next day.

The tankers, now reinforced with infantry, began moving toward the enemy surrounding Governor Scoons's house. They fired a few "demonstration rounds" at the forces besieging the house. Some enemy soldiers surrendered immediately, and some broke and ran. Helicopters were brought in from the *Guam* to ferry the governor general, some civilian staff members, and the Seal team back to the safety of the American carrier. The Marines had relieved the siege almost without firing a shot.

The Rangers had reached the students at the True Blue campus on the first day of the invasion. But U.S. forces had not been briefed that there were two other groups of students on the island. One group of 224 students was at the Grand Anse campus about four miles north of the airstrip, and a second group of 202 students was in a housing complex at Lance aux Epines; they were not rescued until two days later.[31] Enemy forces were in control of both locations and could easily have killed the students. That U.S. forces did not know the location of all the students before launching a "rescue" was one of the main intelligence failures of the Grenada operation. The rescue was stated to be a paramount reason for the invasion. On Wednesday, October 26, a combined assault by Rangers, paratroopers, and Marine helicopters was launched against the Grand Anse campus, to rescue the 224 students there.

The Cubans and Grenadians had thrown up a thin and hasty

line of defense facing the St. George's road, with the campus and their backs to the sea. Thus, they were between the U.S. forces and the campus where the students were housed. According to the students themselves, they never felt in any danger until the Americans arrived and it looked as if there might be a battle. No threats were ever made against either the students or the medical-school staff. Indeed, if the enemy had wanted to kill the students or hold them hostage, they had two full days to do so after the first American forces landed.

From a military perspective, the U.S. force had to find a way to get in behind the defenders and position men between the students and the enemy, so that when the defending line was attacked, the assault would not drive the defenders back through the campus, causing destruction and risking the lives of the students.

The problem was solved by a combined assault. The paratroops assaulted from the ground, keeping the enemy occupied, while six Marine helicopters approached the campus from the undefended seaward side and landed behind the defenders. Why Marine helilift was used is unclear, unless it was for political reasons, to include all the forces in the rescue. Prior to the assault, a number of air attacks were brought to bear on targets near the defense line and the houses where the Cuban construction workers lived. The volume of fire seems to have been intended to intimidate rather than to kill. Many of the targets struck by air attacks were neither occupied nor in the line of defense. The amount of fire placed in and around the defense line was such that two nearby motels were leveled.[32] After U.S. forces were helilifted over the defense line and positioned behind the enemy, smoke grenades were used to guide the Marine CH-46 helicopters onto the beach. As the helicopters approached the beach, one CH-46 was knocked down by ground fire, and another was severely damaged when it crashed into the surf after its rotor blades struck a palm tree on the beach. The 224 students were ordered to run for the helicopters; they scrambled aboard and were evacuated to safety. Once the assault began, the enemy broke and ran, without putting up a great deal of resistance. A few stayed behind to snipe at the Americans, but no strong resistance was encountered. Surprise and overwhelming

firepower carried the day. There were no Grenadian or Cuban prisoners or casualties.

However, the assault did not go quite as easily as the JCS report has it. As the Rangers were boarding the assault helicopters for the move to Grand Anse, the helicopters came under small-arms fire from the bush. It appears from conversations with U.S. soldiers who witnessed the event that the pilots may have panicked and lifted off with Army troops hanging from the doors. Moreover, the command element of the assault unit was left on the ground. After a short time, the helicopters returned to complete the loading, while the Army forces suppressed the fire from the jungle with return fire. The actual assault did not go well, either. As they approached the landing zone, the pilots began to take small-arms fire and, apparently, refused to land, forcing the Rangers to jump from moving helicopters. The landing was successfully completed, but there was difficulty getting the helicopters back onto the landing zone because of the sporadic small-arms fire from the remaining defenders. In the opinion of some Army officers I interviewed, the performance of the Marine pilots at Grand Anse left much to be desired. Again, some officers wanted to file charges against the Marine pilots but were "counseled" out of doing so by their superiors.

By 6 p.m. on Wednesday, October 26, the situation on the island had moved in favor of the American forces. The students from both True Blue and Grand Anse campuses had been evacuated. Marine forces in considerable strength had been placed on the ground behind St. George's, cutting off the enemy's retreat. Richmond Prison was now in the hands of the Marines, and they were positioned for an attack on Fort Rupert. Fort Frederic, occupying the highest tactical terrain in the capital, still had to be taken. At dawn on the third day, Thursday, October 27, American forces were in command of the situation, although the 82nd had not yet moved the four miles from the airport to the capital. The only remaining enemy strongpoints, so they believed, were Calivigny barracks and Fort Frederic.

The assault on Calivigny barracks occurred in late morning on Thursday and involved both Rangers and paratroopers of the 82nd. The Rangers were helicoptered in on the initial assault, while the

82nd acted as the command element and moved its forces on the ground to provide the heavy fire and manpower that it was expected would be required to take the position. It had been thought that Calivigny barracks held a large Cuban force, and so the assault was preceded by heavy air attack from Navy A-7s. In preparation for the assault, light observation aircraft coordinated fire from a battery of 155mm guns belonging to the 82nd. The A-7s from the carrier *Independence* made repeated bombing and strafing runs as AC-130s poured fire into the surrounding hills. When the assault occurred, however, it was discovered that the camp had been deserted some time before.[33] As the troop-carrying helicopters approached their landing zones, the pilot of the top left helicopter was slightly wounded. In reaction, he threw up his hands, relinquishing control of his machine as it was settling to the ground. It crashed into the helicopter below and to his right. Both machines then crashed into a helicopter already on the landing zone which was unloading its troops. At least twelve Rangers were injured and three killed.[34]

With Calivigny barracks now in the hands of the Americans, the one remaining strongpoint to be dealt with was Fort Frederic, perched high on a mountaintop overlooking the capital. It was a French fort built in the eighteenth century and during the invasion was manned by a small mixed garrison. However, this garrison was able to hold off a force of platoon strength for almost five hours. U.S. forces had to call for air strikes and helicopter gunship support. During the fight for the fort, two helicopter gunships were hit as they made repeated passes over the position's defenses. Unfortunately, the attacking aircraft mistakenly hit a mental hospital about three hundred yards to the north, killing and wounding more than a score of patients and staff. Grenadian eyewitnesses whom I interviewed say the defenders of the fort had moved the garrison's flag from the fort to the flagpole in front of the hospital and had set up a machine-gun position at the hospital gate.[35] Because of poor intelligence support, the Navy attack aircraft mistook the hospital for the fort and attacked it. However, conversations with officers responsible for settling damage claims on the island bring out a different story. According to them, the military knew full well that a machine gun was positioned on the mental-hospital grounds, and

they decided to attack the facility because it had become a combat area.[36] Whatever the case, and we may never know, the paradox is that the mental hospital was leveled, but neither the garrison's barracks nor the headquarters building located very close to the fort was touched. The size of the enemy garrison defending Fort Frederic may also never be known. Not a single prisoner was taken. The only dead soldier found was a Grenadian who was killed behind his ZSU-23 machine gun. Other than that, enemy opposition had vanished by the time the Americans took the fort. By the end of the day, U.S. troops were in complete command of St. George's and the surrounding hills.

The first C-141 transporting lead elements of the 82nd Airborne Division landed at Point Salines at 2 p.m. on October 25. They off-loaded one battalion on the first day. This unit came under fire and was deployed essentially as runway security. The buildup of the 82nd's troop strength proceeded relatively slowly. This may be attributable to the use of a single runway with no parking aprons. With limited ramp space, the aircraft had to be unloaded on the runway itself, temporarily precluding its use by other aircraft. By the 26th a second battalion of the 82nd had arrived, and on the 27th a third battalion deployed. By the end of the 28th, there were six battalions in Grenada, suggesting that the 82nd had committed some of its reserve forces.[37]

In addition to providing airfield security, the 82nd was required to detain some six hundred prisoners and to help some Grenadian refugees while the Rangers pressed the attack along the airport road. On the 26th, the second brigade attacked to the east and seized a small village complex, killing sixteen Cuban soldiers and capturing eighty-six others. Also on the 26th, the 82nd acted as the command and control headquarters for the rescue of the students at Grand Anse. On the 27th, the second brigade conducted combat operations along the road to St. George's and supported the air assault against Calivigny barracks. If one can fault the 82nd, it is for moving very cautiously and slowly along the St. George's road. A major criticism leveled by Army officers themselves is that it took the 82nd three days to move a mere four miles against what, by any standard, can only be considered marginal opposition. Moreover, on the third day, their move to contact Marine forces

to their north almost resulted in their firing on the Marines. Only the quick action of the Marine company commander prevented this.[38]

By late Thursday night, October 27, Admiral Wesley Mac-Donald could report that "all major military objectives on the island were secured." By that time, some five thousand paratroopers, five hundred Rangers, and five hundred Marines had been deployed on Grenada. All that was left was to mop up a few pockets of resistance, and this was taken care of by the 82nd. A few Grenadian soldiers took to the hills, but their resistance quickly petered out. By the end of the third day, Operation Urgent Fury had come to an end.

WHY THINGS WENT WRONG

The best wars are those you cannot lose. Certainly, the invasion of Grenada falls into this category. From the beginning, there was never any doubt about the outcome. Given the great troop strength of the United States, its enormous technological superiority, its complete control of the skies, its ability to mass helicopters, air strikes, ground artillery, and, if necessary, fire from nearby ships (including two aircraft carriers), there was little likelihood that a force of some five hundred Cubans and another thousand or so Grenadians could hold out very long. Even so, the Grenada operation was carried out with a large number of blunders. Had the operation met a slightly larger force that was more determined to fight and slightly better armed (say, with SA-7 shoulder-fired missiles or even a few modern antiaircraft guns), the United States would have had much greater difficulty subduing the defenders. From the perspective of military technique, the operation was full of flaws, some symptomatic of deeper pathologies within the American military structure.

Among the most glaring shortcomings was the intelligence failure. Despite access to the most advanced technology and to the complete resources of the American intelligence community, intelligence failed to provide adequate information about the location and strength of enemy positions. According to the Rangers, not

even the positions around the airport landing zone were adequately known in advance. Ground units found the enemy's positions the hard way, by stumbling on them. Moreover, adequate maps were not available to U.S. ground units, and they did not become available until they were captured from the enemy. The Marines went into battle carrying old British maps, and the Army had tourist maps with improvised grid coordination systems.[39] No terrain contours were shown. These maps had been hand-made and reproduced the night before the invasion. And the maps used different grid systems for locating points on the ground. According to the JCS, one consequence was that the air attack on Fort Frederic also destroyed the mental hospital, because the hospital was not shown on the commander's maps.[40] In another case, an air strike called in by a Marine captain hit an Army command post, because the grid coordinates on the maps did not match. In this attack, one soldier was killed and seventeen others wounded.[41]

Although the major purpose of the operation was supposedly to rescue the medical students, the U.S. forces had almost no idea where the students were. They knew that there were students at the True Blue campus just yards away from the east end of the Point Salines runway. But only after reaching them on the first day did they learn (from students) that there was a second, larger group of students at the Grand Anse campus, four miles from the airport. Apparently, U.S. forces did not know about the students at Lance aux Epines until the fourth day, when units conducting routine clearing operations stumbled on them.[42] Yet President Reagan had delivered a television address announcing his concern about events in Grenada in March 1983—seven months before the invasion—and the island was open to anyone who wanted to visit it right up to the invasion. The telephone system worked, so that anyone could have called the medical school to obtain a list of dormitory locations. The inability to gather correct intelligence on enemy positions and the locations of the students is so great a failure as to border on criminal incompetence.

Intelligence failures seem to be a continuing part of U.S. military operations. The one constant in the *Mayaguez* rescue, the Iran raid, and the Lebanon incursion is intelligence failure. Each represents a failure of intelligence to describe correctly the situ-

174

ation that friendly forces would face, or the failure to adequately locate the position, strength, and intentions of enemy forces. The same intelligence failures happened in Grenada. Just why such failures are chronic is unclear. But they have caused great difficulties and, if not corrected, will cause severe problems in the future.

Major shortcomings in the conduct of ground operations were also evident in Grenada. There is rather widespread agreement among military analysts that the overall employment of ground forces left much to be desired. Even after the 82nd was committed, and the ground forces enjoyed a substantial numerical advantage, the Army ground advance was much too slow to effectively neutralize enemy opposition. These conditions were outlined by the FORCECOM commander, General Richard Cavacsos, in a presentation at Fort Devens, Massachusetts, four months after the invasion.[43] He noted that a major error was the piecemeal deployment of U.S. forces, which allowed the Cubans to deal piecemeal with the larger U.S. force. This permitted a much more effective defense than the enemy's numbers and equipment would normally have allowed.

In addition, there was a clear failure on the part of the U.S. forces to seize enemy strongpoints suddenly and in depth. They dealt with each enemy strongpoint as it was encountered, a condition which further enhanced the enemy's ability to mount an effective defense. This was the failure to execute a coup de main, to strike in depth. As noted, none of the special operations missions had any military significance, since they were not aimed at seizing, neutralizing, and holding enemy strongpoints in a way that would have reduced the ability of the enemy to resist. One sees in Grenada a large ground force moving ponderously and cautiously to encounter and reduce enemy positions one at a time.

Another shortcoming of U.S. ground-force operations noted by the FORCECOM commander was the employment of cautious and timid ground tactics, which tended to forgo fire and maneuver while waiting for air and artillery to destroy points of resistance. The slow advance of ground forces was often due to this style of tactical operations rather than to the resistance of the Cubans and Grenadians, who, after all, were armed with only a handful of

World War II antiaircraft machine guns, had no air or missile cover, and had no possibility of reinforcement. The effectiveness of their defense was enhanced because U.S. forces used essentially the same ground tactics used for ten years in Vietnam, with the same results.

U.S. ground tactics in Grenada were simple enough. When an advancing unit came under fire, it stopped. Fire was returned, but no effort was made by the unit to overcome the resistance by fire and by maneuvering its units. Fire was returned to fix the target while air strikes and artillery were called in to "neutralize" it. Commanders were quoted as saying that in order to minimize civilian casualties in Grenada they decided against full-scale ground assaults, choosing instead to deploy small units backed by heavy air and artillery power.[44] Just how such tactics would reduce damage and civilian casualties is unclear. Indeed, one would suspect exactly the opposite. The fact is that troops not properly trained to execute small-unit fire and maneuver tend to smoke out enemy positions and then neutralize them with superior air or artillery fire.

This tactical approach works well as long as the attacking force has air superiority and as long as the enemy does not mount any kind of air defense. In Grenada, even the very poor enemy air defense gave U.S. aircraft, especially helicopters, great difficulty. And in Vietnam, where U.S. forces had complete command of the skies, such tactics failed to kill the enemy in sufficient numbers. In the long run, this cautious approach decreases the ability of ground forces to fight on their own; it trains them to be heavily dependent on conditions that in fact may not pertain in battle. Moreover, such tactics instill excessive caution in small-unit commanders, who may be unable to develop and implement the much heralded "combat initiative" that would supposedly provide the winning edge in any conflict with the Soviet Union—a country that would enjoy great numerical superiority in any war with the U.S.

Further, such tactics can be costly, and in Grenada they were. In the battle for Fort Frederic, for example, U.S. forces were stopped cold by a small enemy force well placed around its position. American ground forces of platoon strength were brought to a halt by heavy small-arms fire. Unable to move against the strongpoint,

they called in air strikes from Navy jets and helicopter gunships. After almost half an hour of bombing and strafing runs, the defenders of the fort had shot down two helicopters with nothing more than AK-47 rifles and machine guns. Essentially, they used the Vietcong tactic of putting up a hail of small-arms fire and letting the helicopters fly into it. The U.S. responded by intensifying its bombardment. Yet, when U.S. forces finally assaulted the position, all they found was one dead Grenadian soldier next to his ZSU-23 antiaircraft machine gun. Either all the others had escaped or a single soldier had done an awful lot of damage.

In Grenada, the ability of U.S. ground forces to move rapidly and boldly against the enemy and to demonstrate effective small-unit fire and maneuver was absent. Should U.S. ground forces ever engage in El Salvador or Nicaragua and use the same tactics, the war will be long—and bloody.

Another factor noted in the FORCECOM commander's presentation was that since the U.S. forces—the first Delta Force—were discovered, the operation lost the element of surprise from the very beginning. The entire invasion depended heavily on surprise and the ability to seize the airport quickly and hold it until reinforcements arrived. By and large, this failure put the whole operation at risk. The airdrop was an improvised attempt to compensate for the fact that the airport had not been seized by Delta Force. Instead of exploiting the element of surprise, U.S. forces faced an enemy that was waiting for them with a surprise of their own. Fortunately, the enemy did not have either the manpower or the firepower to exploit his advantage.

Inadequate medical facilities and treatment emerged as another problem. There seems to have been very poor planning and positioning of medical supplies on the ground. In the initial parachute assault, some medical supplies had to be left behind, and medics on the ground quickly ran out of morphine and plasma and had to requisition what they could from the nearby medical school.[45] Described by one medical officer whom I interviewed as "a near medical disaster," the situation does not seem to have been anticipated by the logistics planners, who were not prepared for the number or the kind of wounds that had to be dealt with. This was especially so with regard to the crush and cut injuries resulting

from the helicopter accidents. Also, the cases of heat exhaustion caused in part by the new heavy battle dress fatigues were almost overwhelming. Because the operation was limited and casualties were light, the logistics planners got away with these shortcomings, but, in fact, these are problems that, according to most military analysts, plague U.S. military forces, which lack the medical supplies and personnel that would be needed in a larger, conventional war. It is a matter that needs much greater attention than the JCS have given it.

Problems of command, control, and coordination were not confined to the JSOC's special operations missions. Command and control of forces on the ground seem a perennial problem of the U.S. military, at least since the early days of the Vietnam war. In Grenada, there were problems in the coordination of movements by rival services. Navy air strikes were delivered against Army positions at Frequente on at least one occasion. U.S. forces fired on one another elsewhere as well, it appears. Army ground units and Marine units are not able to talk directly to each other even though they may be deployed in the same area, because their radio frequencies are different. Nor can Army units talk directly to Marine or Navy aircraft which may be called on to deliver air strikes in support of ground operations. Any request for air support must go through an air controller operating from a light aircraft over the battlefield. But the modern battlefield has become so lethal that the survivability of observation aircraft where the enemy has significant antiaircraft defense is very much in question. It is ridiculous for each of the four services to have different radio frequencies for controlling air-to-ground strikes. During the initial days of the Grenada operation, Army ground units had to send calls for air strikes back to their headquarters in Fort Bragg, North Carolina. The messages would then be relayed via satellite to the Navy commander, who passed the requests on to the air controller aboard the aircraft carriers.[46]

It seems, unfortunately, characteristic of U.S. military operations to use forces comprised of elements from all four services. Whether any given operation should involve mixed forces seems to take second place to the desire of all four services to be involved. In the case of Grenada, at least one congressional military analyst,

Bill Lind, has suggested that this was done in order to give each of the services an opportunity to get in on the show.[47] The same consideration applies to the decision to combine elements of both Ranger battalions, with two command elements, instead of using one unified battalion. The decision to employ the Rangers at all seems to have been pressed by the Army in order to increase support in Congress for a third Ranger battalion. In November 1984, a third battalion was authorized by Congress.[48] The decision to use JSOC seems also to have been made for political reasons. In truth, none of the special operations missions executed by JSOC in Grenada, with the possible exception of the Delta Force drop on the airstrip hours before the official invasion, had any significant military value. The invasion plan would have been none the worse if they had never been staged. As it was, all but one of them failed. But JSOC pressed for the opportunity to demonstrate that it could function well (Grenada was its first test), and Grenada provided a chance for the special operations community to rescue its prestige from the disaster in Iran.

Even the use of the Marines seems to have been largely a political decision. The Marine landing force at Pearls airport was essentially a demonstration operation which anticipated no resistance and found none. It is difficult to determine the tactical significance of seizing the airstrip. The point has been made by Marine officers that the entire Grenada operation could more logically have been assigned to the Marines, who, after all, had the manpower and support facilities in place and who are trained for precisely this type of small assault. The tendency to use combined operational forces goes back at least to Vietnam. And in almost every military operation involving a combined force, beginning with Vietnam, the results have been either failure or poor performance, due to the complexity of such operations and to the military political problems entailed. These problems surfaced in Grenada, and they will show up again and again, as long as the JCS remains a jousting ground for parochial services and interests rather than an efficient planning mechanism.

A finding which emerges from almost any objective analysis of the Grenada operation concerns the poor survivability of the helicopter in battle. Analysts who followed Vietnam and Iran closely

know that the helicopter is a poor battlefield vehicle for anything except transport. During ten years of war in Vietnam, over ten thousand helicopters were destroyed, and even this number is probably low as a consequence of the military's accounting system.[49] In accounting for Vietnam losses, if the numbered tail rotor of a downed helicopter was recovered from the battlefield, then that helicopter was carried on the books as damaged, not destroyed. Even so, the loss of helicopters was staggering. In a single operation, Lam Son 71, over a thousand helicopters were thrown into the battle. A week later, 107 had been destroyed and 608 damaged.[50] The helicopter is a very fragile machine, as demonstrated once more in Grenada, where they proved very vulnerable to the enemy's simple weapons. The military is sensitive on this point, however, since it has made a major investment in new helicopters to counter the Soviet advantage in armored vehicles and tanks. The Grenada experience does not bode well for this investment.

Of the 107 helicopters the JCS claims were deployed in Grenada, it says only nine were lost.[51] Yet, of the total deployed, nineteen, or 17 percent, were OH-58 observation helicopters which took no part in the actual fighting. (Generals and senior political observers watched the war from high above the action, as they had in Vietnam.) Of the eighty-eight combat machines within the battle zone, nine, or about 10 percent, were lost. This is a loss rate equal to the appalling daylight bomber losses in World War II. However, even this loss rate can be disputed. *Time* magazine noted some months after the invasion that the JCS sent the Department of Defense a bill, not for nine helicopters lost in Grenada, but for eighteen,[52] suggesting that the loss rate was almost 20 percent, double that admitted in official reports. Those nine additional helicopters were probably Blackhawks and OH-6s assigned to Task Force 160, the secret aviation battalion sent in to support Delta Force. Military policy is to designate all special operations as "black" and thus omit mention of any losses of either machines or men from official non-classified reports. However, the Gaylord film shows at least one Blackhawk crashing into a ridge above Prickly Bay. Further, civilian eyewitness accounts of the assault on Richmond Prison suggest that as many as five additional Blackhawks may have been lost in that operation. The Army made a budget request in

the 1985 congressional budget hearings which it defined as a "major initiative" in its special operations budget, to "backfill" losses incurred by Task Force 160.[53] Given the fact that Task Force 160 was the unit that flew the Blackhawks and OH-6s, it seems reasonable to suggest that the additional nine helicopters unlisted in the official acounting may have come from this unit. Curiously, although national news networks have aired the Gaylord film showing OH-6 helicopters making gun and rocket runs against enemy positions in Grenada, the Defense Department continues publicly to deny that any OH-6s were on the island.[54] The same is true for the Hughes 500 Defender helicopters shown in press photos.[55] These machines do not appear on any official listing as being part of the inventory; they are, in the terminology of the trade, "deniable" machines, insofar as they are used almost exclusively for clandestine operations.

The loss rate of the new Blackhawk is outrageous. Of the thirty-two Blackhawks the JCS admits were deployed in Grenada, six, or 18.7 percent, were lost, making the Blackhawk the most vulnerable machine used in the invasion. The JCS fully admits that all the helicopters lost to ground fire were knocked down by pop guns, 7.62 rifle fire or 12.7 machine-gun fire of World War II vintage.[56] Against any modern army equipped with machine cannon, radar-controlled antiaircraft guns, and shoulder- and platform-fired missiles, it is likely that the Blackhawk would suffer very high losses. Should such machines be used in large numbers in even a conventional limited war, say in Nicaragua or El Salvador, the chances are great that helicopter losses would approach the losses experienced in Vietnam. The small operation in Grenada seems to prove the point.

Some mention must be made of casualties. There seem to be discrepancies in the casualty data admitted to by the JCS. The military admits to nineteen soldiers killed in Grenada. Of these, however, fewer than one-third were actually killed by hostile fire. More than two-thirds were killed by friendly fire, mistaken bombing attacks, helicopter crashes, and other accidents.[57] In addition, 20 percent were wounded in these incidents.[58] Although the "friction of war" always takes a toll, no army can expect to sustain itself in battle when more than half of its dead and one-fifth of its wounded

are the result of its own fire. Such a high proportion of non-hostile fire deaths also reflects poor military training and inadequate readiness in basic combat skills.

The casualty numbers appear to have been deliberately falsified initially by excluding from public reports those men killed and wounded in the special operations missions. If special operations casualties are included, the death toll jumps from nineteen to twenty-nine, including the six Delta Force soldiers and the four Seals killed before the invasion officially began. That the military deliberately tried to conceal the true number of dead and wounded seems obvious. Originally, the JCS listed eighty-seven men as wounded. In response to press reports that the number of wounded was at least twenty-eight more than the number released, the military adjusted its list to 115 wounded. When it was later reported by the press that the number who received Purple Hearts was higher than the number listed as wounded,[59] the JCS again adjusted the number of wounded upward, to 152.[60] While the number of men wounded in special operations remains uncertain, it seems evident that the special operations missions account for at least one-third of the dead and at least twenty percent of the wounded, suggesting that the creation of JSOC has done little since the Iran raid to improve the quality of U.S. commando operations.

It might seem outrageous to some that the military would cover up the true number of dead, but the U.S. military has a long history of covering up casualties taken in "black" operations. It was normal practice in Vietnam to assign different causes and places of death to servicemen killed on missions in Laos, Cambodia, and even North Vietnam. There are any number of officers and men still in service who were the recipients of "classified" decorations, not included in their personnel files, for actions performed on special operations. This is common knowledge among military men. In the case of Captain Keith Lucas, a helicopter pilot assigned to TF-160 who was shot down on the morning of the invasion, the military took deliberate steps to conceal his death because his unit was in support of a "black" Delta operation. As reported on national television news, Lucas's father was told by the military that his son's death would not be reported as having occurred in Grenada because he was on a secret operation.[61] Mr. Lucas went public

with his story and the military finally admitted that Captain Lucas had died in Grenada on the morning of the invasion.

The policy of concealing deaths in special operations missions extends to deaths resulting from training accidents. Again, the 160th provides an example. Army records reveal that in the six months prior to the Grenada operation, TF-160 lost twelve men in training accidents. Six of the men were killed in two separate night helicopter accidents on July 7, 1983, in South Fox Isle, Michigan. Another member of the unit, a Seal attached for training, was killed when he fell out the door of a helicopter at Marana Air Park in April 1983. Three more men were killed in a helicopter accident at Fort Campbell in October, and two others were killed in Panama, also in a helicopter accident. These men were all assigned to a "black" unit, and although they died in training accidents, they are all listed in the Army's records as having died in automobile crashes. The two men killed in Panama are reported as having died in a vehicle crash on November 4, the same day the casualties in Grenada were announced. There is strong suspicion among some analysts that they may have been killed in Grenada and their bodies "laundered"; that is, given another cause and place of death by the military.

There is also some question about the number of Grenadian civilians who lost their lives in Operation Urgent Fury. According to Pentagon records, twenty-five Cubans were killed and another fifty-nine wounded. The Pentagon initially admitted to having killed forty-five Grenadian civilians and wounded another 358.[62] However, after the *Providence Evening Bulletin* reported a discrepancy in the numbers, the military admitted to sixty-seven Grenadian civilians killed.[63] Even if the Pentagon's figures are accepted as accurate, the number of civilians killed and wounded is far too high for an operation of the size and intensity of Urgent Fury. Conversations with U.S. claims-settlement personnel on the island as well as with Grenadian civilians suggest that there was a good deal of indiscriminate shooting, mostly from the air, at targets that were not clearly identified. A favorite sport of helicopter gunship pilots in Grenada on "roam and kill" missions seems to have been to machine-gun livestock from the air. In one instance, an old woman was killed from AC-130 gunship fire, and in another, an infant was

machine-gunned in her crib by helicopter gunship fire. The high number of Grenadian civilians killed (three times as high as the number of U.S. combat soldiers killed) as well as the high number of civilians wounded (more than twice the number of U.S. combat soldiers wounded) has never been properly explained by the Pentagon.

CONCLUSIONS

Whatever else the invasion of Grenada was, it was a political success. From the perspective of military bureaucracy, it was also a success, insofar as almost every unit and officer that took part (and even many who did not) was able to enhance his career by being awarded a medal. It took the U.S. seven full battalions plus elements of two others to defeat fewer than 679 Cubans, fewer than fifty of whom were trained combat soldiers. By contrast, the British Army defeated more than eleven thousand Argentine soldiers with just eight infantry battalions in the Falklands war. And Great Britain awarded only 679 medals among the 28,000 soldiers, sailors, and airmen who participated in the conflict. That conflict lasted seventy-four days and cost the British 255 lives, six warships, and almost a dozen aircraft. By comparison, seven thousand officers and men took part in the three days of Operation Urgent Fury, and in the weeks immediately following the end of hostilities the Pentagon awarded 8,633 medals.[64] Some were given to officers who never set foot on the island but stayed behind in the Pentagon or in bases from which the U.S. invasion was launched.

The medals issued by the Army included one Silver Star, three Distinguished Flying Crosses, four Legions of Merit, ninety-four Purple Hearts, forty Bronze Stars with V device, 680 Bronze Stars for service, four Soldiers Medals, twenty-two Defense Meritorious Service Medals, 173 Air Medals for Achievement, fifty-one Air Medals for Valor, 301 Joint Service Commendation Medals, 101 Army Commendation Medals for Valor, 4,581 Army Commendation Medals for Achievement, and 2,495 Army Achievement Medals, with authorization for another five hundred pending.[65] Some who received medals undoubtedly deserved them. But, in fact,

simply showing up for the invasion and in some cases simply being in the Pentagon and tangentially related to the planning qualified one for a medal.

The Navy and the Marines have been historically far more circumspect in the awarding of medals. So far, these services have issued only seventy medals, all of them Purple Hearts. Fewer than two hundred medals await approval.[66] Yet a unit commendation was awarded to the 1,800-man Marine Amphibious Unit that remained on the ships offshore and never saw action. As Grenada fades into memory, moreover, the military continues to issue medals to individuals who were never on the island or who were there for a very short time. A report in the *Boston Globe* notes that the Army continued to award Armed Forces Expeditionary Medals to almost anyone involved in any way in the invasion. If the medals already awarded are added to those pending, the number approaches 19,600![67]

The military has learned nothing from its experience in Vietnam, quite obviously. In 1968, for example, 416,693 awards and decorations were handed out, while the number of Americans killed in all services was 14,522. Almost every soldier who "stayed clean" and survived his tour of duty in Vietnam received multiple awards. As Woody Allen has remarked, eighty percent of success is showing up. That certainly was the case in Vietnam. In 1970, there were 522,905 medals awarded, more than double the number of U.S. military personnel deployed in South Asia, despite the fact that Americans were then disengaging from the war and the casualty rate had declined markedly.[68]

For the successful officer, medals are the visible currency of success. Since the United States mounted an operation in Grenada, it was important that the "victory" be touted in the most visible manner possible. Awarding medals is a symptom of this policy. The military resorted to its old habit of awarding great numbers of medals, earned or not. This surely reflects the continuing corrosion of the ideal of military valor. In terms of career advancement, it is far more important to receive a medal for doing nothing than to have done something worthy and not received a medal.

In the end, Grenada was a military success largely because it could be nothing else. The disparity of manpower and firepower

guaranteed success. However, Grenada is more correctly viewed not as a legitimate success against a significant enemy but as a political operation orchestrated to convey the impression that the U.S. has military credibility. The fact that the operation was marred by a number of military failures has generally gone unnoticed. What is intolerable—and dangerous—is that these failures have gone unnoticed by our military planners. It may be true that nothing succeeds like success, except when that success is used to obscure serious flaws. That is a formula for future military disaster. We refused to learn from Vietnam; our refusal led to a decade in which the U.S. application of military force, five times in all, was marked by the same flaws. Our refusal to learn from Grenada does not bode well for our future.

7

REFORM AND THE FUTURE

THE thrust of the argument presented so far is that the American military, at least over the last fifteen years, has failed to meet the test by which armies have historically been measured. It has repeatedly been unable to engage in military operations that succeed or at least demonstrate an application of military technique that in most armies would pass as acceptable. The test is battle. If a military force cannot perform well on the battlefield, then anything else it might do well doesn't really matter. It might be argued, for instance, that the American military is fairly good at taking advantage of developing technology, or that its officer corps is the best educated in the world, or that its values clearly reflect those of the larger society which it defends, or any number of other things. But if it cannot fight and fight well, if its operations go wrong consistently, then all the rest is pointless. It is a sad fact that in the last fifteen years every time the American military has gone into action it has been an embarrassment.

The American military has failed to meet the test of battle because its structure is so deformed that it cannot produce officers—planners and leaders—who are well versed in the arts of war. Throughout history, the focus of responsibility for developing and executing successful military strategies and tactics has rested with the nation's officer corps. As the Duke of Wellington is supposed to have remarked, "there are no bad troops, only bad officers." More recently, the director of Advanced Military Studies at the Army's Command and General Staff College expressed similar sen-

timents when he said: "Military excellence has always depended upon an officer corps which could think creatively about war—one which understood and practiced the art of war."[1] Thus, by any historical standard, the failure of the American military to fight well and win must be laid at the feet of the officer corps which leads it. Anything else amounts to special pleading.

The failure of American military officers to learn and practice the art of war and to succeed on the battlefield is a consequence of a system of officer development which has become deformed over the years, so that its product, the officer corps itself, can no longer function as military advisors and leaders. The American officer is far more a military bureaucrat than he is a combat leader, and is far more adept at mastering the imperatives of the system that provides his promotions and career security than he is at learning and executing the imperatives of battle. It is simply unrealistic to blame the political or civilian leaders for this condition. In the last fifteen years, the U.S. has had four Presidents, more Secretaries of Defense, and even more Chiefs of Staff. In this same period, the defense budget has grown enormously. But, as more and more money is spent for the purchase of new weaponry, the amount of money spent on training the soldier and maintaining the weaponry has declined. On balance, then, the resources and the political will have been more than adequate. If the American officer corps cannot do what is expected of it, if it cannot fight and win, the fault does not lie with the nation's political or social institutions but with the system of officer selection, promotion, assignment, training, development, and education that the military itself has devised and operates. In the American case, bad officers are the result of a wound that has been inflicted by the military structure itself.

In the first chapter I discuss some of the major institutional pathologies which have worked to undermine the quality of the officer corps. These same pathologies have increased the probability that the officer corps will perform badly under fire. If the nation is to have a corps that will be able to design and execute military plans successfully, or at least with an acceptable degree of military precision, as is expected of other armies in the West,

then the officer corps must be drastically reformed. To allow the military to continue as it has been for the last fifteen years is to guarantee future failure. In a properly designed military system, the natural talent of the American citizen-soldier ought to develop to advantage. There is no reason to believe that Americans by nature make better or poorer officers than citizens of any other country. The talent is present and is guaranteed, if by nothing else, by the law of large numbers. The problem is to reform the system so that this talent is developed properly. What, then, must be done in the way of reform?

In the first place, the value structure of the military must be changed. The military must relearn what it once knew; namely, that it is a true profession, and not just one more enterprise awash in the sea of a free society. For the last twenty-five years and most certainly during the last fifteen years, since the advent of the All-Volunteer Force (AVF), members of the military have come to perceive what they do as just one more occupation, a career in which benefits to the individual have come to outweigh the need for selfless service to the Republic. The process began in 1960 with Robert McNamara's attempts to make the military more "modern" by incorporating a number of business practices and techniques designed to make the Pentagon bureaucracy more efficient. Such techniques in themselves are no danger. However, with them came the habits, values, and practices of civilian business enterprises, especially the belief that motivation within the military is no different from motivation in the larger business community. That motivation, as in the larger society, is rooted in self-interest rather than self-sacrifice.

In consequence, the military began to change. It began to lose the perception of itself as a true profession comprised of a corps of officers and men whose reason for existence rests in something higher than the pursuit of self-interest; namely, in the task of defending the freedoms of the Republic. The professional ethos and habits of the military began to change, until, twenty-five years later, it is more than difficult to distinguish the military and its officers from a civilian business enterprise and its executives. Somewhere the military forgot that a true profession is distinguished

from a business enterprise by its scope of service. The military serves the common good, not the sum of the individual interests of its members. The military's service is to the society and the government that created it. No business or social enterprise in the society (private or public) has the same scope of service as the military.

In military service, the assumption is that the officers and men do not serve the common good in addition to their self-interest, as in business enterprises, but that they are required in a number of circumstances to subordinate their self-interest to the common good. A military that pursues the common good only when it co-incides with the private interests of its individual members risks becoming a danger to the society it serves. If it is only the con-gruence of self-interest with communal interests that motivates that soldier—that is, if the motivation for soldier and civilian is the same—then there is nothing to distinguish soldiers from armed thugs. Such a military will come to resemble the military of Latin American countries. It is precisely the military's service to higher communal goals at the expense of self-interest that separates a true professional from other social groups in a free society.

The self-sacrifice demanded of members of the military is qual-itatively different from any sacrifice that may be demanded of members of an entrepreneurial entity. General Sir John Hackett has described the life of the soldier as having at its center the "clause of unlimited liability," the expectation that the soldier will keep his commitments even unto death. There is every expectation that, if the need arises, soldiers will be required to make the ultimate sacrifice—death in battle. No one in his right mind would require this of members of a business corporation or even of profes-sionals in medicine and law. (Since law and medicine do not de-mand this kind of special sacrifice, they are professions but of a different order.) This expectation of sacrifice as a normal part of the profession of arms is fundamental to the life of the soldier and never very far from the minds of his loved ones. Paradoxically, although the civil society may in many ways encourage the military to become like a business corporation, that same society harshly punishes the soldier who does not live up to the expectation of

sacrifice. Those who run in battle or who refuse to lead under fire are subject to military law.

Finally, there is no civilian business which levies upon its members the same degree of moral responsibility that the military routinely demands. A duly sworn officer carries moral responsibilities beyond anything the civilian business executive can imagine. An officer is given the moral authority and obligation by his political superiors to expend the lives of his fellow citizens in pursuit of legitimate military objectives. No civilian enterprise confers such a terrible burden and responsibility. Death on the battlefield is only rarely accidental. More commonly, an officer in command of men must understand that his actions, even when flawless, will result in death and injury among the men he leads. It is the state which confers this authority upon the officer, and it is the state that will hold him responsible if he fails to bear the burden.

The military seems to have forgotten these things, so that the first step in any attempt to reform the military must be a change in values. Every officer and soldier must be made fully aware that he is not a politician, a bureaucrat, or a manager. The officer must know in his bones that his role as a military professional requires different values from those of business executives and, in some cases, even from those of the society at large. It should be obvious that there is a whole range of values and behavior that are perfectly legitimate in a civilian society but cannot be tolerated within a military organization if it is to function well. The military must relearn that its true profession entails special obligations and responsibilities.

There is a need to state clearly the ethical responsibilities of the military, to make that statement a code through which to socialize young members to the profession and punish and expel those who cannot or will not observe a code of ethics. There is a need for a code of military ethics to be taught and enforced throughout the military. Without it, the military cannot resist the pressures of the larger society to make it resemble a civilian business corporation.

Even after the values of the military profession are revived among the officer corps, there remains much else to be done. Much

of our military talent is wasted. Millions of dollars are spent each year training officers in all sorts of skills, only to fail to assign them to positions where they can use these skills. One has only to look at any graduating class of the Army War College. The Army alone educates over thirteen hundred senior officers a year, at considerable cost, but assigns only a fraction of them to positions where their new skills can be used. Moreover, the assignment turbulence is so high that it almost guarantees that officers will not remain in any assignment long enough to acquire expertise and to use their skills effectively. In most cases, any given officer will be learning his job, rather than putting experience into practice. The degree of amateurism in the military is outrageous and terribly wasteful of professional talent. What is needed is a degree of assignment stability within the personnel structure that will allow the military to take better advantage of the talent on which it spends so much money.

To achieve stability in the assignment structure, the services must begin by changing the present twenty-year career system to a thirty-year system, as in most major armies of the West. A thirty-year system would halt the hemorrhage of talent from the officer corps that now occurs as each year thousands of trained, qualified officers leave after twenty years of service, at a relatively young age. A longer career span would allow the military to retain thousands of qualified officers at least until age fifty and would eliminate the disruption of having to begin a second career at the comparatively young age of forty-two. It would also reduce the number of years benefits are paid to retired officers, which would lighten the burden on the defense budget. If an officer remained on duty thirty years, until age fifty, the taxpayer would be getting experienced service for his money. As things now stand, once the experienced officer leaves the service, the taxpayer and the Republic gain nothing except another pensioner.

If officers were required to remain on active service for a thirty-year period, most of them would regard military service as their primary career, as perhaps the only career they would have. This would further enhance the attractiveness of the military as a true profession. A thirty-year span would bring retirement age closer

to that required on average in government service and private industry. Most important, it would provide personnel stability and allow the military to address a number of other problems that have contributed to military amateurism. In the first place the military would be able to staff the present-sized force with far fewer officers. At present, the officer corps comprises about 11 percent of total strength. Under a thirty-year career system, it should be possible to reduce the number of serving officers by about 21 percent and possibly as much as one-third, especially if general officer ranks are reduced to at least World War II proportions. The virtues of a smaller officer corps—historically associated with excellence and with victory on the battlefield—have been discussed in the first chapter. Suffice it to say here that a smaller officer corps has greater cohesion, expertise, better communication, and a focusing of responsibility.

A smaller officer corps would permit the stabilization of officers in their assignments for much longer periods than is now the case. This would be particularly true of staff officers, who could occupy their positions for as long as four to five years, rather than eighteen months, as is now common. Combat leadership would probably improve most of all. Platoon leaders might serve for as long as three years before being considered for promotion to company executive officer, where they might serve for as long as five years. No one would be promoted to captain and serve as company commander who has not served at least ten years with troops. The time in position could be extended all the way through the chain of command, so that a battalion commander would have perhaps eighteen years of experience with troops before taking command and might remain there for four years. Clearly, this would allow the development of a corps of small-unit combat leaders that would be distinct from the rest of the staff officers in the military, who are also moving along in their careers with longer assignment periods. In combat units, unit cohesion would be greatly enhanced, as well as the trust soldiers need to have in their officers but which recent military studies show they all too readily lack.

A smaller and more stable officer corps would, of course, require slower and more competitive promotions. It would also re-

quire the military to rid itself of officers who cannot or will not meet the standards of rigorous combat-oriented excellence. A smaller corps would provide fewer opportunities for an officer to hide himself in the system and stay for a full career. At present, officers compete for promotion and assignment over a twenty-year period. There is nothing inherent in a thirty-year system, however, that would make such competition any less onerous, unless promotion is slowed down and assignment turbulence decreased.

If the U.S. military reverted to a thirty-year career system, with a smaller officer corps with longer time between promotions, it would come into line with most of the military establishments of the West. There is nothing revolutionary here. Historically, it is this type of stable, long-term system that has produced military excellence, high-quality officers, and relatively good combat armies.

Promotion, especially to the higher ranks of lieutenant colonel and colonel, should be linked to age, as is the case in the Soviet and German armies. An officer who is raised to the rank of major, for example, might be required to remain in service for an additional six years, or until the age of, say, forty. In the German Army, a lieutenant colonel must serve until age forty-six. A colonel must serve until age fifty. The point is that promotion is linked to expertise and performance, which depend on extended service and more stable assignments. Once an officer reaches a certain rank, he would serve for a specified number of years and could be assigned to a position that would benefit from his expertise and experience.

Even if it is possible to assemble and keep a corps of officers in military service long enough to stabilize their assignments, it would still be necessary to develop a system to educate and train officers so that they would truly be "warrior poets." The ideal officer is one who understands and can apply the skills of war but who is also concerned with and trained in the human dimensions of our society. An officer must know intimately and appreciate the human dimension of war. The education of the military officer cannot be limited to the acquisition of technical expertise, something which the present military training and education system seems unable

194

to do well in any case. An officer's education must include (and develop) an ethical viewpoint as well. Men cannot be "managed" to their deaths; they are not objects to be moved about for the benefit of the system. Men on a battlefield, when their instincts and senses tell them to flee, must know and respect—or, in the words of S.L.A. Marshall, love—one another and their superiors who have placed them at risk. Only an officer who appreciates these human dimensions and who has developed a sense of how important his task is can ever lead men in battle well. Such are the characteristics of a leader, not of a manager or a bureaucrat, and it is these characteristics that a military educational system must develop in addition to technical expertise.

The education of the American officer is sorely lacking in both elements. All too often, the moral dimension is lacking or is subordinated to military technique. At the service academies, the stress of the curriculum is on the hard sciences, engineering, and other such skills, with little in the way of poetry, history, languages, ethics, philosophy, or writing. The liberal arts, which engender an understanding of the human dimensions of tragedy and destruction, are often ignored or reduced to secondary importance. Many of our senior officers are the products of a military school system that no longer teaches war and military arts but rather teaches management and bureaucratic skills. It is sobering to note, for example, that in the 1950s the Army Command and General Staff College curriculum devoted 665 hours to tactical and operational skills. By the late 1970s, only 173 hours were spent on these skills.[2] The rest of the time was taken up, not with the liberal arts, but with courses and instruction in management, finances, and general politics. Today, at the Army War College in Washington, D.C., the number of courses devoted to military tactics and operations is dismally low, and those devoted to an understanding of the human dimension of war are almost nonexistent. The stress is on "the big picture," once again on economic and managerial subjects so useful in a bureaucracy. The curriculum offers so little challenge that many officers earn an additional master's degree by attending the nearby state college in their spare time! At the National Defense University in Washington, D.C., one of the military's most senior

schools, the curriculum offers courses on how to testify before a congressional committee; apparently, the simple injunction to tell the truth to one's political superiors no longer suffices.

Our system of military education fails to educate the whole officer, and often produces officers unlearned in the skills of war but remarkably apt at management and the skills required to survive and prosper within the military bureaucracy. It is a frightening fact that a staff psychologist at the National Defense University who has been doing personality testing on the university's classes since 1979 can find no differences between the military men at the university and the executives of business corporations whom he also tests. If the officers and executives all wore similar clothes, he notes, it would be impossible to tell them apart. Moreover, he notes that the present military system selects out those officers oriented toward combat skills and battle; he says "the peacetime military does not have the George Patton type. They've been weeded out. I know a number of them who have 'early-outed' in the last ten years."[3]

Even after the officer corps is reduced in size, its assignments stabilized, and promotions slowed, even after it is instructed in a code of ethics and the school system reformed so that it stresses both the skills of war and the human dimensions of battle, it would still be necessary to devise a military planning system that would permit the officers' skills to be brought to bear on the planning and execution of military operations. This means ridding the military of the institution of the Joint Chiefs of Staff. The JCS should be abolished or at the very least removed from the planning process for military operations. The critique of the JCS made earlier need not be repeated here. Of the five military operations that have failed in the last fifteen years, three were planned in the JCS. Whenever the JCS gets involved in planning, its very structure assures that interservice rivalry and bureaucratic pressures will influence the plan. In the past, that has spelled disaster. No less an authority and supporter of the military than Senator Barry Goldwater has wondered just why it takes some two thousand officers to support a group of five men (the JCS) who meet twice a week! Like Cromwell's parliament, it has sat too long for the good it has done, and should have the grace to disband.

With the JCS abolished, it might be possible to follow the example of the Western European armies and even the Soviets and create a stable general staff for each of the military services, including the Marine Corps. A stable officer corps comprised of experts in the art of war can be institutionalized in a general-staff system which would serve as a permanent repository of expertise for each service. It would also serve as an institutional memory, a repository of the lessons learned from history and past military experiences which could be brought to bear on the formulation of future military plans. A small general staff, perhaps no larger than twelve hundred officers for each service and organized along the lines of the German general staff, would go a long way toward ensuring that future military operations would be planned by men tested and experienced in the arts of war. Their long periods of assignment would remove them from the scramble for promotion and future assignment which now afflicts the American military. As in other armies, the preeminence of military considerations over managerial or bureaucratic ones in the formulation of operational plans would be increased.

Yet even a general staff might have difficulty planning military operations if the commanders of the combat units themselves are not trusted and competent. Stabilizing the officer corps for longer periods of time ought to do wonders in increasing competence. Unit commanders with operational missions should be brought directly into the planning process. Recent American military history clearly demonstrates the need for close contact and coordination between planners and unit commanders. Except for the Sontay raid, none of the men who planned the other four American military operations I have described was directly involved in their execution. Worse, none of the mission commanders was involved in the planning process. The separation of planning from execution diffuses responsibility for failure. What is needed is a form of the German and Israeli practice of "mission order" planning, where the staff planners issue a general mission plan to the commanders and the commanders then design the details of the operation for the forces which they will personally command. The operational plan is then reviewed by the general staff together with the mission commanders to iron out any difficulties. Once the plan is final, the

mission commanders execute it. Unless the American military devises some means to ensure that the planners command and the commanders plan, the result will be more military failures. If our recent history demonstrates anything, it is that a military bureaucracy cannot plan successful military operations.

Finally, it is unlikely that the problems of manpower and quality within the ranks can be solved without a return to the draft. With a draft, the American military would have higher-quality recruits from whom to forge capable soldiers. The law of large numbers would ensure that a fairly representative cross section of mental and physical abilities would be drawn from the society at large. Under the AVF, recruit quality has been a perennial problem. In addition, a draft would allow the military to obtain better-quality material at a much lower cost, since wages for non-career enlisted soldiers might be lowered considerably once the need to compete for their abilities with private industry has been eliminated. Also, a fair and equitable draft would allow the reinstitution of a number of military social practices—such as barracks living—which were done away with under the AVF and which would increase the cohesion of American units. The threat of being drafted would also increase the number of students who enroll in officer-training programs on the nation's campuses. Draft calls would be made on a lottery basis, with no exemption except for medical reasons, for the sole surviving sons of families whose fathers or brothers had been killed in military service, or if the person called was the sole support of his family. Further, draft calls would be made biannually, rather than on a monthly or, as is now the case, almost a daily basis, which allows the recruit to choose his time of entry into service. Biannual draft calls would reduce turbulence in the ranks to 25 percent a year, turbulence which would be foreseen and planned for. Better units with greater stability would almost certainly result. The Soviets draft biannually, apparently with good results.

There are also ethical reasons for returning to a draft. Military service is often a heavy burden and one which involves the risk of death or injury. In a society which prides itself on equal opportunity and equal responsibility under the law, an equitable draft would

no longer permit the more fortunate to escape the burden of defending the very nation which provides so much of their good fortune. Under the AVF, the wealthy and well educated have been able to escape the burden of defending the nation, and the responsibility has fallen disproportionately upon the poor, the uneducated, and the nation's minorities. Such a condition constitutes a stain on one of the world's greatest democracies. It also disproportionately distributes the burden of death when it is time to do battle. All American citizens have equal worth in the eyes of the law; they should also have equal responsibilities when it comes time to die for one's country.

The American military is in serious trouble. Its recent historical record, to say nothing of its disastrous performance in Vietnam, has been marked far more often by failure than by success. Its military plans and execution have been unrealistic and unsuccessful. The officer corps by any historical standard is lacking in the spirit and expertise that have characterized the more successful officer corps in history. Worse, it is infected by habits and values which are characteristic of many of the worst officer corps in history. The record is clear that the officer corps has failed the single test of a successful army, the ability to perform well on the field of battle. Either some program for radical reform is adopted, or future American military operations will meet the same fate as those of the recent past. There is no alternative except defeat.

NOTES

1: WHY THINGS GO WRONG

1. Richard Gabriel, "Professionalism Versus Managerialism in Vietnam," *Air University Review*, Jan.–Feb. 1981, pp. 77–85.
2. Ibid.
3. Richard Gabriel and Paul Savage, "The Environment of Military Leadership," *Military Review*, July 1980, p. 56.
4. Richard Gabriel, *The Antagonists: A Comparative Combat Assessment of the Soviet and American Soldier* (Westport: Greenwood Press, 1984), p. 87.
5. "DOD Appropriations for 1984," U.S. House of Representatives Committee Report, 98th Congress, 2nd session, vol. 2, p. 696.
6. Army Training Study, 1979. Cited in a letter by Paul L. Savage to Lt. Gen. Robert Elton, March 27, 1984, p. 2.
7. Lewis Sorley, "Turbulence at the Top: Our Peripatetic Generals," *Army* magazine, March 1981, pp. 14–24.
8. Ibid.
9. Paul Savage and Richard Gabriel, "The JCS: An Institution Whose Time Has Come . . . and Gone," pending publication in *Canadian Defense Quarterly* (1985).
10. General Yasotay, "Warriors: An Endangered Species," *Armed Forces Journal*, Sept. 1984, pp. 16–21.
11. Ibid.
12. Ibid.
13. Savage and Gabriel, "The JCS," p. 12.
14. Richard Gabriel and Paul Savage, *Crisis in Command* (New York: Hill and Wang, 1978), Table II.
15. Soldier Report III, Human Resources Development Directorate, ODCSPER, Washington, D.C., pp. 26–27.
16. Ibid., pp. 43–44.
17. Ibid., pp. 34–35.
18. U.S. House Committee Report, p. 695.

19. Ibid., p. 698.
20. Ibid.
21. Ibid., p. 981.
22. Ibid.
23. Ibid., p. 699.
24. Ibid., pp. 717–19.
25. Ibid., p. 983.
26. Ibid., p. 984.
27. Ibid., p. 706.
28. Ibid., p. 709.
29. Ibid., p. 918.
30. Ibid., p. 919.
31. Ibid., p. 922.
32. Ibid., p. 904.
33. Ibid., p. 927.
34. Ibid., p. 923.
35. Ibid., p. 929.
36. *Boston Globe*, Sept. 20, 1984, p. 3.
37. House Committee Report, p. 941.
38. Ibid., p. 902.
39. Ibid., pp. 804–5.
40. Ibid.
41. Ibid., pp. 805–6.
42. Ibid., p. 801.
43. Ibid., p. 830.

2: THE RAID ON SONTAY PRISON

1. Benjamin F. Schemmer, *The Raid* (New York: Harper and Row, 1976), p. 2. Schemmer's book is the only major work ever done on the Sontay raid. The official after-action report remains classified. The account which appears here draws heavily on Schemmer's work and a number of interviews with individuals involved in the planning and execution of the raid.
2. Ibid.
3. Ibid., pp. 8–10.
4. Ibid., p. 59.
5. Ibid., p. 91.
6. Ibid., p. 207.
7. Ibid., p. 237.
8. Ibid.

3: THE *MAYAGUEZ*

1. Donald E. Carlile, "The Mayaguez Incident: Crisis Management," *Military Review*, Oct. 1976, p. 4.
2. *Newsweek*, May 26, 1975, p. 20.

NOTES

3. Ibid., p. 21.
4. Ibid., p. 19.
5. J. M. Johnson, R. W. Austin, D. A. Quinlan, "The *Mayaguez*," *Marine Corps Gazette*, Oct. 1977, p. 26.
6. Ibid.
7. Ibid.
8. Ibid.
9. Ibid.
10. Ibid., p. 27.
11. Ibid.
12. Ibid., p. 28.
13. Ibid., p. 29.
14. *The New York Times*, May 26, 1975, p. 20.
15. *Newsweek*, May 26, 1975, p. 20.
16. Ibid., p. 25.
17. Ibid.
18. Ibid.
19. *Marine Corps Gazette*, p. 30
20. Ibid.
21. Ibid.
22. Ibid.
23. Personal interview with one of the helicopter pilots involved in the attempted operation on the beach.
24. *Marine Corps Gazette*, p. 30.
25. Ibid.
26. Ibid., p. 31.
27. Ibid., p. 32.
28. Ibid., p. 33.
29. Personal interview with Marines who participated in the battle.
30. *Marine Corps Gazette*, p. 32.
31. Ibid.
32. *Military Review*, pp. 10–11.
33. *Newsweek*, May 26, 1975, pp. 25–26.
34. *Marine Corps Gazette*, p. 34.
35. Ibid.
36. Ibid.
37. *Military Review*, p. 12.

4: THE IRAN RESCUE MISSION

1. *Time*, May 5, 1980, p. 17.
2. Interview with a member of the Iran rescue force.
3. Ibid.
4. Interview with a member of the team who tested the security of the American embassy in Iran in 1974.
5. *Time*, May 12, 1980, p. 33.

6. Richard A. Gabriel, "A Commando Operation That Was Wrong from the Start," *Canadian Defense Quarterly* 10 (Winter, 1980–1981), p. 7.
7. *Time*, May 12, 1980, p. 33.
8. "The Holloway Report: Iran Rescue Mission #3," *Aviation Week and Space Technology*, Sept. 29, 1980, pp. 84–85.
9. Ibid., p. 85.
10. Ibid.
11. "The Holloway Report: Iran Rescue Mission #2," *Aviation Week and Space Technology*, Sept. 22, 1980, p. 143.
12. Ibid., p. 144.
13. "The Holloway Report: Iran Rescue Mission #1," *Aviation Week and Space Technology*, Sept. 15, 1980, p. 69.
14. "Iran Rescue Mission #3," p. 89.
15. Ibid.
16. Ibid., p. 85.
17. "Iran Rescue Mission #1," p. 69.
18. "Iran Rescue Mission #2," p. 144.
19. Ibid.
20. Ibid.
21. Ibid.
22. "Iran Rescue Mission #3," p. 89.
23. Ibid.
24. Ibid.
25. Ibid.
26. Ibid.
27. Ibid.
28. Ibid., p. 90
29. Ibid.
30. Ibid.
31. "Iran Rescue Mission #1," p. 70.
32. Ibid., pp. 68–70.
33. Ibid., p. 70.
34. "Iran Rescue Mission #2," p. 140.
35. Ibid.
36. Ibid.
37. Ibid.
38. "Iran Rescue Mission #1," pp. 68–69.
39. Gabriel, "A Commando," p. 8.
40. Ibid.
41. "Iran Rescue Mission #2," p. 143.
42. Ibid.
43. Ibid.
44. "Iran Rescue Mission #3," p. 84.
45. Ibid.
46. Ibid., p. 87.
47. Ibid., pp. 84–85.
48. Ibid., p. 85.
49. Ibid., p. 89.

50. Ibid.
51. Giorgio Apostolo, *The Illustrated Encyclopedia of Helicopters* (Rome: Ervin S.R.L., 1984), p. 88.

5: DEATH IN BEIRUT

1. The Long Commission Report, *Congressional Record*, Jan. 30, 1984, p. 365.
2. "Adequacy of U.S. Marine Corps Security in Beirut," Hearings of the Committee on Armed Services of the U.S. House of Representatives, Dec. 19, 1983, p. 27.
3. Interviews with Marines who served in Lebanon.
4. Interviews with the MAU S-3 operations officer who coordinated these events.
5. Long Commission Report, p. 358.
6. "Lebanon: The Anatomy of a Foreign Policy Failure," *Newsday*, April 8, 1984, p. 34.
7. Ibid., p. 36.
8. Long Commission Report, p. 374.
9. Ibid.
10. "Adequacy of U.S. Marine Corps Security in Beirut," p. 21.
11. *Boston Globe*, Oct. 27, 1984, p. 19.
12. *Newsday*, April 8, 1984, p. 4.
13. *Time*, Dec. 19, 1983, p. 25.
14. Long Commission Report, p. 365.
15. Ibid.
16. Ibid., p. 366.
17. Ibid., pp. 367–68.
18. Ibid.
19. Ibid.
20. "Adequacy of U.S. Marine Corps Security in Beirut," pp. 34–35.
21. Long Commission Report, p. 370.
22. Ibid., p. 368.
23. Ibid., p. 369.
24. Ibid.
25. Ibid., p. 371.
26. Ibid.
27. "Adequacy of U.S. Marine Corps Security in Beirut," p. 36.
28. Long Commission Report, pp. 361, 379–80.
29. Ibid., pp. 379–80.
30. Ibid., p. 380.
31. Ibid., p. 368.
32. "Adequacy of U.S. Marine Corps Security in Beirut," p. 47.
33. *Newsday*, April 8, 1983, p. 5.
34. *Time*, Dec. 19, 1983, p. 25.
35. Interviews with a number of Air Force and Navy pilots who flew combat missions during Vietnam.
36. Ibid.
37. *Time*, Dec. 19, 1983, p. 25.

38. Ibid.
39. Ibid., p. 25.
40. Ibid.
41. Michael Gordon, "Aegis: A High Priority Naval Defense Project . . . But Will It Work?" in Dina Rasor, *More Bucks, Less Bang: How the Pentagon Buys Ineffective Weapons* (Washington, D.C.: Fund for Constitutional Government, 1983), pp. 207–9.
42. Ibid.
43. Ibid.
44. *Boston Globe*, Feb. 18, 1984, p. 1.
45. *Boston Globe*, Feb. 10, 1984, p. 1.
46. Ibid.
47. Ibid.
48. *Boston Globe*, Feb. 18, 1984, p. 1.
49. *Boston Globe*, Feb. 10, 1984, p. 1.
50. Ibid., p. 6.
51. Ibid.

6: GRENADA

1. Interview with high CIA official, Oct. 1, 1984.
2. *Time*, Nov. 7, 1983, p. 28.
3. Neither Delta Force nor the Seal teams are trained for combat assault or combat seizure missions. Both are essentially counter-terror organizations to be utilized to rescue hostages and neutralize terrorists in aircraft or small buildings. Using Delta and the Seals in a combat assault was completely inappropriate.
4. The JCS report on events in Grenada can be found in "JCS Replies to Criticism of Grenada Operation," *Army* magazine, Aug, 1984, p. 30.
5. Ibid., p. 29.
6. Original estimates of Cuban regular force strength have fluctuated wildly since the first days of the Grenada invasion. Originally, the JCS claimed that as many as six hundred were Cuban regulars. Later that figure was dropped to fifty-four. Robert Healy of the *Boston Globe* (Nov. 14, 1984) suggests it was about seventy-five. If one adds the Cuban dead and wounded together and assumes they were all Cuban regulars, the figure comes to just under two hundred.
7. *Newsweek*, Nov. 7, 1983, p. 75.
8. After denying for a year that there were any advance units on the ground at Point Salines, the Pentagon finally admitted to the presence of a forty-man advance unit on the runway prior to the invasion. See *The New York Times*, Oct. 25, 1984, p. 12.
9. On the day of the invasion, an American civilian living on Grenada filmed about ninety minutes of videotape from his home directly across Prickly Bay near Point Salines. The tape, equipped with sound track and time points, records the events around Point Salines airport in the first few hours of the invasion. This film—the Gaylord film—was purchased by NBC and shown

on national television, although not in its entirety. I have had access to the entire film. It clearly shows an AC-130 Spectre gunship making firing runs at the west end of the runway some twenty minutes before the Ranger parachute assault. The pattern of flight and the sounds of miniguns and automatic howitzers make it plain that the aircraft is delivering suppressive fire on the ravine where the Delta Force is trapped. If the Spectre gunship is not supporting Delta—whose presence had been discovered—then its appearance over the Point Salines runway before the Ranger assault was a major error that compromised the element of surprise for the entire operation. It is hard to believe that Pentagon planners who did not use air strikes against Cuban positions for fear of compromising the element of surprise would send a lone Spectre gunship in. The Pentagon continues to deny that Delta Force was at the Point Salines airport that morning.

10. *Army* magazine, Aug. 1984, p. 31.
11. See comments by Michael Burch, Pentagon spokesman, on ABC *Nightline*, Oct. 24, 1984, in which he admits for the first time that Delta Force assaulted the prison in nine Blackhawk helicopters.
12. The Gaylord film records in brutal detail the crash of Captain Lucas's helicopter and the rescue efforts immediately thereafter.
13. The sound track of the Gaylord film recorded the broadcast appeals of Radio Free Grenada in the background. It was still broadcasting appeals to resist until mid-morning, long after the Seals should have knocked it off the air. Interviews with civilians on the island confirm that RFG was broadcasting at least until 10:30 that morning.
14. A good account of the rescue attempt appears in John Fialka's "In Battle for Grenada Commando Missions Didn't Go As Planned," *The Wall Street Journal*, Nov. 15, 1983, p. 1.
15. *Newsweek*, Nov. 7, 1983, p. 75.
16. This information was gathered in an interview with the six civilian employees of the power plant who were held by the Seals that morning. The story is confirmed by the proprietor of a small store next to the power plant, who also witnessed the capture of the power station.
17. See the article on the Ranger deployment in *Soldier of Fortune* magazine, Feb. 1984, p. 60.
18. Ibid. Also confirmed by the Pentagon spokesman on ABC *Nightline*.
19. *Soldier of Fortune* magazine, p. 60.
20. *Army Times*, Nov. 5, 1984, p. 46. The Ranger commander says that the Rangers parachuted from five hundred feet because intelligence reports indicated a number of ZSU-23 antiaircraft machine-gun positions on the hills surrounding the airport. The Ranger commander says that, given the height of the hills, the enemy guns could not be depressed to fire lower than six hundred feet. Accordingly, the decision was made to jump at five hundred feet, below the plane of fire of the guns. Some questions arise. First, there are only two small mounds, hardly hills, around the west end of the Point Salines runway, neither of which is more than forty feet high. Any guns placed on those hills would easily have been able to cover a drop at five hundred feet. Second, if the Rangers knew the guns were there, why were the emplacements not attacked by air strikes before the Rangers parachuted

in? Certainly, air strikes were readily available from the jets of the carrier *Independence*. The answer seems to be that there were no ZSU-23s on the hills above the airport. Rather, the Rangers were hit by small-arms fire from the Cuban force besieging Delta in the ravine at the west end of the runway.
21. This explanation was offered by the Pentagon spokesman on ABC Nightline.
22. The Gaylord film.
23. Information about the cowardice charges was provided by sources inside the Ranger units.
24. *Army Times*, Nov. 5, 1984, p. 47.
25. *Time*, Nov. 7, 1983, p. 23.
26. Ibid., p. 22.
27. *Army*, Aug. 1984, p. 32.
28. Ibid.
29. *Time*, Nov. 7, 1983, pp. 23–24.
30. *The Wall Street Journal*, Nov. 15, 1983, p. 1.
31. *Army Times*, Nov. 5, 1984, p. 34.
32. *Newsweek*, Nov. 7, 1983, p. 22.
33. *Army Times*, Nov. 5, 1984, p. 34.
34. Ibid., p. 50.
35. Interview with the gatekeeper at Fort Frederic, who witnessed the event.
36. Interview with U.S. military claims-settlement personnel on Grenada.
37. *Army*, Aug. 1984, p. 32.
38. Interview with the Marine commander involved in the incident.
39. *The Wall Street Journal*, Nov. 15, 1983, p. 1.
40. Ibid.
41. *Newsday*, July 2, 1984, pp. 2, 15.
42. *Army Times*, Nov. 5, 1984, p. 34.
43. I was not present at this briefing. Its contents as reported here were assembled from several sources who did attend the presentation and have firsthand knowledge of what was said.
44. *Newsweek*, Nov. 7, 1983, p. 72.
45. *Time*, Nov. 7, 1983, p. 24.
46. *Army Times*, Nov. 5, 1984, p. 34.
47. Interview with Bill Lind, congressional military analyst.
48. *Army Times*, Nov. 5, 1984, p. 46.
49. Gregg Easterbrook, "All Aboard Air Oblivion," in Dina Rasor, *More Bucks, Less Bang*, p. 57.
50. Ibid., p. 58.
51. *Army*, Aug. 1984, p. 37.
52. *Time*, July 23, 1984, p. 49.
53. Hearings for Defense Appropriations: 1984, House Appropriations Committee, March 1984, p. 796.
54. ABC Nightline.
55. For some excellent photos of OH-6 helicopters on the runway at Point Salines, see *Newsday*, Aug. 13, 1984, p. 13. Neither these nor the Hughes 500 Defenders are in the JCS official list of helicopters deployed in Grenada.
56. *Army*, Aug. 1984, p. 37.
57. *Providence Evening Bulletin*, Nov. 7, 1984, p. C-7.

58. Ibid.
59. I first raised the question of casualty figures in an NBC news interview on Oct. 22, 1984. The next day, the Pentagon responded by adjusting its figures upward, to 115 wounded.
60. *Newsday*, Nov. 7, 1984, p. 2.
61. NBC Nightly News, Oct. 22, 1984.
62. *Providence Evening Bulletin*, Nov. 7, 1984, p. C-7.
63. Ibid.
64. Jeffrey Record, "More Medals Than We Had Soldiers," *Washington Post*, April 15, 1984, p. B-4.
65. Ibid.
66. Ibid.
67. *Boston Globe*, Aug. 28, 1984, p. 16.
68. *Washington Post*, April 15, 1984, p. B-4.

7: REFORM AND THE FUTURE

1. Colonel Huba Wass de Czege, "How to Change an Army," *Military Review*, Nov. 1984, p. 45.
2. Ibid., p. 48.
3. Emily Yoffe, "Study War No More," *Washington Post Magazine*, Nov. 4, 1984, pp. 18–21.